AF597233

THE ATTACHÉ IN MADRID.

THE

ATTACHÉ IN MADRID;

OR,

SKETCHES OF THE COURT OF ISABELLA II.

TRANSLATED FROM THE GERMAN.

NEW YORK:
D. APPLETON AND COMPANY,
346 & 348 BROADWAY.
1856.

PREFACE.

The translator of the following pages has attempted nothing more than to render the original German text into English. The work, if we may judge from its general aspect and structure, was not at first intended for publication, and when it was finally prepared for that object, it underwent but slight modification. At all events, what was doubtless its original form—that of a series of rapid, but sincere and earnest notes, made by a young German diplomate in the whirl of fashion, and amid the agitations of political and social revolution at Madrid, during the recent changes there—was still preserved, and a multitude of fashionable phrases, chiefly French, were permitted to stand. These the translator has not deemed it well to alter, as they are generally current among intelligent readers of all countries, and more truly express the ideas of the writer than any translation could do.

With many of the views entertained by the author of these sketches, most American readers will not agree; yet his pages will nevertheless prove amusing and instructive, inasmuch as they present a vivid panorama of the Spanish capital at a period of the highest political excitement, together with the living and breathing portraits of the notabilities of the Court—foreign as well as domestic—seeming to pass before us like actors starring for our special delight. The translator, therefore, commits the work to the public, in the hope that it will meet with favor, alike from those who read for entertainment, and those who are more exclusively interested in studying the developments of truth and history.

NEW YORK, *December*, 1855.

CONTENTS.

THE ATTACHÉ IN MADRID.

TRANSLATED FROM THE GERMAN.

CHAPTER I.

My parentage—Destined to a diplomatic career—Proceed to Madrid as Attaché to Count A.—First impressions.

MADRID, September, 1858.

LORD BYRON awoke one morning and found himself famous. I have no doubt the sensation was delightful; but I would not exchange for it the joy which I feel this morning, on opening my eyes after a short and hurried sleep, at finding myself in Madrid. From my earliest years Spain has been the land of my day-dreams—romantic, chivalrous Spain! Its very contrast to my native land, with its cold blue lakes and frozen mountains, made it charming to my imagination. Land of cloaked Caballeros; of Señoras, with dark eyes gleaming from beneath black mantillas; of serenades and adventures, of love and song; land of the Cid Campeador! how often have I lain at the bottom of my boat, covered with my cloak, wrapped in the adventures of Gil Blas, puzzling over the delightful Don Quixote, or mystifying myself with the pages of Calderon; and so completely forgetting all external objects, that the sound of the dinner-bell ringing a tremendous peal through the woods surrounding our chateau, and intended solely for my ear, had scarcely power to startle me from my reveries, till the thoughts of my father's grave reprimand, my mother's gentle reproach, and the bantering inquiries of my young sisters, forced me to shut the fascinating volumes, spring hurriedly on shore, climb the hilly path amidst the pine trees, and arrive heated at the dinner table, just as the venerable butler was handing round the soup!

My mother was born and bred in Italy—my cradle was rocked to the sound of Neapolitan ballads—my father represented his sovereign, not many years ago, at the Court of Madrid. I spent that time, and, indeed, many years previous, at Ascott, but when I returned for the holidays, I had no pleasure equal to that of listening to my mother when she spoke of Madrid, of Aranjuez, of the Escurial. In short, Spain was my vocation; and there is no struggling against manifest destiny. So my father, finding that neither Ascott nor foreign travel had cured me, procured me, through his interest with the prime minister in ——, an attachéship to Madrid—not with the fond notion of my becoming distinguished in the diplomatic career, but with a view to the facilities thus afforded of obtaining the entrée into good society, under the wing of my respectable minister and chief, Count A——.

Behold me, then, taking a hurried leave of my family, and receiving injunctions from each individual to write by every courier. My father desired me to give him an account of the state of political affairs; my mother—a strict and pious Catholic—of the state of religion, of the churches, and charitable institutions; my sisters, of the court, the balls, and especially of the dress and manners of the Spanish ladies; my younger brothers, of the clubs, the sport, the horses, the bull-fights, &c.; in short, I was to write a kind of modern history of Spain, and if I had obeyed all their behests, his Majesty's service would have suffered greatly in the neglect of the diplomatic duties destined to be performed by his loyal and faithful attaché. However, I promised faithfully to write frequently; and when my venerable grand-aunt, the Baroness L——, said, as she leant upon her gold-headed staff, "Don't plague him with more nonsense—let the boy write when he has time, and whatever he likes—never make a toil of a pleasure,"—I thought her the most sensible woman in my fatherland. In short, as my Irish friend in this capital remarked, "After all, you have only come out for a lark," by which I suppose he meant to indicate my joyous and soaring aspirations; I certainly have arrived here more intent upon amusement than diplomacy, while hoping to combine the two.

To Madrid I came via France. Every one knows the journey. My chief, who has lived many years in Madrid, but has lately been in Paris upon *congé*, travelled in all the state of his own equipage and servants. I came with the English courier, not the shadow of an adventure on the way. When we crossed into the Spanish frontier, my companion probably had doubts of my sanity, from the extravagant demonstrations of joy in which I indulged, whilst he philosophically smoked his cigar. He allowed me ten minutes to run into the cathedral at Burgos, where I would gladly have lingered for hours. When I returned, full of enthusiasm, I found him gravely devouring a sandwich, of which he had a goodly pile in his hamper, and washing it down with a glass of old port. He invited me to join him, and begged to know what interest I could take in watching a group of Spanish soldiers, of dirty peasant women, and whining beggars. Not a bit whining, however, were they. They asked for alms as independently as if they conceived themselves to be rather conferring a favor than otherwise. They evidently acted upon the principle, that "more blessed is he that giveth than he that receiveth," and gave so many blessings in return for a *cuarto*, that, after all, they were cheaply purchased. Amongst the peasant women, there were several worthy of figuring on the canvas of Murillo; and, in fact, from the moment of entering Spain, I could not but remark that we scarcely passed one object which would not have afforded a good subject for the pencil.

The lucky derangement of a wheel gave me half an hour to enter a *fonda*, and with my head full of the *ventas* of the immortal Cervantes, I was surprised to find a number of diligence travellers seated before an excellent breakfast. The bread was especially commendable. The repast was plentiful; stewed fowls and roast meat following the soup and *puchero;* vegetables, chocolate, grapes, plums and pears in profusion; and, moreover, two beautiful girls in waiting. I sketched the head of the handsomest, and even my companion allowed that she was good-looking and *quite clean;* but he persisted in abstaining from all food, insisting that every thing was full of rancid oil and garlic, even the grapes, of which, together with bread, I carried off a large supply.

It was late when we entered Madrid, a beautiful moonlight gilding the houses and churches with a silvery light, and gleaming upon the distant mountains; but no one seemed to have gone to rest. Bright forms were on the balconies, sounds of music issued from open casements, the streets were still crowded. Groups of men stood at the doors of the cafés, talking, laughing, smoking; and it was with some reluctance that I took the advice of my sage companion, and followed him to a *casa de huespedes* (Anglicé, boarding-house) in the Calle de Pontegas, where he kindly and with some difficulty procured for me a small bedroom, looking out upon the court-yard, and left me to my reflections. *Couleur de rose* they were. No young damsel about to make her debut, at her first ball, can ever have had brighter. I respect sleep as did Sancho Panza, when there is nothing worth keeping one's self awake for. As this was decidedly my case, I addressed myself to slumber, dreamt that a Manola, with a knife in her garter, was dancing the cachucha in the most bewitching manner, and woke to the sound of the finest military music I have heard since I left.

Having dressed and breakfasted in an almost invisible little saloon which adjoined my bedroom, I proceeded to examine my letters of introduction, and to make my plans for the day, with no small impatience to emerge into the air and sunshine. First, as in duty bound, I repaired to my Legation.

CHAPTER II.

Aspect of Madrid—the Legation—My reception—Arrangements—Diplomacy—My droll acquaintance—Pails of champagne for horses—A drive with Count A.—The French Legation—The Italian Legation, &c.

2 A. M.—Impossible to sleep when all Madrid is still astir, so for an hour or so I address myself to my journal. To arrive betimes at the Legation, I took a *berlina*, a little horse carriage, like the *remises* in Paris. Though early, all Madrid seemed to be in movement. It appeared to be a *jour de fête*, but I found that this is the general aspect of the city. Bells were ringing, military bands were playing, blind men were hawking about papers, containing wonderful news, fair ladies in mantillas were going to mass, others were engaged in the feminine occupation of shopping; the streets through which I passed were thronged with a busy, happy-looking crowd. Numerous carriages were already passing along the Calle Mayor, in some of which were officers in uniform, who were driving in the direction of the palace. I had but a momentary view of this magnificent edifice, perhaps the most noble of all royal residences. The Legation stands in the Plaza del Oriente, and fronts the eastern side of the palace. I found the minister installed in very comfortable quarters. He was at his toilette when I arrived, and was shown into the *chancellerie;* nor was I disposed to find the

time long, as I took my post of observation at the window, and looked at the solid, colossal work of the architect, Sagneti, which I have been told was twenty-nine years in building.

My reception by Count —— was most kind, and even paternal. He spoke of my father with all the respect which his character deserved—of my dear mother, with enthusiasm. He had known her when she formed one of the chief ornaments of the court at Naples. He spoke of Caroline's husband, my well-beloved brother-in-law, as a rising young man, likely to become distinguished as a statesman. In short, I found myself completely at home; and some slight feelings of *heimweh*, which, in spite of my Spanish mania, have now and then come over me since I left, vanished as by magic. The count is slight in person, infirm in health, with one of those countenances which the Spaniards call *simpático*. He seems precisely as my father described him—severe in requiring the strict observance of their duties from his subordinates, yet of an indulgent disposition, not inclined to cavil at the faults or follies of youth, and though fond of retirement himself, ready to encourage them in the enjoyment of all the pleasures of society natural to their age. As the secretary of Legation is absent in Vienna, he told me that, for the present at least, I could have an apartment in the Legation, and presented me with a key, by means of which I can make my exit and entrée independently, at all hours, through a back door leading to the garden. "For I know by experience, my dear count," said he, "that *surveillance* is not particularly agreeable to young men of your age. At seven you will always find a place at my table, but no remarks made if you do not occupy it, except on extraordinary occasions, which, let me warn you, frequently occur in Madrid (though that, I confess, sounds something of an Irish bull), your business hours are from ten to four, generally speaking. But now, as your father's friend, you will, I am sure, excuse me if I give you some advice upon one subject. I know by his letter that you have obtained your appointment more as an advantage to your social position than with any view of becoming a diplomatist. This is an error. Diplomacy is a noble profession, but were it less so than I truly consider it, you will lead but a useless life, and fritter away the best period of your existence, if you adopt a profession without striving to excel in it. Endeavor to understand its duties. Make yourself master of the political condition of this extraordinary country. If, instead of a diplomatist, you had become a village schoolmaster, I should still say: Put your heart in whatever you have undertaken, for whoever does not gain knowledge loses it. There is no standing still. My library is small, but full of the best books upon these subjects, all of which are at your disposal. You will have much spare time, our relations with Spain being unimportant, compared with those of other nations—of England or France for example; but at present, in the absence of the secretary, you will have sufficient occupation; and I am mistaken if you do not speedily discover the importance of applying yourself earnestly to obtain information in all that concerns your present profession; whether you are destined to become a mere man of fortune, living on your paternal acres, or to continue in your present career. I do not mean to read you a lecture, but I earnestly desire to remove from your mind the idea of using your profession merely as a means of obtaining an entrée into certain aristocratic circles."

I thanked the minister warmly, the more so that I felt he was right, and that my object had been a very unworthy one. He insisted, however, upon giving me a few days of complete holiday, examined my letters of introduction, advised me to go to my banker's and to deliver my letters to Mr. M——, an Irish gentleman, of whom he spoke in high terms, and who he assured me knew more of Madrid than any man in town—and desired me to return at four o'clock, when he was going out, and would introduce me to several of his colleagues.

When I saw Don José Salamanca, I wondered at my hardihood in calling him *my* banker! Some day I shall give you an account of this extraordinary man, one of the most striking characters in this or in any other country—daring, energetic, spurning all obstacles—a millionnaire at one time, at others, *criblé de dettes*—a man of business, a man of pleasure, royal in his expenditure—according to his enemies, unprincipled—according to all, generous; sometimes living like a prince, at others hidden in a garret and escaping for his life—full of talents, inexhaustible in resources—a kind of practical Monte Christo, only that his resources lie in his own abilities, rather than in any hidden treasure.

But at present it is with his *personnel* alone that I have to do. I found a tall, gentlemanlike man of a certain age—extremely handsome, rather gravely dressed—with a simple, frank expression of countenance, a quantity of brown hair very negligently dressed, and falling a good deal over his forehead; good penetrating eyes, and almost a boyish smile. How my Irish friend, to whom I have not yet introduced you, laughed afterwards, when I gave him my first impressions of Salamanca! He received me with great kindness, and when we had despatched our business, entered into conversation with me. His manners are extremely agreeable; and as he also knows my father, and even received some service from him during his residence in Paris, we have many subjects in common. He made me many offers of service, apparently sincere, offered to introduce me to the Casino, to the *tertulia* of the Señora B——l, and invited me to dine with him on Sunday next, besides putting his house, in general terms, *à mi disposicion*. His *study* was beautifully fitted up, even luxuriously, but in excellent taste. Fine paintings on the walls, and choice books on the shelves of his library. We smoked a cigar and separated, I will not say *mutually* pleased, but will answer for the good impression made upon myself.

I then carried my letter to Mr. M——, who lives in the Plazuela de la Villa, rendered illustrious, as he afterwards told me, by the ancient house of *los Lujanes*, where the tower is still standing in which Francis I. was confined after the battle of Pavia. I like the *grandiose* air of the streets in the vicinity of the palace, and even prefer them to the more modern and commodious part of Madrid. I was fortunate in finding Mr. M—— at home. He received me at first rather coldly, for like all Irishmen educated in London, he has adopted some of that stiffness and formality which characterize the Englishman in his first reception of strangers. But he thawed rapidly, and frankly confessed to me, that he is so much bored by constant letters of introduction, that in self-defence he has adopted a system of reserve until he knows something of the individual presented. In age he appears about forty; tall, and athletic in figure, with a true Irish face; fair hair, blue eyes, and a remarkably good-humored expression of countenance. Slightly sarcastic, or he would not be a free-born Briton, but good-natured *au fond*. He has resided in Andalusia for five years, in Madrid for ten, was educated at an English University, is full of English prejudices, but likes the Spanish character, though he swears against their government as a matter of course. He saw Caroline when she was presented in London, and declares she was so handsome, he supposed her to be an English girl, and was sorry to find she had an outlandish name. He paid me the compliment of saying that I resembled her very much.

M—— lives like a man in easy circumstances, has a comfortable bachelor's establishment, modelled as closely as possible upon an English one; keeps horses, has an English groom, an English butler, and an old Spanish housekeeper, who reigns paramount in the household. He, however, employs a French cook, who has orders to serve up every thing *à l'Anglaise*, which must be excruciating to the feelings of Monsieur Adolphe. He was less profuse in his offers of service than the banker, but told me in a few words that he would gladly be of use to me, and also finished by inviting me to dinner, which invitation I declined for that day, thinking myself in duty bound to keep company with my chief.

At four o'clock I returned to the Legation, at the door of which I found a handsome ambassadorial-looking equipage, with a couple of beautiful bright bays, and well-appointed servants, with the —— cockades. The minister was in the act of drawing on his gloves, and I received commendation for my punctuality, which praise had all the charm of novelty.

We drove in the first instance to the French Embassy, an old palace belonging to the Dukes of Ossuna, known as the Palace of Benavente, where the duchess of that name, grandmother of the present duke, resided, and where, as Count A—— told me, she used to reunite all the distinguished society of Madrid. "Nothing," he added, "could be more charming than these tertulias; no one was ever more graceful or more witty than the duchess, no one more generous and splendid. She was also very eccentric and independent. I remember her reading a lesson in her own way to the French ambassador. At a ball which he gave her, the champagne came to a close before the entertainment was over. A few evenings after, his excellency came to visit the duchess, in great state, with a numerous suite. To the surprise of his servants, large pails of champagne were brought from the stable, and set before the horses! But here we are at the Cuesta de la Vega, and on the extremity of this hill stands the Embassy, almost in the country, as you will observe."

We passed through several splendidly furnished salons, commanding from the windows the most beautiful and extensive view of the surrounding country that you can imagine, bounded by the mountains of Guadarrama and Somosierra, their summits even now crowned with snow. We were shown into the cabinet of the Marquis Turgot, who received us with much politeness, and seemed to me a very worthy representative of his Imperial Majesty, and a dignified *doyen* of the diplomatic corps. He and the count had a long political discussion, which my ignorance of persons and politics here prevented me from taking much interest in. They spoke of General Lersundy, the present president of the council, and the probabilities of a change of the ministry before long. I heard him commended as an honest man and a good general, but doubts expressed of his being able to cope with the difficulties of his present position. I learned that Calderon de la Barca had been sent for, to assume the post of minister of state, but that, being at the present time in Washington, where he is minister, he may not arrive for some time. I liked his name, at all events, which recalled my northern reveries to my mind, and my favorite passages of *La Vida es sueño.* I looked down from the western window, and saw the Manzanares creeping along like a silver snake, its banks bordered by apparently all the white linen in Madrid, in such prodigious quantities, that the country around seemed like a vast bleaching-field. From the contemplation of this sovereignty of washerwomen, I was called by the marquis, who kindly proposed to present me "à ses dames," and we followed him into the reception room of Madame la Marquise. A fine-looking woman she is, with features strongly marked, and full of intelligence; nothing common or trifling in her appearance, but such as the daughter of a marshal of France should be. A pretty daughter was with her, who looked so young, I was surprised to hear her addressed *Madame*. She was pleased to compliment me on my Parisian accent, and gave me a gracious invitation to her soirées, of which I shall not be slow to profit.

Italian Legation comes next. Hotel of the Marquis de Biario Sforza—high-sounding Milanese name. A pleasant, gentlemanly old man, three ladylike-looking daughters, perfectly English-looking; work, books, and music scattered about the room—a good many morning visitors, whose names I did not hear—amongst others, some young men of the French Legation, who have promised to show me the lions. We left cards at the English Legation, which is close to the palace of the queen mother. His lordship is absent, but we afterwards met Mr. O., the present chargé d'affaires, a tall, fair, calm, good-looking type of the Anglo-Saxon race. We called at the Austrian Legation, who occupy part of an ancient building called "the House of the Seven Chimneys," at the corner of the Calle de las Ynfantas, now belonging to the Marquis of Somernelos, with a fine old garden, filled with fruit and flowers. Count E—— was from home, but we were received by the countess in her boudoir; pretty and *piquante*, and very spirituelle, belonging to a noble French family, and speaking half a dozen languages in perfection. The Russian minister, who lives in the Calle de Alcalá, was from home—so were several others. I was glad to meet your old friend the Danish minister, Mr. D'Alborgo del Primo, looking as young as I recollect him when I first returned from college for the holidays. He is now Baron del Asilo, a title which he has well earned by the generous protection which he has afforded in his house to a vast number of political refugees. Amongst others, Salamanca was hidden there for weeks; and Count A—— assures me that there is scarcely a public man who has not, at some period or another of his political career, had to escape for his life, and keep in hiding until the storm has passed by.

At length all the diplomatic visits were performed, and it was nearly dark when we went to drive in the Prado. But enough for to-night, I should say for this morning. To my northern family, soft slumbers and bright dreams.

CHAPTER III.

A ride—Gate of Alcalá—Beauty of the climate—Dress of the Spanish ladies—Of the gentlemen—The Duchess of Alva—Obelisk in honor of the Queen—The Salon—The crowd—The sunset.

September —.

We drove in the Prado, as I told you yesterday; but to-day, having procured a good horse, I rode out with Mr. M——, the best of *cicerones*. The heat being intense, few were in the Prado when we rode out at five o'clock. My horse, a black, long-tailed Andalusian, gentle and spirited, I preferred even to the handsome and powerful English bay of my friend. We rode down the beautiful *Calle de Alcalá*, a street of palaces, leading on one side to the Prado, on the other to the Fuente Castellana—the two great promenades of Madrid—and terminating in the graceful and beautiful gate of Alcalá, beyond which is the high road leading to Aragon and Catalonia. This gate, a magnificent triumphal arch, was built in the reign of Charles III., to commemorate his arrival in the "*heroica villa.*" The architect was Don Francisco Sabatini. It has five entries; the three middle ones arches, those at the extremities of a rectangular form. It is adorned with beautiful Ionic pillars, the models of the capitals taken from those by Michel Angelo, in the Roman capitol. Above the cornice is a frontispiece with the royal arms. The gate itself is seventy feet high, built of the finest granite, and on either side is the inscription Rege Carolo III., Anno 1778.

But my Andalusian is curvetting, with every intention of showing off himself and his rider to the best advantage in the Prado; the graver English steed shows signs of impatience, and leaving the regal gate, we ride down to the magnificent fountain of Cybele, where the goddess, seated in her lofty chariot drawn by lions, is surrounded by *aguadores*, filling their barrels from the limpid basin, into which the sparkling waters are gracefully falling. Here making our way between hundreds of gay carriages, now pouring down the Calle de Alcalà, and filled with *élégantes*, we direct our course to the Castilian fountain, on the right.

The sky was of a bright turquoise blue, perfectly cloudless. The day, which had been sultry, was now freshened by a gentle breeze. This beautiful *paseo*, called "*Las delicias de Ysabel Segunda*," had been freshly watered. Numbers of pretty girls, in their graceful amazones, galloped by on horseback, with their attendant *caballeros*. Few actual mantillas were to be seen. They are too warm for this season, and are besides confined to morning costume. Their place was supplied either by light Parisian bonnets, or by a still prettier head-dress; a veil of black lace or tulle thrown over the head, fastened by gold pins, and generally thrown very far back; the magnificent hair beautifully dressed. Certainly this appeared to me the prettiest head-dress in the world, showing to the greatest advantage the splendid eyes, fine hair, and expressive features of the wearers. I was astonished at the richness of the toilettes, and M—— assured me that luxury in dress is now carried here to an extraordinary height; and to show you that I am not so blinded by admiration of what is Spanish as not to see faults, at least when they are pointed out to me, I will allow that

French women have a better idea of the fitness of things, and that there is an absence of simplicity in the dress of the Spanish women, which is out of taste. I allude chiefly to those who were on foot. The rich silks and brocades which trail along the Prado, hiding pertinaciously the exquisitely small feet of the wearers, would, in Paris, be confined to the *élégantes* who promenade the Bois de Boulogne or the Champs Elysées in carriages. Here the wife and daughter of the poorest shopkeeper disdain chintz and calico; nothing short of silk or velvet is considered decorous, except within doors. But having made this confession, I must add, that the general effect is charming, and as for beauty both of face and figure, especially the latter, surely no city in the world can show such an amount of it.

As for the dress of the men, upon which I can speak with greater confidence, they are, in my opinion, the best dressed men in Europe—equally removed from a certain *petit maitreism* observable among Frenchmen, and the assumed negligence of Englishmen. As we rode slowly along from the Puerta de Recoletas to the Fuente Castellana, my companion told me that this beautiful Paseo has only recently been completed—that it was begun in the last years of the reign of Ferdinand VII., slowly continued by various *corregidores* (mayors), until it was inaugurated by the Marquis de Pontejos, under the title of "Delicias de Ysabel Segunda;" that the beautiful fountain of the "Swan," taken from the cloister of the Convent of San Felipe el Real, was placed there by Col. Don Luis Campos; that when the Marquis of Santa Cruz became *corregidor* of Madrid, the central passage for carriages was opened, the walks traced out, and the obelisk which terminates it, constructed—the trees were planted, until gradually the gardens and labyrinths which embellish it transformed the most arid and disagreeable part of the environs of Madrid into one of the most charming promenades in Europe.

I stopped M—— to ask him the name of a pretty woman, to whom he took off his hat. She was lying back in a small open carriage with beautiful horses, the smallest of English jockeys, and servants in the French imperial livery. She was dressed in the most perfect of French toilettes, and the whole turn-out was irreproachable. Half a dozen young men were galloping by the portière of her carriage. "That," said M——, "is the Duchess of Alva, sister of the Empress of France, the greatest *élégante* in Madrid. The Palace of Siria, belonging to the ducal family of Alva, is one of the finest in the city. It was built nearly a century ago, by James Stewart Fitzjames, third Duke of Berwick and Siria, under the direction of Rodriguez, a celebrated architect. The interior is magnificent, and it has been lately re-furnished with, I am told, extraordinary splendor." "Do you not visit the duchess?" "I leave my card at the palace occasionally, but she receives no one. It is three years since I have been admitted. But it is almost a royal residence. I particularly admire the chapel, beautifully paved with marble, and the walls painted with frescoes by Galiano. There is also an immense terraced garden, filled with flowers, and fountains, and marble statues, disposed with a great deal of taste, and a fine gallery of paintings collected in Italy by the father of the present duke." "But why does not the Duchess receive? From pride?" "Not at all. She is as simple in her manners, and as free from pride and affectation as a child. I must do the Spanish aristocracy the justice to say, that whatever their pride of family may be, it is never offensively shown. You will find that the grandees here receive very little, and I will leave it to your own philosophy to discover the reasons, when you become acquainted with

Madrid society." "How superb the Medina-Cœli looks to-day!" said a young German who had joined us. "What a fine specimen of an Andalusian! What jet-black eyes and hair, what white and glittering teeth, what deep-red roses on her cheeks and lips! What a figure, as she leans back in her carriage, with rather a disdainful expression, and a curl upon her coral lip! What a brigand's bride she would make, drawing the trigger of a pistol, or sword in hand like the maid of Zaragossa!" "How amazingly eloquent!" said M——, "why do you not join her?" "I prefer adoring the young duchess at a distance. For humble mortals like me, the Countess de V——s is more approachable. See her walking there, so daintily—so charmingly dressed from head to foot, with such soft eyes, and what a smile!" added he, as the little condesa turned her eyes in our direction, and acknowledged the obeisance of her devoted admirer.

We stopped to look at the obelisk, erected in commemoration of the birth of the present queen, and the fountain of the Sphinxes, from whose bronze mouths streams of clear water were gushing. Many carriages were standing in the circular space winding round the obelisk and fountain, whilst their owners were sauntering in the alleys of the parterre; but as the generality were now moving towards the Prado, we retraced our steps, and followed the multitude. Here also the Madrileños owe a debt of gratitude to Charles III., by whom the vast tract of uncultivated ground, now forming the Prado, was levelled, planted with trees, and adorned with fountains. The Prado begins at the convent of Atocha, and passing in front of the gate of that name, continues in the direction of the Calle de Alcalá, which it crosses, and extends as far as the gate of Recoletas. One wide *paseo* is destined for carriages; one on either side planted with fine trees, for foot passengers. From the street called the Carrera de San Géronimo to that of Alcalá, the space grows wider, and the Paseo is known by the name of the *Salon*. The whole promenade, with the beautiful gardens and fine buildings, that meet the eye in every direction —the noble streets that emerge from it, the beautiful fountains that adorn it, is certainly one of the finest of which any city can boast.

At the entrance of the Salon, fronting the Carrera de San Géronimo, is the fountain of Neptune; in the midst of the basin, the god stands upon his chariot, in the form of a shell, drawn by sea-horses; dolphins and tritons sporting around him; a fine work, by Don Pascual de Mena, as M—— informed me. Further on is the noble fountain of Apollo, crowned with a statue of that god, and adorned with four other statues, representing the Seasons, fronting the four cardinal points, the water, by an ingenious contrivance, flowing from one basin to the other, in measured cadence, in honor of the musical divinity. One circumstance must be remarked upon and commended, namely, the perfect order which reigns in these paseos, in the midst of apparent confusion; due to the strict watchfulness of the mounted guard, who ride up and down, and prevent the slightest attempt on the part of the coachmen to break the line.

An immense double file of carriages extended nearly to the church of Atochia; but the Salon itself, the great resort of those who come in search of amusement, was crowded like any London rout, and offered, certainly, one of the most curious and brilliant spectacles I ever beheld. Between the rows of carriages were hundreds of young men on horseback, many riding close to the carriages, which, owing to the crowd, went at a footfall. The middle of the Salon was thronged with an immense crowd of people, of every age, sex, and rank. Multitudes of beautiful girls, with the graceful lace veil, were walking slowly up and down, gracefully recognizing their acquaintances with a little movement of the fan, as necessary an appendage to the dress of a fair Castilian as her gown or shoes. Companies of young men were enjoying the agreeable spectacle of so much beauty; and if I do not mention the mothers and chaperons, do not imagine them absent; for no Spanish girl ever leaves her house alone, or walks for a moment unattended. But besides the better classes, the whole people of Madrid seemed to be enjoying themselves, and the jacket and *calañes* hat were as common as the well-cut coat and pale kid gloves. Numbers of beautiful children added to the gayety of the scene, and the pasiega nurses, with their babies in long flowing mantles of spotless white, were not the least striking part of the picture. These pasiegas are generally fine specimens of peasant beauty; with bright colored petticoats, trimmed with black velvet, and bands of gold or silver; colored handkerchiefs, and plaits of wonderful hair coming nearly to their feet. The stone benches which are placed all along the Prado, for the accommodation of the tired or lazy, were all taken, as well as long rows of chairs, whose occupants sat talking and fanning themselves, enjoying all the pleasures of society without the stifling atmosphere of a salon within doors.

The setting sun threw a rich glow upon all these varied groups. The sky was, as it usually is in this climate, one vast field of cloudless blue. The hum of human voices, the gayety, the laughter, the shrill cries of the venders of water or bouquets, the sweet perfume of flowers from the neighboring gardens—this mingling of people of all ranks—the beautiful women with their becoming toilettes—the bright coloring of the various dresses—the picturesque costumes of the common people—the handsome uniforms, gay equipages and fine horses; all combine to render this a scene entirely unparalleled in any other country. Hyde Park is a stately promenade for the higher orders. The Champs Elysées is a charming lounge, where one's eyes are fascinated by the sight of the elegant aristocrats, the perfection of whose toilette all the world allows. The Prater of Vienna presents more points in common, but the contrast between the German and Spanish people is too complete to permit any comparison.

The sun had just dipped below the horizon, when we heard at a distance the music of the royal march. The carriages all drew up; the royal guards in their brilliant uniform, escorting three carriages and six, came sweeping round the street of Alcalá, and entered the Salon. Hats were lifted. Ladies in their open carriages stood up, as the young sovereign passed by. She leaned back in an open carriage, smiling and bowing to every one. I saw her but imperfectly, but she seemed a fine-looking woman, with a good expression of countenance. The king sat beside her, with his hat off. His face seemed handsome. They say he is too short, a fault which he shares in common with many of his subjects, the Madrileños especially being generally rather below the middle height, though there are many exceptions. The little Princess of the Asturias, her Majesty's only living child, sat on the knee of her governess, the Marquesa de Povar, and had fallen fast asleep; and I am now going to follow the example of her royal highness.

CHAPTER IV.

Various occupations—The meeting of the aristocracy and the people—Description of the Plaza——The bull-fight—A dinner at my banker's—A ministerial crisis predicted—The Discussion—The Queen—An insight into Spanish hotels.

You must know that, at present, Madrid is, in fashionable parlance, supposed to be *empty*. Of these beautiful young duchesses and countesses, some were taking a drive, as a *parenthesis*, either on their way to France, or to Caramanchel, or other environs of the capital. Many are living out of town, and come in occasionally. In October, it is supposed that the good society begins to pour in once more. No time better then, as M—— remarks, for seeing Madrid. Since I wrote I have been at a bull-fight. I have been at the Casino, I have been at Caramanchel, I have visited the prison of the Saladero. I have studied diplomacy for two hours daily before breakfast. I have been employed in a vast deal of base copying. I have made a number of new acquaintances. I have heard nearly every Spaniard I have met abuse his own country, and have marvelled thereat. I have heard politics discussed till, in self-defence, I have become interested in the state of public affairs, which appear to me to have arrived at a complicated and incomprehensible condition. In a few days I am to have the honor of being presented to her Majesty.

As a *spectacle*, there is, perhaps, nothing in the world equal to a bull-fight. I am not speaking of it in a moral point of view, or as to its influence on the people. No amusement is so ancient in Spain—none so rooted in the hearts of the Spaniards. No government could put down the "corridas de toros;" and within the last twenty years, the daring deeds of the famous Montes, the Cúchares and others, have raised the public enthusiasm for this diversion to a higher pitch than ever. They have been the Keans and Kembles of the "plaza." In former times, these entertainments were celebrated only once or twice a year in the *Plaza Mayor*, and on great occasions; now at least twelve take place annually, chiefly from March to October, and generally on Monday afternoons. For some days previous to the *funcion*, crowds may be seen perusing the handbills where the entertainment is announced, with a programme of the sport to be expected—the names of the owners of the bulls, of the picadores and swordsmen who are to officiate on the occasion. On this one subject there is universal sympathy and union of feeling, and it is said that no dispute ever took place at a bull-fight.

Being invited by Salamanca to accompany him, we drove through the Puerta del Sol, along the Calle de Alcalá, which leads to the *plaza*, as fast as the crowds pouring from every quarter of the city on foot, on horseback, in vehicles of every description, aristocratic and plebeian—berlinas, omnibuses, landaus, &c.—would permit us to go. Impossible to see a more complete blending of interests than exists on these occasions between the people and the aristocracy. The most elegant equipage followed the humblest conveyance: from the manola up to the duchess, there seemed but one feeling of enjoyment and delighted expectation. The queen was not to be present, owing to her situation, but the Ynfante drove down from his palace of San Juan in a state coach, drawn by six mules, and with a well-appointed escort.

The grandeur of the scene within took me by surprise. The immense circular plaza, capable of containing upwards of twelve thousand persons, was entirely filled; the covered boxes by all the beauty and fashion of Madrid, amongst whom the ladies of the foreign ministers were conspicuous; and as every box is appropriated, foreigners who wish to attend these *funciones* must depend upon the *abonnés*. But the most striking part of the scene is the sea of heads on the uncovered benches, rising in gradation to the boxes, of men with jackets and Spanish hats, and women with mantillas and fans and bright-colored dresses. The Manolas, with their flashing eyes; the smart young men with their gay embroidered jackets and bright-colored sashes; the people, in short, in their holiday attire, with their handsome, good-humored faces; one immense dense mass, sit there prepared to admire, to criticise, to applaud, to condemn, and to enjoy themselves with the most perfect and sovereign independence.

Upon a signal from the *corregidor*, the alguazils rode into the arena—a strange-looking reminiscence of former times—dressed in black, with short cloaks, Spanish hats with nodding plumes, black silk stockings with knee breeches, somewhat burlesque in their appearance, and looking like caricatures of Philip II. They were mounted upon noble horses, which pranced and reared to the amusement or admiration of the crowd. The gates were thrown open, and the picadores entered on horseback, the matadores and other bull-fighters on foot. Their dresses were truly magnificent; some of green and gold, others of blue and silver, orange and purple, or black and white, with a light scarlet or blue or yellow cloak thrown over the arm. After saluting the Ynfante and the Corregidor, they rode or walked round and round the arena, amidst a low, universal hum of voices from the impatient crowd. Again the gate was thrown open, and a furious bull rushed blindly forward, then stood still to reconnoitre his position. He was a noble-looking brute, as he stood pawing the ground, tearing up the earth, and lashing himself into fury. Suddenly he rushed at one of the picadores, lifted both man and horse from the earth on his horns, and dashed them on the ground. Then the *chulos* came to the assistance of the prostrate picador, embarrassed under the weight of his bleeding horse, but which he soon remounted; shaking their scarlet cloaks in the face of the bull, and leaping over the barrier with extraordinary agility, when within an inch of his horns. In a few minutes seven horses were stretched panting and dying on the arena. This is the barbarous part of the spectacle, as the horses are passive victims. The wonderful skill and agility of the men, and the constant risks they run, keep the interest of the spectators constantly excited. As a mere *chasse*, it is almost equal to our boar-hunts.

This first bull certainly died game, and when the matador gave the final blow, which he did with wonderful skill and coolness, driving the sword up to the hilt in the body of his adversary, the applause was divided between the victor and the vanquished. Heavens, what shouts! what beating of benches! what throwing of hundreds of hats at the feet of the conqueror! How each got back his own, was a matter of wonder to me, as the matador, with a nod of thanks, picked them up and threw them back. Then the dead horses and the dead bull were dragged out swiftly by mules. Sand was sprinkled on the bloody traces, the magnificent band struck up an air from Ernani, and in a few moments another lordly bull made his appearance upon the scene of action.

All were not equally brave. Frequently the bull was hissed by the public, and *banderillas*, sharp arrows containing fireworks, loudly shouted for, and applied to him to increase his fury; upon which the poor brute, maddened by the noise of the crackers, and by the pain of the fire, blindly attacked his adversaries as he roared in savage desperation. When the bull appeared to be an irredeemable poltroon, and no means would avail to induce him to come forward in fair fight, he was finished by the *media luna*, a sharp instrument of a crescent form, fastened to the end of a long pole, with which he was hamstrung, and on falling received the final blow. This is a vulgar finale, and like seeing an ox slaughtered by a butcher. Seven bulls and twelve horses were killed. When calmly written down, it sounds frightfully cruel. I am far from denying that it is so; and I am sure that my mother, who never was present at a bull-fight, and my sisters, who have never been in Spain, would shudder at the idea of attending so barbarous a sport; yet, unless they are different in their feelings from every foreign lady with whom I am acquainted here, they would do so if in Madrid. I looked round now and then, and observed that the most eager and most interested of the spectators in the boxes, were the ladies of the foreign ministers—of course all belonging to different countries. That Spanish women, born and bred to the amusement, should attend bull-fights from habit, I can easily understand; but I was surprised, without pretending to blame them, at observing this *aficion* in German, French—no matter to what country these ladies belonged. As they are perfectly feminine, and I have no doubt would not willingly hurt a fly, I leave it to wiser heads than mine to explain this phenomenon, and only mention it as a proof of the injustice of those who rail against the Spaniards on account of the barbarity of their favorite diversion.

I returned to dine with Salamanca—a bachelor's party, though he is married; but his wife, who is said to be almost a saint from her goodness and charity, and still very handsome, was, I believe, absent. A gay party we had, and a banquet that Lucullus would not have sneered at. I confess that it required a glass or two of sparkling hock to purify my imagination from the remembrance of bulls' horns and blood—of prostrate picadores and gored horses; but the conversation, even more sparkling, was a still more efficacious antidote, and soon banished from my mind these sanguinary ideas, which proved me to be but a tyro in *tauromachia*.

There was a young Andalusian, handsome and witty, whose every word was a *bon mot*. He had none of the strained witticism of a professed sayer of good things, but a natural fund of cleverness and good humor, which seemed to make it impossible for him to say a stupid thing. There was a grave professor, evidently a man of the world, dealing in powerful and polished sarcasm. There was an editor, one of the opposition, who scarcely spoke until his inner man was satisfied, when he launched forth in tremendous diatribes against the government. There was a young grandee, good-natured and gentlemanlike, guiltless of having invented gunpowder. We were in all twelve persons, and did justice, like any honorable jury, to the case under consideration. There was no dissentient voice as to the excellence of the table, on which was collected every imaginable luxury, in or out of season, worthy of the superb gold plate on which they were served. But when the wine had circulated briskly, and the table was piled with a dessert of purple grapes, plums, green figs, melons, every species of fine fruit, and every possible kind of *dulce*, only to be imagined in Spain; and when the servants had withdrawn, then every one spoke at once; every voice was raised in argument, and no one could have believed that such vehement discussions were carried on in reality with perfect good humor. Excellent cigars were handed round by our host, and we were soon enveloped in a mingled cloud of smoke and metaphysics.

Place aux dames! They were first upon the tapis. What anecdotes! What gossip! What scandal! What stories of husbands hoodwinked, of hair-breadth adventures, of lovers' escapes! and as the heroes of half of these adventures were political and public men, the transition was easy to the politics of the day. After coffee, we adjourned to the Casino, the fasionable club of Madrid, where I was presented to several characters of note, and invariably received with that cordiality which all strangers find so great a charm in Spanish manner. In the various groups of men who were collected together, and talking eagerly, the same style of conversation was carried on as at dinner; gossip and politics. All seemed to be discontented more or less with the present state of things. A ministerial crisis was predicted. The conduct of the present cabinet was freely discussed. Men in power were as openly accused of robbery and corruption, as women of want of virtue. Spain painted by the Spaniards would present but a sorry spectacle. I allude chiefly to those young political aspirants, whether employés or *cesantes*, as men out of office are called, who wish for any change, in hopes of either bettering their situation, or of obtaining office. This habit of wholesale abuse seems to have become a kind of epidemic, and entirely contrasts with that noble, chivalrous character which seems to belong by right to the true Spaniard.

I ventured to express my opinion to a clever young senator, the Marquis of ——, the moderation and good sense of whose remarks had frequently struck me. "You are, unfortunately, quite right," said he. "These are the results, first, of long civil war, and then of constant ministerial changes, which lead every young man to hope that his turn for taking a part in the government may come next. This place-hunting mania is the ruin of our country. Personal interest has taken the place of patriotism. Accusations against men in power are made without a shadow of foundation; and the multitude are always ready to give credit to those high-sounding declamations which they believe to be prompted by a genuine love of liberty, and a desire to promote the interests of the people. Thank heaven, there are many noble exceptions; but in all countries, men of sense and moderation make themselves less heard than the noisy malcontents and declaimers." "One thing more still surprises me," said I. "The queen, so young and inoffensive, for whom so many swords were drawn in her childhood, who, I am told, is generous and charitable even to a fault, and royal in her munificence, —how has she become a mark of calumny, so that even the false accusations against her which stain the columns of the Times, hardly excite indignation?" "You are judging," said the marquis, "from the surface of things. All the wise and good men of this country are indignant at these base attacks against our sovereign. These people still adore their generous queen. But there is a party in Spain who endeavor systematically to undermine all monarchical institutions. Finding that a vain attempt (for Spain is essentially monarchical); unable to destroy the principle, they have turned their attacks against the person of the monarch, and if they cannot destroy monarchy, they would at least degrade the sovereign. These infamous stories are carefully prepared, insidiously propagated, and a superstructure of guilt raised upon any slight imprudence natural to a young princess, who a queen at thirteen, after an education interrupted by civil wars, was not endowed with a supernatural insight into character.

"Of the truth or falsehood of these accusations we can judge as well as the public. We can see that, in her public conduct, her Majesty is a model of decorum. They can see no further. If these stories are propagated by her servants, what reliance can be placed on them? The correspondent of the "Times" was never admitted within the palace walls; therefore in all that he relates he can only draw upon his own corrupt imagination. But if these stories are repeated by any young man who pretends to be the queen's favorite, can he be worthy of credit? and is the queen to be denied that justice which we extend to the lowest of her sex?"

"Yet I well remember," said I, "after her Majesty's attempted assassination by the monster Merino, reading an account of the universal enthusiasm with which she was greeted at her first appearance in public." "Yes, there the heart of the people spoke. Every sentiment of chivalry and loyalty was aroused within the breasts of the whole nation. The moment that was chosen for this horrible attempt—the sublime courage and charity shown by the queen—every thing concurred to awaken that loyalty, which then indeed had hardly slumbered.

"I remember that day well. The queen was leaving the royal chapel, at the head of the grand staircase, her face beaming with happiness, hardly lifting her eyes from the face of the infant, whom she had just consigned to the arms of its governess. Her dress was truly gorgeous; but it was easy to see that, under her royal robes, her heart was beating with maternal feeling, and with no sentiment of gratified vanity. Yet at the moment when the miserable suppliant approached, and kneeling down, tendered her a petition, she stretched out her hand to receive it.

"It was like a flash of lightning. The whole passed in a moment. She was seen to put her hand to her heart, stagger to the wall, and all who were near her, could see the blood flowing from the wound. The first words she spoke were, 'My child! my Isabel!' The confusion that ensued was indescribable. Swords were drawn. The murderer was seized in a moment, and with difficulty saved from being instantly torn in pieces. The multitude swayed to and fro, like a living sea. I saw a tall halberdier lift up the child above the mass of heads, that the queen might see it was uninjured, and then she was led away fainting, amidst cries and tears, mingled with groans and execrations upon the cowardly assassin. It is well known that when she recovered from her swoon, she exclaimed anxiously, 'Let him not be hurt on my account;' and it was with the greatest difficulty that she could be persuaded to consent to his execution.

"That day was held like a jubilee, and it was soon discovered that the regicide had no accomplices, but was possessed of a solitary mania. I saw him led to execution, commenting upon various indifferent matters as he went along; observing, for instance, that a church was off the perpendicular, and was unsafe. He expressed no regret for his crime, but much surprise upon learning that the blow had not been fatal. I was present at a horrid scene—the burning of his body. The executioner refused to perform the office—said it was not his business; so several respectable individuals were forced to take it upon themselves. His head, which had fallen off, was kicked, shudderingly, into the flames, and his ashes scattered to the wind. It was a frightful spectacle.

"The day the queen drove out for the first time after all this was past, with the little princess in her arms, through the streets towards the church of Atocha, to return thanks for her miraculous escape, you would have thought that the whole people were possessed by one general madness. Their shouts rent the air. The guards could not keep them from pressing round the carriages. The ringing of the bells from every church and convent—the loud music of the military bands—nothing could drown these wild and joyful acclamations, and it seemed as if every heart in Spain joined in the Te Deums' offered up in gratitude for the queen's recovery.

"It is since then that calumny has been slowly doing its work, and with that effect which calumny never fails to produce; that is, leaving an impression like the slimy trail which the venomous serpent leaves on the flowers over which it crawls. But I trust she may outlive it. Youth and generosity are popular attributes, especially in princes!"

CHAPTER V.

Fall of the Ministry and formation of a new Cabinet—Reunion of Señora B——, —Plaza del Oriente—Puerta del Sol—Marquesa of Alcañices—Buenavista and the Retiro: its former grandeur—The Prado: its Palaces—Plaza de las Cortes.

THE Lersundy ministry has fallen. The new minister of state arrived a few days ago, and, it is said, will continue to occupy the same post in the new cabinet. Sartorius, count of San Luis, *dit on*, will be president of the council; the Marquis of Gerona, minister of grace and justice; Don Esteban Collantes, of *Fomento;* the Marquis of Molins, better known by his family name of Roca de Togores, minister of the navy; General Blaser, minister of war; and Don Felix Domenech, minister of the treasury.

After a day or two of suspense, during which every other topic was laid aside as comparatively insignificant, the cabinet was formed, and now, according to custom, is criticised—matter for a long dispatch from my chief. All the world is talking politics more than ever, and discussing the characters of the new ministry. I think this kind of discussion never ceases except in church, and during the "small hours" of the night. The liberty of the press is as nothing compared to the invaluable privilege of liberty of the tongue. That the Spaniards enjoy to its fullest extent. That the Conde de

San Luis is no ordinary man, is evident. His friends adore, his enemies abhor him.

The only one of the ministers I have yet seen, is Don Esteban Collantes, who occupied a place in the last cabinet, and whom I met at a tertulia given by the Señora B——, a celebrated beauty, but who now seems to occupy herself more with politics than with intrigues of a softer description. She is still very handsome, her figure perfect, and her manners agreeable. Her tertulia consisted only of men, none of whom arrived until one o'clock. Nothing could exceed the ease and laissé-aller of the society. They came in and went out without sign or salutation; smoked, lounged, talked, or were silent, as best suited their inclination; some even fell asleep, the less astonishing that the hostess does not open her doors till after midnight. As I entered, I caught a glimpse of a fair vision, in the form of a very young and lovely girl, niece, I am told, of Mme. B——, but who does not assist at these reunions.

The extreme freedom of the conversation, in a society composed of men of every party, particularly of members of the opposition, was original and amusing. No sort of restraint was imposed by the presence of a member of the cabinet. On the contrary, this circumstance seemed to render the conversation more piquante. "I cannot imagine," said Mr. de ——, "how a conspiracy is ever carried through in Spain: for rather than not retail the news, a Spaniard would mention it before the very persons conspired against." "It is precisely for that reason," said G——, "that these plans succeed. So many false reports are got up, that no one believes any thing he hears, and when a truth ekes out, it shares the fate of falsehood. For instance, a report is circulated that an outbreak will occur on a certain day. The government get word of it, precautions are taken, and nothing occurs. Then every one laughs and says, "Nothing happens in Spain which is predicted." But meanwhile the plot which has been smothered continues to gain ground. The most minute circumstances concerning it are detailed—the plans of the conspirators are publicly spoken of, but no one believes in the truth of these rumors. Precisely at the moment when no one believes it, and when the government is unprepared for it, it breaks out. It had been true all the while, smouldering like a concealed fire, checked by a few precautionary measures, and known more or less to every one, because every thing is known in Madrid; but those who should have been better informed remained incredulous, because they had so often found themselves deceived. Then, when the blaze breaks out, everybody says, "I expected it." This is not the fact. Everybody had heard of it, but amidst the mass of truth and falsehood, no one could discern fact from fable, and no one felt sure of what was about to occur, but those who were positive agents in the affair. I have seen this sort of thing happen a hundred times.

"In France it is different. Police and spies mean something in that country. There is less liberty of tongue, as you call it, and if such conversations as we are indulging in to-night were to take place in any salon in Paris, half the company would be arrested by daybreak. We have no spies here, and besides, in fact, half of this talk means nothing." "And the other half?" When reduced to very small dimensions, by depriving it of the dilution of nonsense and braggadocio, which form its principal ingredients, there is no doubt to be found a small modicum of reality in the centre. But here comes chocolate, a sign that it must be three o'clock! I received a cordial invitation from the hostess to repeat my visit, with an assurance that the house was at my disposal.

The Plaza del Oriente, where we live, is in my opinion one of the finest parts of the city, though said to have been in former days one of the bleakest and most disagreeable, and I can believe that in winter the situation may be somewhat exposed to the piercing air from the snow-capped Guadarramas. It forms a semicircle of fine buildings fronting the palace. In the centre is a garden or *glorieta* as it is called, of an elliptic form, raised somewhat above the level of the *plaza*, planted with fruit trees, and filled with flowers of every color, and of the most delicious fragrance. All around it is a broad walk, bordered by trees, and terminated by forty-four collosal statues, representing the monarchs of Spain —executed in the reign of Philip V.—designed to ornament the roof of the palace, consequently out of place in their present position. There are the kings of the Gothic line, Astolfo, Theodoric, &c.—the monarchs of the Asturian race, beginning with Don Pelayo. Ferdinand and Isabella, of course, occupy their appropriate place amongst these colossal representations of sovereignty.

A lofty pedestal stands in the middle of the *glorieta*, with inscriptions purporting that Doña Ysabel Segunda erected that monument "for the glory of the arts, and for the adornment of the Capital;" and one of the basso relievos represents Philip IV. investing the painter Velasquez with the Order of Santiago. Four pedestals, with large bronze lions, stand at the four angles, and two fountains at the base, each with the statue of a river, represented by an old man pouring water into an urn.

But the crowning beauty of the monument is the equestrian bronze statue of Philip IV., which was brought here from the Buen Retiro, and is the work of the Florentine artist Pedro Lacca, as may be seen by an inscription on the horse. The proud attitude of the noble animal, the dignified air of the rider, and the perfect finish of the work in its minútest details, render it one of the most remarkable of modern equestrian statues.

I made these observations at an undue hour this morning; for at six o'clock, M—— presented himself at my door, and insisted that *bon gré, mal gré*, I should rise and take a walk. An indefatigable pedestrian, and scorning the Madrid system of turning night into day, he would take no excuse, and the morning air was so fresh and balmy, that I forgave him before we had reached la Puerta del Sol. We were, besides, fortified by two cups of foaming chocolate, which the respectable Doña Andrea, housekeeper or *ama de llaves* (mistress of the keys) of Count A—— insisted on our partaking of, before starting on our expedition. She herself in all the dignity of a mantilla, followed by a small girl with a large basket, had already returned from market.

The *Puerta del Sol*, the great forms of animate life in Madrid, was crowded even at this early hour, though not by the class of cloak loungers who bask there in the sun at mid-day. Certainly it is neither spacious nor handsome, nor worthy to be styled "The Gate of the Sun," which name, my *cicerone* informed me, was bestowed upon it in consequence of an image of that great luminary having been painted upon an ancient castle which stood there in the 16th century. Its advantage, I presume, consists in its being central; as it is in fact formed by the conflux of the principal streets in Madrid —the Calle Mayor, that of Alcalá, Carretas, San Gerónimo, Montera, Carmen and Arenal.

Fronting it to the west, is the Church of Buen Suceso, a poor and unimposing edifice, on which is placed a clock, illuminated at night, serving to show the *flaneurs* who spend their time there in hearing the news and gossip of the day. How many hours they have wasted in that employment!

We passed several palaces of the grandees, almost all of which are distinguished by an ancient and massive appearance; amongst others, that of the Counts of Oñate, an immense building, dating back to the 16th century, from whose principal balcony the kings of Spain used in former days to view the processions as they passed up the Calle Mayor.

We passed along the Calle de Alcalá, a true street of palaces. I admired, amongst, others, that of the Marquis de Casa Riera, a rich banker. It is a splendid house, built more than half a century ago, as a dowry-house for the Duchess of Abrantes, and called at that time *La Casa de los alfileres* (pins), alluding to its being given for her grace's pin-money. After her time, it was occupied by the Russian ambassador, *Latischeff*; and ultimately bought by the present proprietor, who has improved and embellished it, adding to the beautiful and extensive gardens, which we could only admire imperfectly through windows cut in the wall bounding it towards the Calle de Alcalá.

The house of another banker, the Señor Santamarca, has a rich and opulent look, and overtops the palace of the Marquis of Alcañices, situated at the end of the street, and turning the corner of the Prado. But the latter has the interest of antiquity to recommend it, having been built in the 16th century, upon that vast scale in which the nobles of former days constructed their houses, each forming a small world within itself; with innumerable suites of rooms—chapel-gardens, &c. M—— tells me that the marquesa is one of the most beautiful women in Madrid, daughter of the late Marquesa de Santa-Cruz, mistress of the robes of her majesty, and grand-daughter of the Duchess of Benavente, of whom he related to me an anecdote, forming a good *pendant* to the pails of champagne When playing at cards one night with a foreign ambassador, his excellency dropped a piece of gold, and took up a candle to search for it—upon which she coolly took up a parcel of bank-notes that lay beside her, lighted them, and helped him to search for his missing coin. Imagine what a piece of civil contempt!

To the left of the street, standing upon an eminence, is a remarkable building, the Palace of Buenavista, now the War Department, but originally intended for an abode of almost royal luxury. Built by the famous Duchess of Alva, a court-beauty of the days of Charles IV., celebrated alike for her beauty, splendor and enormous wealth; she and her husband, the Marquis of Villafranca, directed the construction of the palace, and bought up a vast extent of surrounding land, with the intention of laying out gardens and orchards upon a corresponding scale of magnificence.

But two conflagrations broke out during the construction of the palace—the duchess and her husband died—the town of Madrid bought the property from their heirs, and bestowed it upon Godoy, Prince of Peace. At the fall of the favorite, it passed successively into different hands. It was occupied by Espartero during his regency; afterwards by the Turkish ambassador, Fuad Effendi, and is now the department of the minister of war. The views from the balconies, commanding all the Prado, Retiro, the Calle de Alcala &c., must be beautiful and extensive, sufficiently so to justify the appellation of Buenavista, bestowed upon it by the duchess.

We continued our walk to the Retiro, and entered by the gate of La Glorieta, close to that of Alcalá. We wandered for hours amongst these beautiful groves and gardens, occupied at this time of the day chiefly by nurses and children, and a few early risers who had the good taste to prefer the delicious air of the morning to the heated atmosphere of the afternoon, when these walks are filled with a fashionable crowd, previous to the hours when it is alone considered correct to appear in the Prado or Fuente Castellana.

I especially admired the beautiful garden called the *Parterre*, filled with roses of every variety—with jasmine, heliotrope, violets, and flowers of almost overpowering fragrance We walked by the great tank of water, on the opposite side of which are the private gardens of her majesty. This tank is sufficiently deep for little boats, several of which are kept in the Chinese boat-house fronting the lake, for the use of the royal family. At present, however, it was abandoned to a flock of white ducks—and a number of pretty children were amusing themselves by feeding them with bread. Round the lake are broad walks for the public in general—and further on are others leading to the site formerly occupied by a famous porcelain manufactory.

Turning from thence to the left, we arrived at a house containing a fine collection of wild beasts, but had not the curiosity to enter—as wild beasts, like civilized men, are the same all the world over. We saw the tower for the telegraph, and the Astronomical Observatory, terminating that part of the Retiro, with its broad and extensive promenades, which includes within their limits the garden, convent, and Church of St. Gerónimo.

The private gardens of her majesty are said to be beautiful and curious, with ponds, fountains, belvedere, &c., but as M—— had not brought the order without which strangers cannot be admitted, we reserved our inspection of them for some future day; and I can assure you, that when we left the Retiro, bythe gate fronting the Calle de San Gerónimo, I was convinced that these gardens are as extensive as they are agreeable.

But I was even more interested by the account which my companion gave me of the Retiro as it was in former times, than by its present beauty; for there is no building or garden in Madrid, of which M—— does not know the history, and there is no city richer in traditions.

He told me how, in the gallant and chivalrous days of Philip IV., and of the famous Conde Duque of Olivares, the king held his court at Buen Retiro, with a magnificence worthy of those palmy days of Spanish monarchy. He described, as if he had lived in those times, all the splendor and beauty of the woods and gardens, the regal dwellings, theatres and temples—the brilliancy of the fetes, masques and entertainments which enlivened this royal retreat; how poetry, music and painting lent fresh charms to these courtly amusements—and how, amongst the *habitués* of the court, figured such names as those of Lope de Vega, Calderon, Quesada, Murillo, and Velasquez. In short, he described Spain as I have imagined it still might be.

From the days of Philip V., the monarchs preferred the delicious gardens of Aranjuez, and the cool breezes of San Ildefonso as retreats from the heat of spring and summer; but still there are many living who can remember the court of the Charleses as held in the Retiro, with all its etiquette of powdered wigs and swords; as well as the Italian Operas executed in its beautiful theatre—the magnificent manufactory of china, destroyed by the English; and who have assisted at the debates of the Cortes, which were held in the *Salon de los Recinos*, then adorned with paintings by the best masters.

But when the French left Madrid, after having made their citadel in the Retiro for four years, they left behind them nothing but a mass of ruins and destruction; the palaces destroyed—the gardens devastated—the trees cut down. At an immense expense, it has been gradually restored by Ferdinand VII., and the present queen, to its actual condition, and rendered one of the most beautiful and extensive places for public recreation that can be imagined.

Before passing through the Prado, M—— made me stop to admire the elegant pyramid erected by the order of the Cortes, on the very spot where the patriots of Madrid fell on the glorious *dos de Mayo*—bearing on one side the following inscription: "The ashes of the victims of the second of May, 1808, repose in this Field of Loyalty, watered by their blood. Eternal honor to patriotism." And on the other, "To the martyrs of Spanish Freedom, a grateful nation. Concluded by the heroic city of Madrid, in the year 1840."

He pointed out the noble palace of the Dukes of Villahermosa, forming the corner of the Prado and of the Carrera de San Gerónimo, built by the grandmother of the present duke, but of which he only occupies an apartment; an immense edifice, where, a few years ago, the Society of the Lyceum was held, and where the great public masked balls were formerly given. He tells me that the interior is magnificent, and the ducal chapel well worthy of a visit. The principal apartment is now in course of preparation for the reception of the Peruvian minister, who has not yet arrived, but whose servants were, at this very moment, carrying in enormous cases full of French furniture.

Exactly in front of this house stands the palace of the Dukes of Medina Cœli, with thirty-five balconies looking on the Prado. It is, in fact, a street, built without taste or any pretensions to architectural beauty, but covering an immense extent of ground. It was formerly the residence of the famous Cardinal Duke of Serma, the minister of Philip III. Within its vast enclosures, besides the palace and gardens, he founded a house for Jesuits, a church, and convent, afterwards belonging to the Capuchins, and another for the Trinitarian fathers. At a later period, it served as a residence for Philip V. and his court, when, grieving for the loss of his queen, he could no longer bear the sight of his own palace.

M—— says that Don A. B——, who was the duke's agent some years ago, showed him over this enormous building, and that he remained lost in astonishment at the curiosities which it contains. It has an armory, a rich and valuable collection; a library containing fifteen thousand volumes, with the rarest old manuscripts; a collection of the finest paintings, statues and busts, ancient and modern; the most curious and beautiful Flemish tapestry, &c. It is inhabited by hundreds of *dependants*, who live there with their wives and families. The present duke and his brother, the Duke of Feria, have lately married two beautiful girls, sisters, from the provinces; one of whom, the Duchess of Medina Cœli, called forth the admiration of our German friend, at the Fuente Castellana.

Towering above this ancient palace, are the houses of the banking aristocracy; rich, sumptuous, and elegant, with gilded balconies, and a gay and modern look. M—— passed them by in dignified silence. I admired the *Plaza de las Cortes*, so called from the Chamber of the Cortes, which it fronts. The houses, which form it, occupy the site of the Convent of Santa Catalina, destroyed by the French. In the midst stands the fine statue of Cervantes, in bronze, placed there by orders of Ferdinand VII. Here, much to the disgust of my companion, I hailed a *berlina*, in which I persuaded him to accompany me home, as the sun was intolerably hot; and I only trust that you will not be as tired of my description as I was (physically) of our long walk.

CHAPTER VI.

Diplomatic Dinner at the Countess de Montijo's—The Countess—Eugenie—Dramatic representation at Caramanchel.

September —.

SOME days ago, Count A——, having received an invitation to a diplomatic dinner at the Countess de Montijo's, at Caramanchel, recommended me to ride out in the cool of the evening, when he would, he said, present me to the countess. I set off about eight o'clock, together with B——, and others of the French Legation, on one of the most beautiful evenings imaginable; crossed the fine solid bridge of Toledo, with its nine bold arches, and entered the pretty village of Caramanchel, when it began to grow dusk. When we arrived, we found some of the guests playing at billiards, but the greater part, amongst whom was the countess, were enjoying the cool breezes of the evening in the beautiful and extensive gardens and shrubberies, in the arrangement of which she takes the greatest pride and pleasure.

We walked out through a labyrinth of trees and flowers, until we met the party returning in different groups, almost all laden with large bouquets of roses. I was presented by the Count to the mother of the Empress Eugenie, and received with that kindness and cordiality for which she is remarkable, even amongst Spanish women. In conversation she is delightful, perfectly unaffected, and extremely *spirituelle.* I think that in almost any other country the mother of an empress would consider herself as rather elevated by her position above her *peers.* Not so here; if any difference is to be remarked between the Countess de Montijo and other ladies of her rank, it is that she is even more simple in her manners, and more anxious to please than they are.

Since I came here I have heard a thousand anecdotes of Eugenie when Countess of Teba; of her eccentricities, her charity, her courage, and her talents. Of her beauty I can judge, having seen her on the memorable day of her marriage, when the deep emotion of her feelings made her deadly pale. It is said that she was always ambitious, and would have been contented with no ordinary fate; but in spite of all the wild dreams that may have filled the heart of a beautiful and clever girl, raised by her talents and position above her associates, spoiled and capricious, generous and fanciful, what strange sensations of unreality and wonder, and even of fear, must have made her heart throb when she heard herself hailed as the empress of a mighty nation, and felt her brow pressed by the diadem that had encircled the head of Josephine and that of Marie Antoinette!

The country house of the Countess de Montijo is large, airy, and furnished with great simplicity. Nearly all the foreign ministers and their ladies had dined there; also the President of the Council. There were also a number of pretty girls, who live there at present, and by whom the countess takes pleasure in being always surrounded. Nothing can be more sociable and unceremonious than these reunions, which take place weekly. A good many ladies arrived from Madrid, amongst others the Dowager Duchess of Alva, and a number of young men. Music, dancing, and billiards for those who preferred it, made the time pass quickly. Some of the foreign ladies expressed their regret at having arrived too late in Madrid to be present at a representation which had been got up at Caramanchel, in honor of the empress, in which the actresses were those young girls who had been the friends and companions of the former Countess of Teba. The piece was composed by Rubi, the famous dramatic writer. It is called a *Loa*, and is written in verse. The music is by Heradier, a celebrated composer. Its title is *La Perla del Genil*, the pearl being, of course the fair heroine. Love, glory, beauty, &c., had each an appropriate representative.

The Pearl has been carried from her native shores by the Imperial Eagle. The verse is easy and flowing, and the music so well adapted to it that it is in its way, a little *chef d'œuvre*. As Heradier was present, and also several of the performers, the countess complied with the general request; and some of the choruses were sung with a spirit and taste that would have done no discredit to professional singers. There is one part of the *Loa* particularly pretty. The young maidens approach the Temple of Time, and ask what the future fate of their Pearl shall be. Time answers, in melodious verse, that the future is unknown to him, but that whatever be her fate, the descendant of the Guzmans will never be found unworthy of her high destiny.

CHAPTER VII.

Soirée at the French Embassy—Gen. José Concha, the Marquis of Molins, Calderon de la Barca, Bravo Murillo, &c.—Impressions of Spanish Beauty—Extravagant Costume.

October.

HAVING received an invitation to attend a soirée dansante at the French Embassy, I accompanied his excellency there last evening. It was very brilliant, not a regular ball, the music consisting of one piano, and the refreshments of a buffet and tea-table. The long suite of rooms, *tapissés* with red and gold, are difficult to light; and, notwithstanding the size of the hotel, and that the company was supposed to be extremely select, it was crowded, though not disagreeably so. I was amused to find myself included under the head of the *pollos* of Madrid, which being translated *chickens*, seemed to me a strange nomenclature. For your benefit I must explain that all the *jeunesse dorée* of the capital—all young men capable of dancing and flirting, are *pollos*. I think one ceases to be a *pollo* after thirty.

Nothing can be better than the way in which the marquis and his lady do the honors of their house. As a polka had just struck up when we arrived, I requested, without introduction, the honor of a turn from the pretty little Condesa de ——, who, having just entered, had not yet marked her engagements upon her tablets, and who waltzes and polkas *divinamente*, as the Spaniards say. In an interval, during a long and tiresome quadrille, I told her the difficult position in which I was placed, from having two young sisters full of curiosity at the mode of dressing of the Spanish ladies, my desire to store their minds with useful knowledge, and my ignorance of the mysteries of the toilette. I entreated her to take pity on my ignorance, and as a preliminary, to tell me what her own dress was composed of. "Que tonteria!" (What folly!) said she, laughing, you surely *must* know that this is *glaçé* rose-colored silk—that these are point-lace flounces—that these are roses in my hair—that these jewels are—" "Diamonds; yes, I know that. It was only the *glaçé* silk that puzzled me. I flatter myself even that I am a judge of lace, and that I know something of fine jewels, yet I have seldom seen a greater display of both than to-night." "That is nothing; wait until you go to court, or attend a real ball. No one wears half of their diamonds to-night."

I asked the name of a very *joli garçon*, whom I had heard talking English, some moments before, with Mrs. S——, an English lady who resides here. "He is the son of a rich Irish banker," said the condesa, "yet he has a Spanish ducal title, and is married to the daughter of a grandee of Spain, whose son is the husband of one of the Ynfantas. That pretty person who has his arm, dressed in blue, and so extremely fair, is the Countess of ——, a German by birth. That silk, you must observe, is *moire antique*—very handsome, though rather heavy for dancing. But here comes Mr. de —— for a waltz. If you do not wish to find a partner for yourself, I shall put you under the charge of the Marquesa de ——, who knows everybody." She beckoned to a pretty, good-humored looking personage, and told her to show me the carte du pays, and giving her my arm, we commenced a tour of the rooms.

The marquesa certainly knew every body, and we made slow progress in our voyage of discovery. She was, however, an excellent *cicerone*, and showed me all the notabilities, generals, senators, statesmen—amongst the latter the Count of San Luis, whom I had yet scarcely seen, as he was leaving Caramanchel when we arrived. I was surprised to see so young a man. He is rather under the middle size, and stout, his head handsome. His eyes are dark-blue, and expressive. He has an air of great energy, and of unmistakable intelligence, with an extremely sweet and gentle smile, which gives a peculiarly pleasing expression to his face. His hair, whiskers, and moustaches are light brown. He was dressed to perfection, almost too well and too carefully, with the finest linen and most brilliant studs.

We met the Countess de Montijo, leaning on the arm of General José Concha. The marquesa went up and kissed her on each side of the face, which custom of kissing prevails to a notable extent amongst the fair portion of the society. Where, in England or Germany, two women shake hands, here they always kiss each other, and on each side of the face. The condesa asked the marquesa and me to accompany her into the supper-room. The marquesa spoke familiarly to General Concha, calling him *Pepito*, Pepe being the diminutive of José! and Pepito a little *less* familiar than Pepe.

The general is a gentlemanly-looking man, extremely polite, slight, dark, and with a way of bending forward, which gives him an extremely deferential air. His brother, the Marquis of Duero, is very handsome, but looks bilious and out of health. He was sitting beside a strikingly handsome girl, one of the *entourage* of the Countess de Montijo, whom she addressed, I think, as *Sofia*.

The marquesa pointed out to me the Marquis of Molins,

who has a kind of picturesque, antique air, which I liked; rather tall, grave, with masses of dark hair, great eyes, something melancholy and *fastidious* in his expression. He is a great patron of literature, and has weekly reunions of poets and authors. I also saw Calderon de la Barca, who seems the oldest member of the cabinet; has white hair and whiskers, and a peculiarly good face. He came up to speak to the Marquesa de C——, who was standing at the tea-table near us, and who attacked him violently for having joined the ministry. He laughed good-humoredly, and turned the conversation apparently to some passages of her early days, for they talked of the tertulias of the Duchess of Benavente, &c., and the marquesa told him he was the oldest friend she had; when suddenly the minister, taking advantage of the first pause in the conversation, slipped off. I saw General Blaser, a grave-looking *militaire*, who seemed to have encamped upon a sofa for the whole evening, beside the handsome Countess ——. Domenech was there also; and the marquesa pointed out Mons. Pidal, Bravo Murillo, and other names well known to those who have taken any interest in Spanish affairs, of late years. The Marquesa de Molins, Madame Calderon de la Barca, Madame Collantes, and Madame Domenech, were all present; but as most of my time was spent in the waltzing circle, in which none of these ladies joined, I had no opportunity of seeing them very near.

I was presented to the Duchess of ——, and danced with two of her daughters. The Duke of —— is well known both as a literary man and a statesman. He is a great patron of literature and literary men, and upon the whole, I conclude that literature is his province rather than politics, though he is said to maintain an entirely contrary opinion. He is still a handsome, fashionable-looking man, very juvenile for his age, both in appearance, manners, and ideas. It is said that he does not hesitate to talk openly of his own merits as a statesman, and to express his conviction (like the Marquis of M——) that *he* is the only man capable of saving the country. As a poet and dramatic writer, I am told he has a good deal of merit. His son is one of the handsomest and most distinguished looking young men in Madrid, resembling his father in appearance, and also, like him, a poet.

I waltzed several times with the Countess E——, an indefatigable dancer. The Count is a tall, stiff, gentlemanlike man, extremely polite, though cold and reserved.

As a general impression, I should say that there is more beauty both of face and figure to be seen here, than in any other capital—that the toilette in Paris is more tasteful, in London less so. In London there is, perhaps, a greater air of high breeding in the highest circles, but incomparably less grace. No such feet and figures were ever seen at St. James, nor, in spite of all the accessaries of dress, at the Tuileries. A Frenchwoman's graceful *tournure* is the result of art, education, and the toilette. An Englishwoman's elegance proceeds from her high breeding and *pur sang;* but the grace of the Spanish woman is pure nature; nowhere can such eyes be seen as in Spain, whether for size, color, or expression. As an Englishwoman advances in years, she generally grows thin—the Spanish señora is apt to become unwieldy. The one contracts—the other expands; and the expansion system, though it must be inconvenient, preserves the beauty of the face to a later period of life.

I was presented last night to the Marquesa de A——, the beauty *par excellence* of Madrid, and, in spite of all I had heard, was not disappointed. Not having known her in her youth, I can hardly imagine her to have been handsomer. Soft brown hair, beautiful eyes, teeth like pearls, a beautiful complexion, the finest arms and hands imaginable; had she not shown me her son, the Duke of S——, a living proof that she has reached a *certain age*, I could not have believed it. The Marquesa de M—— is another, though much older, instance of beauty, respected by time. Her daughter has a fine figure, but, as all the old people say, is not to compare with her mother, as they remember her, at the same age, which is generally said of the daughters of all great beauties.

As for dress in general, the married women wore a profusion of fine lace and diamonds; the girls were well dressed, but too richly, in my humble opinion. "This luxury in the toilette," said an old general, the father of half a dozen pretty daughters, to the Marquesa de V——, "is ruinous and absurd. I say nothing of the lace and jewels of the married women. Most of them are heir-looms. I find no fault with that pretty little Duchess of A——, who, my wife tells me, wears a new and expensive dress at every party; her fortune and rank permit her to indulge her taste; but that the wives of poor *empleados* should adopt the same style, or that the daughters of the most needy grandee should appear every night in dresses from Paris, embroidered in gold and silver, I consider positively wrong." Until I had observed this universal taste, I was somewhat astonished at what appeared to me the undue severity of a learned priest, who delivered a sermon last week against luxury and extravagance, especially in dress, which no doubt went home to the conscience of many a fair damsel in the congregation. And this reminds me that I have not yet written to my mother, as she desired, upon the state of religion in this country, nor given her an account of the churches and charitable institutions. For this she must give me time, and the opportunity of making inquiries, and I promise her a long and serious document upon the subject one of these days.

CHAPTER VIII.

The Drama in Madrid—Italian Opera—A Scandal-monger—The Opera—Norma—Señora Gazzamga—The Marquesa de B——.

As there are as yet few balls or evening gayeties of a sociable description, I have been making a round of the theatres. There is no taste more developed in Madrid than that for the drama—nowhere more excellent actors, more brilliant pieces, whether ancient or modern, or a more just and discriminating audience. The royal theatre, as the Italian opera-house is called, is now open, under the direction of the favorite *empresario*, Don Fernando de Urries. Already every box is taken. I have secured for myself a *stalle* for the season. This superb theatre was begun in 1818, and had already cost the government twenty-one millions of reals, but for want of funds remained unfinished, until the Count of San Luis became minister *de la gobernacion*, and pressed on the work with so much zeal, that, to the astonishment of the public, it was completed in five months. It was opened on the birthday of Queen Ysabel, on the 19th of November, 1850, with the representation of Donizetti's *Favorita*, the Alboni being then *prima donna*.

For beauty, spaciousness, comfort, and elegance in its

decorations, I know of no theatre superior to this. There is a noble simplicity and richness in the interior arrangements, which give it the appearance of a splendid drawing-room. The rich crimson damask of the boxes, the handsome velvet arm-chairs of the parterre; the elegant lustres, splendid gilding, all are at the present day unsurpassed in any European theatre. The sums expended upon this great work, during the former administration of the Count of San Luis, have furnished his enemies with a handle of complaint against that minister. For my part, I made none, feeling much indebted to the caterer for my pleasure, as I found myself luxuriously established in my comfortable arm-chair, listening to the charming voice of La Gazzamga, and to the best orchestra and choruses that can be heard out of Paris.

Every corner of the house was full, from the pit to the highest gallery. The queen has two boxes, one in the centre of the house, on the first tier, and another upon the stage, which she usually occupies, except on state occasions. Both are elegantly fitted up, with crimson hangings and mirrors, and regal-looking chairs. Opposite the stage-box is that of the Ynfante Don Francisco. The queen was not present that evening; but the Ynfante, with his daughters and their governess, occupied their box. One of the young Ynfantas, the Princess Amelia, struck me as being pretty, with a good, intelligent expression. They were very simply dressed, and had but one attendant, the Marquis of Bassecour, a fine looking man, whom I recollect seeing at Turin, where he was minister when I made my continental tour, under the auspices of my reverend tutor.

Below the Ynfante's box is that of the cabinet ministers, and opposite theirs is the box of the Duchess of Alva. The ministers' box was empty during the first two acts. Afterwards the minister of war came in, and took up his position with his back to the scenes, seeming to find metal more attractive in the boxes. "Il n'est pas dégouté," said M. de ——, to whom I made this remark. There were indeed a wonderful number of pretty women in the four tiers of boxes and in the galleries. Bright eyes seemed to gleam forth even from the ethereal regions of the *Paraiso*. In the entr'actes, the occupants of the *butacas* (arm-chairs) in the pit, take an opportunity of ascertaining this fact, either visiting the boxes or turning their *lorgnons* in that direction.

The French ambassador and his family occupied a box next that of the queen, on the first tier. I recognized the Duquesa de A——s, the pretty Duchess of S——s, the Countess of S——i, the Duchess of F——a, the Countess de V——s, &c. I happened to be seated next a wealthy *parvenu*, with whom I had made acquaintance at the Casino, and who, knowing everybody by sight, though probably not admitted into the circles of the aristocracy, undertook to tell me not only the names but the history of the occupants of each box. If I had believed him (but since I came here my ears have grown strangely incredulous of slander) I should have been shocked at the disclosures of my communicative neighbor. His histories generally ran in this style: "That lady with feathers in her hair and a rose-colored shawl, is the Countess of ——. Next her is seated her lover, General ——. In the next box is the Marchioness of ——, a celebrated beauty. That is her husband, and his chère amie is in that box on the pit tier, that tall woman with the yellow shawl and black eyes. She herself has *relaciones* with Don ——, that little man with moustaches, looking through his opera-glass, and so on, through each row of boxes. Scarcely one escaped; if the lady happened to be old and plain, he had still a story to tell of her former conduct.

As I found this wholesale scandal extremely distasteful,

I made my escape to the box of the Countess of C——, whom, by the way, my neighbor had passed over without comment, and indeed it would seem impossible that the most determined slanderer could find in her character a weak point on which to found his calumnies. Pure and gentle-looking, with soft and amiable manners, and such a look of repose and dignity withal, I found it refreshing to bask in that atmosphere, after the air I had been breathing. Yet Don —— —— is by no means an ill-natured man. It is the fashion to speak in this manner, and often means nothing, and it is more especially the fashion amongst those who have no opportunities of judging of the truth or falsehood of these stories.

The Opera this night was Norma. The Gazzamga, besides being an exquisite singer, is a perfect actress, but the music of Rossini is evidently not in her style. She will show to more advantage in the trumpet-toned notes of Verdi, and her triumph is expected to be complete in the *Trovatore*, which is announced for representation in a few weeks. She is fair and blue-eyed, with nothing tragic in her features, nothing likely to produce dramatic effect; but her genius conquers that difficulty, and it is impossible to see a more expressive countenance. The arrangements for leaving the Opera are defective. There is no cloak-room, and the fair señoras stand shivering in a kind of open vestibule with their handkerchiefs before their mouths, waiting for their carriages; their attendant *caballeros* smothered in their cloaks. The only carriages which drive into the vestibule, are those of the royal family.

I was recognised while standing there by the Marquesa de B—— and her three pretty daughters, whom I knew in Italy. The second, C——, I found more lovely than ever, with her glasses covering her pretty eyes, stuck in after a fashion which in any thing less fair and feminine would look independent.

The Marquis of —— asked me to sup with him at his rooms in the *Calle Ancha de San Bernardo*, to which I agreed, more for the sake of his conversation than of his *cuisine*.

CHAPTER IX.

Female Charity in London and Madrid contrasted—Slanderers, their social position and character—The Fair Penitents of Madrid and London compared.

October —.

Seated at my friend's table, with cigars and claret beside us, I ventured to propound a delicate question; knowing him to be at once a man of the world, a man of a certain age, and a sensible and honorable gentleman. "Do you believe that the conduct of married women in Spain is worse than it is in other countries, as I have generally heard it asserted in England?" "You have been listening to ——. I saw him talking to you in the pit, and can easily believe what a *chronique scandaleuse* he was getting up for your entertainment, doing the honors of his own country to a stranger." "I found him very *un*-entertaining, but after all, you give no answer to my question." "Well then, to answer you decidedly, I firmly believe that *it is not.* You know that the greater part of my life has been spent in London, consequently it is chiefly between that city and Madrid that I can form a comparison. Two evils exist in this country, or rather in this city, (for remember that Madrid is not Spain,) which combine to give a stranger a false impression upon this point. One is the unchecked propensity to calumny which so generally exists here, and the other, the indifference with which these calumnies are listened to. Besides this, no one who has resided for any length of time amongst the aristocracy of Madrid can deny, that women of doubtful character are received and welcomed in general society. This is another great evil, though perhaps unavoidable.

"Here, as in all great capitals, there exists a certain number of women of the highest rank, whose position, beauty, and fashion, render them more open to observation than their neighbors. If their conduct is entirely above reproach, their example is all important. If they are imprudent, careless of the opinion of the world, distinguished by the magnificence of their dress, jewels, equipages, &c.; but above all, if they are constantly surrounded by dissipated young men of fashion, they are, to a certain extent deservedly, in the mouths of the public. Stories concerning them are built up on a very slight foundation. Their characters become as it were public property, and though possibly nothing serious can be proved against them, there gradually arises a general feeling that society receives them on *souffrance*, and merely because they continue to live with their husbands, the general touchstone of respectability.

"The *dashing* style has gone out in England; but the mothers and grandmothers of the present generation can tell us of feats performed by the beautiful Lady —— and the Duchess of ——, who were nevertheless the leaders of fashion some thirty or forty years ago, but which in the days of Queen Victoria would suffice to ruin the reputation of any high-born dame. Hypocrisy, the homage which vice pays to virtue, must now be practised in England, to enable a woman of doubtful virtue to keep her place in society. She has besides the dread of divorce before her eyes. Here, the worst she has to dread, is a legal separation. There, she may be coldly received in society—here, she finds herself on a level with the most virtuous of her sex."

"But why should this be so?"

"Probably from the very circumstance that reputations are assailed on the slightest grounds, and that if one half of the world is indifferent, the other half remains incredulous. I do not justify, but only mention the fact. But besides, you must bear in mind, that only those whose imprudence has given cause, however slight, for evil interpretation of their actions, are spoken of. Those whose lives are at once blameless and circumspect, and these are certainly the largest portion, excite no observation. Their names are not to be heard at the clubs, at the Casino, at Doña ——'s tertulia. It is my firm belief that in Madrid, the number of women who have failed in their duties, present only exceptional cases; and even in regard to these, as they give no public scandal by their conduct, we may consider the stories propagated concerning them, as at least doubtful.

"A woman who lives in the gay society of Madrid, and whose character has never been traduced, must be a model of virtue as well as a prodigy of prudence. A young man of fashion dances half a dozen times with a beautiful young married woman—goes to her opera box—rides several times beside her carriage—publicly expresses his admiration of her. It is enough—the Countess de—— has a lover. If she is prudent, and foresees what may be said, or is informed of what has been said, she avoids the snare, and the report dies away; but if through vanity or carelessness she continues to permit these attentions, however innocently on her part, she becomes a mark for scandal; and however irreproachable her conduct may be in after life, it will generally be believed that at one time she had *relaciones* as it is called, with that individual." "And her husband?"—"Is good-naturedly supposed to be either blind or indifferent, the usual story with the world; while in fact he is naturally the last man to hear these reports. I will give you an instance of the justice of 'the world,' in a case that occurred lately in a family where I am intimate.

"A very short time ago, one of the principal ladies of Madrid, young, beautiful, lately married, a native of Andalusia, her high position somewhat envied on account of the latter circumstance, she having carried off this great *parti* from the rival beauties of the capital—hitherto irreproachable in her conduct, and somewhat proud in her demeanor, suddenly became the object of what, to me at least, was an unaccountable report. It was affirmed that she had fallen from her high estate, and had a lover—one of the most elegant and distinguished *pollos* of her acquaintances. The story was told circumstantially, asserted in every club, repeated in every circle. But in this case it was added, that the husband had discovered his dishonor, that a separation was to take place the following day, and the lady returned upon the hands of her parents.

"A pathetic picture was drawn of the despair of the mother-in-law, of the desolation of the husband, who had adored his young wife, of the projected duel &c., and had I not known the parties intimately, I confess that I could hardly have doubted the truth of these rumors. Meanwhile the story fortunately reached the ears of the noble couple. Astonished and indignant, they took the best means of silencing the slanderers. The very next day, that announced for the separation and public disgrace of the duchess, she and her husband appeared together in an open carriage in the Prado, before the eyes of *all Madrid* there assembled. The calumniators were crest-fallen, but only for a moment. That species of human animal knows no shame. They admitted that they had been mistaken, and prepared to attack another and more assailable reputation. Hundreds of similar instances take place," continued my friend, warming with the subject, and only stopping to light a fresh cigar. "Idleness, envy, the love of gossip, and perhaps the conviction that the object of their calumny will not lose her place in society, in which case it is to be presumed that they would pause to reflect on the evil they might inflict, all contribute to this prevailing spirit, amongst a certain class of young men, who in nine cases out of ten, are not even admitted into the society of their victims. I speak my sincere opinion, when I affirm, that with the exception of a very few fashionable persons, whose lives do indeed seem to pass in one constant round of dissipation, whose time is spent in driving in the Prado, attending the theatres, the opera, the ball-room, precisely as their compeers do in every other great city,—the Spanish women are the most domestic in the world—the most devoted to the care of their children—the most truly pious and the best *ménagères*; which latter circumstance may arise from the fact that their fortunes are rarely equal to their rank, and that a lavish expenditure would soon bring ruin upon the possessors of the most ancient names and most splendid palaces of Madrid. I repeat that I believe all other cases to be exceptional, and when they do occur, to have been the results of a *marriage de convenance*, or to have arisen from the carelessness of a dissipated husband, who seeing his wife well-dressed and admired, amuses himself after his own fashion, and leaves her to do the same."

"After all," said I, "I can only wind up with the philosophical reflection, that men and women are the same in all countries."

"No doubt," said the marquis, "but the end is not the same. In England Pope's lines still hold true, and generally speaking the 'youth of pleasure' is followed by 'an old age of cards.' Here it is rarely so, and no doubt the different results are owing to the difference of religion." "How so?" "In England, if the once far-famed and beautiful Lady —— retires from the world, attends the sermons of the Rev. Mr. ——, goes regularly to church every Sunday morning and afternoon, to evening lectures, and puts her conscience under the charge of the reverend pastor, all her dear friends and fashionable acquaintances discuss the subject with alarm." "Poor Lady —— has become very odd. She has given up parties—she has taken a serious turn—she distributes tracts—she goes on charitable errands—she really carries it too far—they are afraid there is something wrong—her eldest brother had something peculiar about him, &c. It requires some courage to bear the brunt of these remarks, especially when coming from those who knew her in her dissipated youth. Her house becomes gloomy—she herself sad and severe. It is attributed to the influence of the Reverend Mr. ——.

"But here, many an instance is unnoticed and uncommented upon, where the dissipated beauty, whose youth and loveliness has nearly departed, returns with penitence to her religious duties, earnestly and quietly, and spends the last years of her life in endeavoring by contrition to expiate her former errors. She is, indeed, seldom seen in the world, but no gloom or severity marks her demeanor. A calm and placid serenity can alone be observed on that face formerly lighted up by gratified vanity. Her conversion cannot fail to be sincere, for in the world it is unnoticed. No liveried footman attends her—no velvet-lined pews or soft cushions, make her devotions comfortable. Kneeling on the floor, in a retired corner of the church, enveloped in her mantilla, with nothing to distinguish her from the poor by whom she is surrounded, the sincerity of her contrition is known to God alone.

"She has nothing to dread from the world's opinion, for the world no longer occupies itself about her; and it is certain, be the cause what it may, that the race of old dowagers, with rouged cheeks, false ringlets, and shaking pendants, forming so prominent a feature in London society, is almost entirely unknown in Madrid."

I write down the remarks of the Marquis de —— as I remember them, both because his opinion has great weight with me, and because they form a *pendent* to the observations of my censorious acquaintance at the opera.

CHAPTER X.

Official reception of the Attaché by her Majesty—The Queen, her appearance and memory—The King—The Princess—Her Nurse—Murillo's Santa Ysabel—The Alcazar.

October —.

YESTERDAY, my chief received a note from the minister of state, informing him that her Majesty would be pleased to receive us this evening, at 7 o'clock, when I am to have the honor of a presentation. To-morrow I shall write you an account of it.

We arrived at the palace at the appointed hour, in uniform of course, and ascended the grand staircase, which is entirely composed of white marble, the roof adorned with fine allegorical paintings. A white marble statue of Charles III., and two lions of the same material were all I had time to observe as we passed. Upon these lions it is said Napoleon laid his hand when he reached the first landing of this noble staircase, and exclaimed: "Je la tiens enfin, cette Espagne si desirée." In the first *salon* we found the *Introductor de Embajadores*, and the minister of state. Having been told that the queen is proverbially unpunctual, I prepared myself for a long examination of the paintings and objects of taste and luxury of these splendid apartments; but we had hardly entered the antechamber, when we heard the music of the "*Marcha Réal*," and the tramp of horses, and immediately after, the royal carriages drove into the court-yard, stopping at the foot of the grand staircase.

A few moments after, we were desired to enter the queen's private cabinet. She was accompanied only by the king, the little princess of the Asturias and her governess, and by the mistress of the robes. The queen, who had been at the church of Atocha, where she assists every Saturday at the office of the Virgin (a custom of the sovereigns of Spain since the time of Philip III.), was still in her carriage-dress—a silk gown I think, with a black lace mantilla. She received us most graciously. I was struck by the sweetness of her smile, and the beauty of her expression. Without being handsome, she is certainly a fine looking woman, and though very large for her age, yet being tall and with a very regal port, carries it off well.

She asked in the most gracious manner after my father, whom she said she remembered perfectly, though but a child when he was in Madrid; spoke of my mother's beauty, and of having heard her sing at a concert in the palace, during the regency of Queen Christina. In short, she has that royal memory, which is so important a gift in a sovereign. There is a kind of honest simplicity in her manner, which is very charming. The king conversed with me for some time in French, which he speaks like a Parisian. He spoke a great deal of my country, and seems thoroughly versed in its literature. His face is handsome, with a fine open expression. His figure is somewhat insignificant, and he has a high-toned voice which sounds effeminate, but he would certainly be considered as an agreeable and well-informed man in any rank of life—and his manners are both prepossessing and dignified.

The little princess is a fair, sweet looking, rather delicate child, very tall for her age, which is not yet two years, and extraordinarily intelligent. She held out her little hand to be kissed, with the air of a miniature queen. Her Majesty, who seems wrapped up in that child, could hardly take her eyes off her for a moment. Her nurse, who came in while we were there, is the finest specimen of peasant beauty I have ever seen. She had a regular Grecian profile, with eyes like dark stars, and splendid black hair. One of the first artists here has taken her portrait, which hangs in the palace. It is considered a great stroke of good fortune to be chosen as nurse of one of the royal children. A certain number of peasant women from the mountain country of the Asturias are sent for before the queen's *accouchement*, and it must be with a beating heart that the candidates present themselves before her Majesty. Those who are not chosen, are sent home loaded with presents, as some compensation for their disappointment, but the happy individual who is selected, may consider her fortune made.

After again kissing hands, we backed out, and I must confess that I came away entirely fascinated by the kind and gracious manners of *Doña Ysabel Segunda.* I observed in the antechamber, Murillo's beautiful painting of St. Elizabeth of Hungary, Santa Ysabel as it is called in Spanish, dressing the wounds of the poor. All the details of their infirmities are rendered with terrible fidelity, and the sweet countenance of the Saint, with its expression of heavenly pity, forms a beautiful contrast to the rude faces of the beggars whom her charity is relieving. The Countess of Toreno was "on guard" as it is called, in the anteroom, and several ladies of the palace stopped to speak to Count A—— as we passed out.

I have been since told by M—— that the St. Elizabeth

in the palace, is a copy, and that the original is in the "Museo;" which he has hitherto pertinaciously prevented me from visiting, assuring me that when I have seen it, I shall think nothing else worth looking at. I am not much inclined to believe this assertion, since a sight of the palace alone might compensate a traveller for the trouble of making a journey to Madrid. It appears that the original design of this royal edifice, which drew from Napoleon the remark, "Mon frère, tu es mieux logé que moi," was upon the most gigantic scale. The ancient *Alcazar* of Madrid, dating back to almost fabulous times, occupied the site where it now stands. There Francis I. was removed after his confinement in the "Casa de Lujanes," and there he received the visit of his royal rival; and strangely enough, upon returning to his own city of Paris, he commemorated his captivity by building a palace in the Bois de Boulogne, upon the model of the Spanish Alcazar, known until the revolution as the *Chateau de Madrid.*

On Christmas eve, in the year 1824, a terrible conflagration destroyed the Alcazar, and Philip of Bourbon resolved to build another palace upon its ruins, more worthy to be the residence of the monarchs of Spain. Juhara, a famous architect, was sent for from Turin, and made a model of a palace, which, had it been carried into execution, would certainly have been one of the wonders of the age. His death, however, put an end to his projects, and his pupil, Saqueti, who was intrusted with the work, reduced the proportions of the projected palace to more feasible dimensions, by the express desire of the king. The first stone was laid on the first of April, 1828.

The palace forms a great square, entirely built of stone, with the exception of the mahogany work employed in the doors and windows. At each angle are projections in the form of pavilions, and on the principal façade are two wings, begun in the time of Charles III., but which even yet remain unfinished. The whole edifice is imposing, from its massive walls and arches, and an air of extraordinary solidity and grandeur. The principal story, which contains the royal apartments, is adorned with innumerable pillars and pilasters, and the whole edifice is crowned with a balustrade of stone. The views from these windows are said to be delightful, especially to the north, looking down upon the Campo del Moro, and the beautiful gardens in the environs.

As for the interior, I can easily believe the truth of the assertion, that it contains riches sufficient to furnish forth half a dozen ordinary palaces—not only in the splendid furniture, the rich carpets, curtains, hangings, &c., but in the intrinsic value of the works of art which it contains—in the paintings, by the best masters, which cover the ceilings and adorn the walls of the innumerable apartments—in the inlaid tables—curious clocks—lustres of rock crystal, admirably cut—great mirrors, fabricated at La Granja, of almost incredible dimensions—walls covered with marble, china, stucco, inlaid woodwork—in short, a collection of all that the most capricious taste and most unbounded wealth could collect at different periods.

The inside court is a great square, surrounded by an open portico. Amongst other apartments to which it leads, are the *bureaux* of the minister of state. Surrounding the second story, is a gallery enclosed with glass, which leads to the chapel, and to the royal apartments.

CHAPTER XI.

Mr. Soulé and Mr. Perry—Calderon de la Barca—Appearance, manners, and polish of Mr. Soulé.

October —.

The great topic of conversation at present in Madrid, is the arrival of the new American minister, Mr. Soulé, a red-hot democrat, whose late speeches in his own country, in favor of the annexation of Cuba, have naturally excited a vast amount of prejudice against him, in this. It seems to us a strange nomination on the part of the President of the United States. Perhaps in a democratic government there was only the *embarras du chois*, as it may be inferred that other public men there have the same sentiments, though less openly and offensively expressed. He is said to be a man of talent, a Frenchman by birth, a *republicain rouge*, who was obliged, on account of his political principles, to leave his native country, where he was known as the editor of a republican newspaper, entitled "The Yellow Dwarf," *le nain jaune*. He will require much tact and prudence to overcome the prejudice universally felt against him. His secretary of legation, Mr. Perry, is married to a very charming poetess, *La Coronata*. Count A—— is of opinion that the nomination of Calderon de la Barca to the post of minister of state, was partly intended as a kind of counterbalance to that of Mr. Soulé, it being supposed that his long residence in America will enable him to see through the political intrigues with which it is supposed that the latter functionary intends to distinguish his diplomatic career.

He called this morning at the legation, when I happened to be present. He has a very remarkable countenance; dark, deep-set eyes; his hair cut after the fashion of the ancient French republicans. He is very polished in his manner, and speaks well—slowly, in rounded flowing periods. As the French say, *il s'ecoute en parlant.* He seems very desirous to make himself agreeable, but is, perhaps, somewhat too confident of his own powers.

CHAPTER XII.

Churches of Madrid—Salesas Reales, its magnificence—Adorned by Works of Art—Church of Santa Teresa—Republicanism at Church—Church of San José; Military at Divine Worship—The General Hospital—Catholic Charity—Hospitals in General—Hospital of St. Patrick.

October —.

I HAVE not yet expressed my admiration of the churches in Madrid; and though every Spaniard assures me, that until I have seen the cathedrals of Toledo and Seville I have seen nothing, I must still hold to my opinion that the churches here are, generally speaking, equally noble and splendid, both as to architectural beauty and to interior decoration. I have had the good fortune to make an invaluable acquaintance, within the last fortnight, of an *ex-employé*, Señor de —— ——, who, after a long and arduous political career, has retired from public life, and even from society, except from that of a few particular friends. Having met him at the house of Señor M——n, ex-minister of the treasury, I mentioned my curiosity on the subject of charitable and beneficent institutions in this city, and found I could not have addressed myself to one more capable of enlightening me on these matters. He was kind enough to propose that I should accompany him next morning to early mass at the church of the *Salesas Reales*, and offered to take me from thence to visit the general hospital.

The convent and church of the Royal Salesas—the name

taken from the founder of the Order of the Visitation, St. François de Sales, with the addition of *Royal*, as having been founded by King Ferdinand VI. and his queen, Doña Maria Barbara—is one of the most noble and beautiful religious edifices in Europe. The object of the royal founders was to provide for the education of girls of noble family. The building was concluded in 1758; and it is said, that in the will of the queen, a note of the expenses incurred in its construction, makes them amount to upwards of eighty millions of reals, without including the splendid diamonds, articles of gold and silver, and rich vestments with which her majesty enriched the church.

As it stands alone, and at the opposite extremity of the city from our legation, I had not yet seen it. Passing along the Calle del Barquillo, and turning to the right, we suddenly came in front of this imposing mass of building, which is said, including the garden and orchard, to cover a surface of nearly eighty thousand square feet. The vast court-yard is enclosed by a strong iron fence with massive iron gates, forming a fitting entrance to the noble church, its *façade* adorned with columns of a composite order, and fine basso-relievos over the principal door.

No one can fail to remark the extreme cleanness of all churches appertaining to convents. Hère the floor, composed of beautiful variegated marble, was spotless; and as the Salesas stands in a retired situation, there was not the usual crowd, which frequently makes it impossible to advance beyond the doors of the other churches in Madrid. Besides, though a fête day, it was early. The high altar is magnificent, with a profusion of massive gold candelabras, fine statues, and rich adornment. Nothing is more remarkable than the pillars, each composed of one single block of the exquisite serpentine marble of Grenada, almost as rare as a fine precious stone. The lofty roof is covered with frescos by the three brothers Velasquez, and the walls with fine old paintings by foreign artists. I particularly admired a Holy Family, by Cignaroli, a Venetian painter.

After mass, Don —— —— called my attention to the sepulchre of King Ferdinand VI., which stands under an arch, in a niche to the right of the altar, and is covered with rare-colored marbles, and adorned with various allegorical statues, one of which represents Time in châins, holding in one hand a sword, and in the other the portrait of the monarch. The tomb of Queen Barbara is placed near that of her royal husband, and each bears an inscription commemorating the virtues of the departed sovereigns.

Certainly I have never seen a temple more fitted for the worship of the Divinity, in its noble simplicity and rich severity. In the extreme quiet and stillness which reigned around, we might have imagined ourselves leagues distant from the populous and noisy city. The only sound that broke the silence was the chanting of the nuns within the iron grating. The early breath of the morning blew in at the open doors, laden with a sweet fragrance of violets from the convent garden. As we came out, Señor —— —— told me that many of the principal families of Madrid still send their daughters to this convent for their education, as well as to a branch of the same order, called the "New Salesas," established a few years ago in the *Calle Ancha de San Bernardo.*

As it was still early, Señor —— —— proposed that we should visit Santa Teresa, a church belonging to a convent of nuns of the Carmelite order, and founded in 1684, by the Duke of Medina de las Torres, directed by the venerable superior, Maria de los Angeles. It is also a fine church, on a much smaller scale than the Salesas, with a few good paintings, and a quiet, venerable aspect. Nothing can have a more devotional effect than the kneeling figures on the floors of the churches, the complete absence of all distinction in dress or place; the women enveloped in their mantillas, rich and poor together. How infinitely I prefer this to the cushioned pews of the London churches, or even to the chairs in Paris! I must say, however, that the fair sex have the advantage over us in one respect. When tired of kneeling they can rest by sitting on the floor; but unless a man can find a bench, he must stand during the whole of the longest sermon, which is very fatiguing. Here, at least, is true republicanism; equality in the worship of God.

As we passed along the Calle de Alcalá, we met a fine body of well-dressed soldiers, with a military band, going towards the church of San José, to attend military mass, their daily custom. To me there is not a more imposing spectacle, and we followed them up the middle aisle. When the troops lie prostrate at the elevation of the Host, the coldest and most unbelieving heart must feel touched at the sight of the brave and hardy soldier falling in mute acknowledgment of the presence of the Deity. This church of San José is large and spacious, yet does not please me as much as many others. It seems ill cared-for, perhaps owing to the age of the curate, who looks like a tall pale shadow of by-gone days. He did not officiate on this occasion, but I saw him looming aloft in the choir, like some old priest of the Middle Ages who had risen from the tomb to survey the scene of his former labors.

San José, which formerly belonged to the Carmelite nuns, was built at the beginning of the last century, and together with their convent, contained a vast collection of fine paintings, of which only a few remain, in the chapel of Santa Teresa, to the left of the high altar. This chapel was founded by Don Rodrigo Calderon, Marquis of Siete Yglesias, minister of Philip III., condemned to death and beheaded in the Plaza de Madrid in 1621. There are two paintings worthy of note in this church; the one representing Our Lady, a beautiful work by Michel; the other, the "Santo Cristo del Desamparo," by Alonso de Mena.

The general hospital, towards which we next directed our steps, is under the charge of the "Junta de Beneficencia," and does honor to their zeal. Its size is enormous; the building consisting of a square of six hundred feet in length, by six hundred in breadth. It receives annually within its capacious walls, eight thousand men and six thousand women We passed through no less than thirty-eight halls, spacious and well ventilated, in which were fifteen hundred and twenty-six beds. The utmost cleanliness and comfort prevailed throughout. This immense establishment was founded in 1587, by Philip II., and cost an annual sum of one hundred and twenty-five thousand dollars. The sick and destitute find there not only the best medical assistance and medicines, but the best and most wholesome food, admirable both as to quality and quantity. The daily ration consists of sixteen ounces of bread, twelve of meat, a pint of wine, an ounce and a half of *garbanzos* (beans), and an ounce of bacon. When the doctor orders it, eggs and chocolate are given, and in extraordinary cases, more delicate meat, more generous wine, potatoes and other vegetables.

Besides being visited morning and evening by the best physicians and surgeons of Madrid, the patients are carefully attended by Infirmarians, by the Brothers of the "Congregation of the Cross," and by the devoted Sisters of Charity; and also receive constant visits from the members of other female corporations. Eleven chaplains are attached to the service of the hospital. Want and helplessness could not meet with more assiduous attention, or more unceasing care. There is also a part of this vast building set aside for the reception of persons of a higher class, who by the payment of from six to ten reals a day, are more carefully waited on and attended to than they could be in their own houses.

"Dickens," said my companion, who having spent ten or fifteen years in London, speaks English like a native, "ought to visit our hospitals, and if he were to write upon the subject of charitable institutions in this country, his able pen would prove that all the liberality and charity of a generous nation, cannot make up for the absence of the true spirit of charity which is alone to be found in Catholic countries—and that hired nurses, however respectable, even though there should be no *Mrs. Gamps* amongst them, will never equal the Sisters of Charity either in care or skill; will never possess the heaven-born devotedness of those who look for no reward upon earth."

The following day we visited several other establishments; and I have now devoted a whole week to this investigation, for which I expect a long letter of approbation from my mother, for whose sake I begun it, though I have ended by becoming deeply interested in the subject myself. A volume, however, would scarcely suffice to give a detailed account of the whole; and you must be satisfied for the present, with the dryest possible list of the principal hospitals. After the general hospital, I may mention the military hospital, where from six to seven thousand soldiers are received annually. This magnificent building was opened in 1841 for the use of the troops; but was originally founded by Philip V., as a seminary for the sons of the nobility. It stands near the gate of San Bernardino, and may be regarded as a model for establishments of this nature. It contains twenty-four spacious and well-ventilated rooms for the patients, with large halls for anatomical dissections, for clothes, medicines, &c., and a superb chapel. Nothing can exceed the cleanliness and order which reigns throughout the whole building; in the long galleries, in the large halls, offices, and dependencies.

Then there is the hospital of San Juan de Dios, under the direction of the Brothers of that order, founded by the venerable Anton Martin, for the reception of persons attacked by contagious maladies, cutaneous diseases, &c. It contains ten halls, two hundred and fifty-three beds, and receives at the rate of fifteen hundred patients annually. It is zealously attended by the members of the Brotherhood, and for its interior government, is provided with a director, two chaplains, physicians, infirmarians, and numerous dependents, the whole supported by the provincial *Junta de Beneficencia*. The church attached to this hospital, is rich in sculpture and paintings, adorned with the rarest marbles, and with frescos by the best masters. Amongst the finest pieces of sculpture are an *Ecce Homo;* the scourging of Our Saviour; Our Lord carrying the Cross, and San Juan de Dios supporting a sick man, all works of Don Pedro Hermoso. There is also a fine Saint Lazarus over the altar, the work of an artist named Contreras, and several other remarkable paintings on sacred subjects by native artists, besides one by Giordani.

Another hospital worthy of notice is that of Incurables for Women, founded in 1803 by the Countess of Lerena, under the patronage of Charles IV., in the street of the Conde Duque, since transferred to the college of Monte Rey, granted to them by the present queen. It is a beautiful institution, destined for women inflicted with incurable maladies, or impotent from nervous or rheumatic pains, paralysis, or old age. It is under the direction of the Sisters of Charity, and contains at present one hundred and nine patients. A similar institution, but for male patients, is the hospital of Our Lady of Mount Carmel, which contains accommodation for upwards of two hundred persons, and is also under the direction of the Sisters of Charity. Both these hospitals depend upon the *Junta de Beneficencia.*

I come now to the hospital of the *Buen Suceso*, situated in the Puerta del Sol. Passing with great difficulty through the groups of loungers, the venders of wares, orange and chestnut sellers, sturdy Gallician porters, and athletic Asturian water-carriers, gay equipages, horsemen, and soldiers, we made our way up to this hospital, founded in 1489, by the Catholic monarchs, Ferdinand and Ysabella, for the relief of servants and dependants of the royal household. Besides these, all wounded men who bring an order from the authorities, are admitted there, and after being partially cured, are transported to the general hospital. Medical assistance and advice are also given daily, at eleven o'clock, to all poor and sick persons who present themselves at the hospital, and medicines suited to their various infirmities distributed amongst them gratis.

The hospital of St. Peter was founded in 1619, for the relief of poor priests, and is supported by the venerable congregation of Presbyters, natives of Madrid, who founded it at their own expense. One interesting circumstance connected with it, is worthy of record. The head chaplains of the hospital, at one time, were Lope de Vega and Calderon de la Barca. There is also the hospital of St. Patrick for the Irish. It appears that when, in the seventeenth century, the Catholic clergy of Ireland were forced to emigrate, on account of the civil and religious wars of which that kingdom was the theatre, and sought protection and asylum in foreign countries, many took refuge in Spain, and received a hospitable reception in Madrid, whence the origin of this establishment.

We visited the hospital of Our Lady of Montserrat, founded in 1616 for the Arragonese, a fine building with a handsome church; that of the Italians, established in 1598, for the poor natives of Italy, whose church is remarkable for its elegance and simplicity; and that of the Flemish, founded in 1606, for the relief of poor pilgrims from Flanders and the Low Countries. We went through the hospital *de la Latina*, founded in 1507 by Doña Beatrice Galindo, surnamed the *Latina*, and her husband, General Francisco Ramirez; now united to the convent of Franciscan nuns. This Doña Beatrice, celebrated for her piety and learning, was mistress of the robes and instructress of Isabella the Catholic, and surnamed *la Latina*, on account of her having taught that language to the queen. Her husband, secretary to the Catholic monarchs, and also general of artillery, lost his life in fighting against the Moors. The tombs of Beatrice and Ramirez are still to be seen, in the fine old church belonging to the convent of La Concepcion Gerónimo, of which *la Latina* was also the foundress.

The hospital of San Luis was founded in 1615 by Don Enrique Saureau, chaplain of Philip III., for the relief of destitute Frenchmen; that of the third order of St. Francis of Assissium in 1678, for infirm laymen of the order. It is a large and handsome building, and contains apartments for the sick and infirm of both sexes, with one hall especially dedicated to consumptive patients.

The hospital of Buena Dicha (good fortune) was founded in 1594, by Father Villosbada, abbot of St. Martin's monastery, for the relief of twelve *enfermos vergonzantes*, as they are called; that is, persons whose position in life makes them ashamed to beg, while they are too infirm to labor. Every infirmity, every class of unfortunate beings, seem to have been taken into consideration.

There is the hospital of actors of Our Lady of La Novena, for the support of the infirm and destitute among the sons of Thespis; and that of St. Catharine de los Donados, the most ancient in Madrid, founded in 1440 by Don Pedro Fernandez de Lorea, for the maintenance of twelve destitute but respectable men, whose advanced age prevents them from gaining their livelihood. A tradition exists here that the emperor Charles V. was lodged in this house, on the occasion of one of his visits to Madrid.

The hospital of San Fermin de los Navarros, belonging to the society of the Navarrese, is situated in the Prado, and was founded in 1684. The church contains some good pieces of sculpture.

I shall conclude for the present with the hospital of San Antonio, commonly called *of the Portuguese*, because intended at its foundation for the poor natives of that kingdom, but which, since the separation of Spain and Portugal, has been devoted to the support of poor Germans, and is under the charge of the brotherhood of the *Refugio*. The church united to this hospital, and to a school for girls, also under the direction of this brotherhood, is one of the most beautiful in Madrid. It is of an elliptic form, the walls and roof entirely covered with fresco paintings, by Lucca Giordano, Ricci, and Carreño. The religious ceremonies are conducted here with an extraordinary degree of pomp and solemnity. The members of the "Hermandad" belong in general to the first families in Madrid. When the sun pours its rich glow upon these paintings, and the sweet voices of the young girls resound in the choir, the effect is both grand and soothing.

So much for the principal hospitals; but as for the other charitable establishments—the brotherhoods, *hospicios*, asylums, colleges—the mere enumeration of them would be entirely beyond the limits of a letter. Nevertheless, I shall attempt to give you some account of them at a future period. I shall reserve it for another rainy day—for, strange to say, the sky is cloudy and the rain pouring in torrents, to which circumstance you owe the above rather long narrative.

I must however, before concluding, say one word of those admirable institutions, called the "*Archicofradías sacramentales*," whose origin dates back to the most remote antiquity. Upwards of two hundred of these religious associations exist in Madrid, under the names of *Hermandades*, *Cofradías*, *Esclavitudes*, and *Congregaciones*. Some are devoted entirely to the adoration of some holy mystery; others add to religious exercises, the most extensive and beneficent charity. Amongst the last are the Brotherhoods of *Refuge—Peace and Charity—Hope—Ave-Maria*, the *Third Order*, &c. One called the "Primitive Congregation for the Lighting and continual Watching of the Holy Sacrament," was founded by Charles IV., and Maria Louisa. Another for the guardianship and prayer of the Holy Sacrament" during the jubilee of "the Forty Hours," contains more than sixty thousand members, who watch by turns day and night before the "*Santisimo.*" The principal personages in Madrid belong to these associations. Then there is the "Congregation of the slaves of the Most Holy Sacrament;" in whose ancient registers may be seen the names of the most illustrious nobles and literary men of the reign of Philip IV. Many are especially devoted to the veneration of the Blessed Virgin. One especially called "the Court of Mary," containing several thousand members, is established in the spacious Church of St. Thomas, where the most splendid religious ceremonies are celebrated, especially in the month of May.

There are also many professional societies, under the guardianship of different patron Saints; that of *Advocates*, dedicated to Our Lady of the Assumption; that of *physicians*, to St. Cosmo and St. Daurian; that of *Architects*, to Our Lady of Belen; that of *Goldsmiths*, to St. Eloy, &c. &c.

CHAPTER XIII.

Opera Comique—Martinez de la Rosa—Spanish love of music—Teatro del Principe—Theatre of Lope de Vega—Count A——.

October —.

TIME passes here swiftly. Between diplomatic duties, tertulias, dinners, the Casino, the opera, the theatres, rides in the Prado or in the country, I find the days too short, even while cutting off, as every one does, a respectable portion of the night. I have been spending most of my leisure time in the *Museo*, of which some day I must endeavor to give you an account, but it is difficult by any description to do justice to a gallery, which I firmly believe to be unequalled in Europe. One of the most amusing little theatres here is the *Circo*, formerly destined for a circus, as its name imports, under the direction of a French company, Messrs. Paul, Avrillon and others, afterwards dedicated to the Italian opera, and now devoted to a new species of entertainment, a kind of Spanish *opera comique*, *la zarzuela* as it is called. It is of an inconvenient form, especially for the occupants of the boxes; but the music is light and pretty, the performance generally good, and it enjoys high favor with the Spanish public. *La Ramirez*, a pretty little actress, with a charming voice, is a great favorite. Her execution of Spanish songs especially, is perfect. Within a few seats of me, in the pit, which as usual in Spanish theatres is furnished with handsome velvet chairs, I almost invariably observe Martinez de la Rosa, ex-minister of state and ex-ambassador in Paris, who has perhaps retained the greatest number of friends, and who has the fewest enemies of any public man living. Amiable, kind-hearted and agreeable, he seems endowed with a kind of perpetual youth; and especially is the general favorite of *le beau sexe*. It is supposed that he will be named president of the Chamber of Deputies in the approaching session of Cortes, having already held in succession almost every great appointment under the crown; never ceasing to be a poet, in the midst of his most arduous political duties as a statesman.

The *zarzuela* last night was *Don Simon*, a laughable farce executed with great spirit. The song by one of the principal performers, "*Soy la nata y flor del amor*" (I am the cream and flower of love), was vociferously applauded and encored; yet strange to say, I think the Spaniards are, generally speaking, rather cold as an audience, or perhaps I should say, critical. Their taste for music is so great, and their judgment so correct, that they will not endure a middling singer. The galleries as usual were crowded with the men of the jacket and Spanish hat, with their families; and I am told that many pass their evenings there from calculation as well as for amusement; finding that it costs them less to sit in a well-lighted theatre, and hear good music, than to light their *braseros* and lamps at home. A seat in the gallery costs three reals, a *butaca* or chair in the pit, ten. The house, which is crowded nightly, is capable of containing sixteen hundred persons.

The *Teatro del Príncipe* is in another style. It is large, and handsomely decorated, and all the best modern plays of the Spanish school are performed there. The principal actress la Madrid, or la Teodora as she is generally called, is deservedly a great favorite. I saw her the other night in a play taken from Adrienne le Couvreur, a system of adapting from the French, much used here. A new piece comes out in Paris. Rubi, and other celebrated Spanish dramatic writers, will not run the risk of translating it, but they adapt the story to the Spanish stage, with a change of names, scenery and places. This has been done with the "fils de famille," and many others which I have recognized as familiar friends in Spanish attire. La Teodora has a singularly sweet, and on the stage, a beautiful countenance; a remarkable combination of dignity and tenderness in her expression, and that chief qualification for an actress, a soft and melodious voice. She speaks low, yet every word is distinctly heard. She is said to have made Rachel her study and model, but she does not recall that phenomenon to my mind. The other performers are all good in their way, particularly *Arjona;* but I did not observe one who was not above mediocrity.

The Ynfante Don Francisco occupied one of the boxes, a plain, good-natured looking man, with a most inexpressive physiognomy. Scandal says that he is about to be married to a woman of low birth and doubtful character, known as La Teresa Redonda, who was pointed out to me in one of the boxes; a handsome face and fine figure, very richly dressed, with a bold *Manola* expression and air. She was in a box not far from the Ynfante's, whose back however was turned to her during the whole performance.

The Theatre of Lope de Vega, has the advantage of possessing the two brothers Romea, both excellent actors. In this theatre are given the best plays of Lope de Vega, Moratin, Calderon de la Barca, and other great Spanish dramatic writers. It may therefore be considered more national than the Principe; while, for a correct representation of the national manners of the day, the manners of the people as they now are in Madrid, there is nothing like the Circo.

I accompanied Count A——, yesterday, on a visit to the Ynfante, Don Francisco, at his palace of San Juan, near the Retiro. The palace is merely a large country-house, such as might be suitable for the residence of a private gentleman. It has pretty gardens, with as fine trees and flowers as the arid soil round Madrid can produce. Very little ceremony—a few liveried servants and an officer on guard in the ante-room. The Ynfante received us very kindly, made us sit down, and talked a great deal, chiefly upon music and theatricals. His daughters do not reside with him; they have apartments in the palace. The only good picture which I have yet seen of the queen, hangs in the drawing-room. It is the work of Madrazo. She is dressed in a morning gown of green silk, with her child upon her knee. There is also a good portrait of the king, by the same artist.

CHAPTER XIV.

Dinner at the English Legation—Don Juan——,—His Vanity—His Discomfiture—His Excuse—The Question of Religious Toleration—The Times and English Policy—The Spanish People, Parties, and Politics—Rigoletto—Female Ease and Grace—Spanish Inborn Politeness.

October.

Dined at the English Legation, a handsome, well-furnished house—the dinner good, the company agreeable. All the cabinet ministers and their ladies were there. Lord H—— very pleasant. He has been, and indeed still is, a remarkably handsome man, known in former days in Paris, as "*le beau C——c.*" He is extremely tall, with a fine figure, particularly well *conservé.* After dinner, while the ladies took coffee in the drawing-room, we adjourned to his lordship's cabinet to smoke cigars.

I think I have never mentioned to you a certain Don Juan——,who, as our Legation does not occupy the whole of this house, which is very large, but only the *rez-de-chaussée* and the first floor, has taken an apartment on the second floor, and whom we frequently see in the *Chancellerie.* He is a young man of respectable family, of tolerable abilities, and good natured in his way, but who has the misfortune to consider himself *a beauty.* He is a large, rather clumsily-built man, certainly handsome, though, perhaps, not of the most distinguished style of good looks. He was at one time secretary of Legation in Berlin, and is now here upon *congé*. He is extremely anxious to distinguish himself in some way, chiefly in public speaking, for which he thinks he has a peculiar turn. When very young, he was taken up by the Marquesa de —— and other amateurs of her description, and his present mania is, that every woman who sees him falls in love with him *right away*, as the American attaché in Berlin used to say. He dined at the Legation yesterday, and laid down the law in culinary matters, giving various pieces of information to the minister which were neither new nor instructive. After dinner he took me into his confidence, showed me a miniature, a piece of hair in a locket, the addresses of several letters in female hands, with a charming *naiveté*, astonishing in a man of his years. "My great difficulty," said he, "is when I meet them together. You can't imagine, my dear fellow, how much diplomacy it costs me. To the marquesa I shall ever feel grateful; but she is past thirty, and that charming little Mariquita is in the very bloom of youth. I have not told you their names. Pray do not insist upon it. But I fear you will soon discover them, for you will observe their eyes constantly following me from different quarters of the ball-room, or at the theatre, or passing in the Prado. By the way, did you observe that lovely girl with fair hair walking in the Salon yesterday? As I passed, she made me an almost imperceptible sign with her fan while her mother happened to be looking in another direction. I followed them into a shop to-day, and she gave me such a glance! What a bewildering place this Madrid is! For these kind of adventures and for politics, it is almost impossible to suffice. But you, with your quiet, demure face, let me hear a few of your adventures." I assured my friend I was not so fortunate as he. "Perhaps not," said he gravely. "I have so much feeling myself, that I think it exercises a kind of magnetic influence upon others. I may cease to adore a woman, but I never cease to love her. I write her an honorable letter, telling her that another has fascinated me, but will never obliterate her from my remembrance, and we always remain good friends, though a shade of sadness marks our intercourse from that period. I consider her as an elder sister, or a young mother." "That must be very interesting, but hard for her, I think." "Not at all; women are strange creatures. I know them thoroughly, and never was deceived in one." "Never?" said M——, who had dined with us, and who appeared to be asleep on a divan near the window. "What was that story of the Italian singer in Turin, and—of the English Legation?" "Oh! that," said Don Juan, growing very red, "was a ridiculous affair. She was a mere coquette, not worth a thought. But, my dear friends, I must leave you. I have a little rendezvous to-night, political I assure you, though M—— looks so knowing. Au revoir!" "I thought I should drive him away," said M——, laughing. "That man has no Spanish blood in him; he is an exceptional character. If he were only amusing! but he is such a terrible bore!"

I should not have troubled you with this long account of Don Juan, but for an amusing incident which occurred last evening at Lord H——'s after dinner, of which he was the discomfited hero. He was there in all the glories of a pale blue waistcoat, opal studs, and a most *recherché* toilette. He had been seated at dinner next the beautiful Marquesa de S——, and appeared to be in a state of intense excitement. When we had got into the cabinet, he took me aside with a mysterious air, and showed me a small corner of a lace handkerchief protruding from his waistcoat pocket. "Do you know whose this is?" said he. I professed my ignorance. "Did you not observe me at dinner? I flatter myself I did not prove a very disagreeable companion. You know I took her in to table. I told her she looked divinely. The marquis was just behind us. She said nothing, but you should have seen her expression! What eyes that woman has!" "And the handkerchief?" "Ah! my dear friend, I must be discreet; but it was easy to draw it from the unresisting hand which rested confidingly on my arm. It shall never leave me but with life!" "Egregious coxcomb!" was my mental ejaculation. "Confess that you are a little envious, my dear fellow," said the bore, following me as I made my retreat to the drawing-room. Just then we observed a slight movement amongst the guests. "Pray do not trouble yourself," said the marquesa, "only I have dropped my handkerchief. I believe I have left it in the dining-room." I looked at Don Juan, whose face was in a blaze. The master of the house despatched a servant to look for the missing handkerchief. Several gentlemen volunteered their services, but returned, saying it was not to be found. All the cushions were turned over; all the sofas searched in vain. The marquesa was shocked at giving so much trouble, yet seemed annoyed. Lord H—— insisted upon going himself, when Don Juan, who had been looking the picture of uneasiness, rushed off, and in a few minutes returned, looking very red and displaying the handkerchief. "Where did you find it?" said several voices. "In the ante-room." "A thousand thanks," said the marquesa. "I am glad you found it, as it has a curious value attached to it." Every one admired the curious old point and rich embroidery of the handkerchief. "That is not its chief value," said the marquesa. "It was given to my grandmother many years ago, when she was a young bride at the French court, by Marie Antoinette herself. You see it has the crown of France with the fleur-de-lis embroidered on it, and the initials of the poor queen. My mother gave it me as a precious relic, and I seldom carry it. In future I must be more careful."

I was malicious enough to look at the discomfited Don Juan, who had the hardihood to whisper—"All this is a mere *ruse*. She saw me speaking to Mme. G—— after dinner, and was jealous; and besides, upon reflection, she perhaps feared the fate of Desdemona. But I have promised to look in upon the little Countess de V—— in her opera-box to-night, so *adios!*" "Now there goes one of the pests of society," said the Marquis de C——, as we were walking together towards the theatre. "Luckily, he has been discovered to-night. He had already shown that handkerchief to M—— and to me; he would have shown it in the same way at the Casino. Although known and laughed at, yet some few would have been gulled by his absurd vanity; and the poor marquesa, against whom scandal has never breathed a word up to this hour, would have been supposed to favor this most insufferable blockhead!"

"We have had a pleasant party," said I; "Lord H—— and the cabinet appear to be on the most harmonious terms." My friend shook his head. "All seeming," said he, "at least on his side. They are at present upon the vexed question of the Protestant cemetery." "I thought that question had been settled." "To a certain extent; that is, the Protestants are permitted to have a cemetery *extra-muros*, surrounded by a wall, but without religious processions, church, or ceremonies, beyond the mere reading of the burial-service. The *Times* calls Calderon de la Barca a second *Torquemada*, in consequence. But, in the first place, there are no religious processions at Protestant funerals; there are only more or less coaches. In the next place, it is the law of the land, which is opposed to religious toleration. Considering, then, that this reservation is made in a country which does not admit the public exercise of any religion but the Catholic, and that the law affects merely a few foreigners, generally transitory, seldom resident, and apparently very indifferent, since as yet they have not even built the wall round their cemetery; whereas, in England, where universal toleration is supposed to be exercised, millions of faithful subjects of the queen, belonging to the oldest and most loyal families, are not permitted to carry their dead to the grave with Catholic processions or ceremonies—it must be admitted that all this vituperation against Spanish bigotry is equally absurd and unjust."

"But between England and Spain, it is the fable of the wolf and the lamb acted out from one year's end to another. The English minister will pay court to the moderado cabinet, from policy; but no true cordiality can exist between them. The *Times* will continue to write offensive articles against the queen, with the tone of an offended sense of virtue and morality, for which its unworthy agent here is well paid—a course of policy utterly unworthy of a great nation. The opposition party will be privately but powerfully encouraged; and no pains spared to bring about the return of Espartero and the liberal party, no matter at what expense of blood and treasure, to this country. And, unfortunately, many of the aristocracy themselves unwittingly play into the hands of their enemies. It is the old story of the French revolution. The abuse of the queen came at first from the higher classes. It was caught up by the vulgar; and when the public passions were let loose the nobles found themselves the first victims, and could no longer stay the tempest they had themselves undesignedly aided in raising.

"Here the grandees will oppose the ministry because the Count of San Luis has raised himself to his present position, and they are annoyed to find a man of yesterday at the head of the government. The Conchas will oppose the ministers, because the ministers are not the Conchas. You will hear something worth listening to when the Cortes opens, if I am not mistaken." "You expect, then, a violent opposition to the government and the defeat of the ministry? Upon what question?" "Upon the first that is discussed, whatever it may be. I expect a violent opposition, though by no means sure that the ministers will be in the minority." "But, generally speaking," said I, "the aristocracy appear to interfere very little in politics."

"There are three classes here," said the marquis, "very distinct in character. The grandees of Spain, from pride or indifference, seldom take any prominent part in public affairs. They are, as you must have observed, the most agreeable, refined, and gentlemanlike men in their manners imaginable. There is no mistaking the *pur sang*, noble birth, and high spirit of the race. But their talents have lain dormant for generations. Their lives pass in the atmosphere of the court, and whatever natural gifts they possess grow rusty from want of use. The second class, the young men who have their fortunes to make, the editors of newspapers, those who come from the provinces, those who fill nearly all the posts at the bar, the magistracy, &c.; those who compose the principal part of the deputies; they possess the talent, the energy, the ambition which the others lack. They are less high-minded, less chivalrous in their feelings, less fastidious; but they are more daring, energetic, and active, and they work the secret springs of every popular movement. The *people* of Spain are the finest in the world. Bold, independent, honorable, they only require the long continuance of a good government to develope all their noble qualities. But they are credulous and easily led; and in every revolution which has hitherto taken place, they have been mere machines in the hands of ambitious and designing men. But I hear the chorus of the dancers in Rigoletto:

> "Tutto é gioja, tutto é festa
> Tutto invitari à goder!"

Let us accept the invitation, especially as our cigars are out."

The theatre was unusually brilliant last night; the opera Rigoletto. Every one knows the horrid plot. La Basseggio sang beautifully, but cannot compete with la Gazzamga, either as actress or singer. The part of Rigoletto by Varessi, was well performed. He is an excellent actor, but has nearly lost his voice. The theatre was crowded up to the highest gallery, and more brilliantly illuminated than usual, owing to the expected attendance of the queen. She came in about ten o'clock. The orchestra struck up the Royal March. She came forward and curtsied to the audience, every one standing of course. She looked better than I have ever seen her, dressed in white satin, with pink flowers. No one accompanied her but the king and the mistress of the robes. Some of the cabinet ministers went up to pay their respects to her majesty.

The music of Rigoletto has already become popular to the extent of being played by every hand-organ, and sung by every little *gamin* in Madrid. "La Donna é Mobile" is played by the military bands, hummed by the loungers at the Puerta del Sol, whistled by porters and cabmen; in fact, the very air seems impregnated with it. Verdi might walk triumphantly through Madrid, perpetually serenaded by his own music. At the scene of the sack, I observed many people rise and leave their boxes, and even half the pit was deserted. "How absurd," said M——; "these people would not leave the *plaza de toros* till the last bull was killed, and the last horse gored; and now they cannot bear to look at la Basseggio in a sack, though they know that she is going home to supper in half an hour; and hungry she has a right to be, after all she has gone through this night."

Went with M—— to see Madrazo's studio. He is a clever artist, and has one great merit. He keeps closely to the likeness, yet *poetizes* the individual. Saw a lovely portrait of a Habana girl in a ball-dress. If as like the original as they say it is, I rejoice for my peace of mind that she is not here. M—— says her voice is even more perfect than her face, and that she made a *furor* here a few years ago. There is also a fine picture of the Duchess of Medina-Cœli, and another of the Countess of Vilches, the latter very lovely. The duchess is represented in a superb Andalusian dress, which exactly suits her style. They say she sent a magnificent one as a present to the queen, who returned her a parure of diamonds.

All the Madrazos are men of talents, born artists. A brother of the painter is a poet of great merit, and unlike the generality of his brethren, looks like one.

I could not help remarking the other evening, on coming from a tertulia at the Marquesa de M——s, that in Madrid, from the queen downwards, I have not yet met an affected woman. This perfect simplicity of manner is, in my opinion, one of the first things that strikes a stranger on his introduction to society here. Affectation seems a quality ignored by the Spanish race, *minauderie* unknown, and what is called giving one's self airs, a thing unheard of.

Count A—— who has lived many years in this country, confirmed my opinion. "It is certain," said he, "that the first duchess in Spain, however young, beautiful and elegant, is as simple in her manners as the wife of the poorest shopkeeper. She is never afraid of letting herself down, or of being too condescending in general society. Lately, at rather a mixed gathering at the Countess of ——s, which the witty Marquesa de —— remarked, was like the Prado with a roof upon it, I observed the old Duchess of S——, certainly one of the most distinguished ladies in Madrid, accidentally seated beside a peculiarly disagreeable, and for a Spaniard, very vulgar man; of low family, and whom she did not know; yet upon being addressed by him with some commonplace remark, reply with the greatest politeness, and continue to converse with him, precisely as if he had been one of the first hidalgos of the land.

"But indeed I have never seen rudeness shown to any one. If such a manner were to be adopted by an individual of the highest, towards one of a secondary class, it would appear to him merely absurd. Whatever the distinctions of rank, there is perfect independence in all classes. You will see the young ladies of the family wish the porter good morning as they step into their carriage, and the porter is not a bit the more familiar, because as he takes off his hat, he says, "*Vayan Vds. con Dios.*" This cordial manner never begets familiarity on the part of servants or dependents. I am aware that it could not be practised in other countries, in the relative position of master and servant; but it is a pleasant thing to see, and speaks well for both parties. Moreover, the result of it is, that in times of danger and trouble, unfortunately too frequent in this country, these servants have constantly proved their unshaken fidelity, their readiness to lay down their lives for any member of the family in whose service they have lived.

Here, there is dignity without haughtiness, a desire to please, without affectation, besides that cordiality and kindness which in society puts every one at his ease. In my opinion, there is no country in the world which might not take lessons in manners from Spain; and I trust it will be very long before foreign fashions are introduced in this particular.

"Moreover," continued the count, "it is a fact which no one acquainted with this country will contest, that as affectation is unknown, so, generally speaking, is vulgarity; but the latter is no doubt, in a great measure, the result of the former. Vulgarity is generally produced by an attempt to seem what we are not. A plain farmer does not strike us as being vulgar, but his fine lady daughters, who murder Strauss's waltzes on the piano, are offensively so. A mincing femme-de-chambre, who wears the cast-off dresses, and apes the manners of her mistress, is vulgar; not so the peasant girl who carries her vegetables to market. The lower classes in this country, as you will find when you have an opportunity of travelling, are quite as independent as the highest grandees, and are neither vulgar nor servile. There seems an inborn courtesy in the Spaniard; a perfect appreciation of what is due both to himself and to others. He is never shy or embarrassed, yet is never insolent. This simplicity of manner in all classes, has to me a peculiar charm. It seems to proceed from real kindness of heart. In this alone they are republicans, since they undoubtedly act upon the conviction that all men are brothers, and equals in the sight of Heaven. The great difficulty in other countries is, that the lower classes would presume upon the familiarity of the higher, of which here there is no danger.

"I have been amused at seeing how little sympathy a fine lady from London or Paris has met with in Madrid. These *grandes dames*, who gave themselves airs, no doubt expected to impress the world with a sense of their grandeur; but no one understood them, and they were considered stupid or silly. Whatever pride of birth may lurk in the hearts of the *sangre azul* in Spain, it is certainly never offensively displayed."

CHAPTER XV.

Pulmonía—Charitable Institutions, how managed—Hospital of San Fernando—College of the Unprotected—Foundling Hospital—Mendicant Asylum—College for Orphan Girls—Confraternity of Refuge and Pity—Other Hospitals and Asylums.

November —.

THE weather here seems to have no *juste milieu;* it is either sunny and dry (this is its normal state apparently), or it rains without ceasing, as it does at present. Nothing is spoken of but the approaching opening of the Cortes. The Marquis of Viluma, now ambassador in Paris, will, it is supposed, be chosen president of the Senate. He will look the thing at all events. Tall, dignified, and imposing, he seems to have been intended by nature to perform the part of a grave ambassador, a dignified lord in waiting; to have been destined, in short, for what he is.

Meanwhile, if I have not come to the end of all the charitable and beneficent institutions in Madrid, it is not that I have felt indifferent to the interest which my mother expresses in her last letter to hear further details on the subject; nor is it that I have been afraid of the rain, or of taking a *pulmonía*, the great bug-bear, by the way, of the Madrileños. This *pulmonía* appears to be a pleurisy arising from the coldness of the air, coming upon checked perspiration. It is very sudden, and often fatal; and owing to the extreme rarity of the air, blowing directly from the snow-capped mountains, is said to be very frequent; so that the proverb says, "The air which would not blow out a candle, will kill a man." For this reason, people are afraid to open their windows on days which seem warm to my northern feelings, devoutly dread a draught, and rush from the theatre enveloped in cloaks which only permit the exposure of half an eye, and the extreme *bout du nez.* Various are the warnings which I have had upon this subject. Yet the fairest half of creation seem to have no fear about the matter; for although the thick mantilla is now more generally worn than it was last month, there are still hundreds who have no other covering to their head but the lace veil. I have taken advantage of a kind of *lull*, caused partly by the bad weather, and partly by the total absorption of the public mind in elections and political affairs, to visit nearly every thing worth seeing in Madrid. I need not say that I have spent hours in the *Museo.*

But to return to the subject of charitable institutions in Madrid, I ought to explain to you that they are under the direction of what are called *Juntas de Benificencia*, and that these juntas are divided into three classes—general, provincial, and municipal; at the head of the first are the cardinal, Archbishop of Toledo, and the Duke of Riansares; the governor of the province is president of the second; and the municipal is directed by the *alcalde corregidor.* The most distinguished persons in Spain compose these juntas. Under the charge of the general junta are all those persons afflicted with infirmities of a permanent character, which require especial attention, such as the blind, deaf, and dumb, the infirm and decrepit. To the provincial juntas belong the care of all ordinary infirmities, and they are charged with the protection and education of orphans, or destitute children. The hospitals for the sick, the houses of mercy, and maternity, are under their direction. The municipal juntas are destined for the assistance of those afflicted with casual maladies or infirmities, for the shelter of the indigent poor, of houseless beggars, &c.; for all which purposes they have houses of refuge and beneficence. It is evident that this system, zealously carried through, must produce incalculably good results.

On a day in which the rain poured in torrents, and even Madrid looked gloomy, I accompanied Don —— to visit the hospitium of San Fernando, in the street of Fuencarral, founded in 1688 by the queen regent, Doña Mariana of Austria. Its object is to give shelter, food, and clothing, together with occupation, to the poor of both sexes. It is a large, spacious, and well-ventilated building, capable of containing eighteen hundred persons. Here all are occupied in various labors. Within the establishment are manufactories of linen, cloths, embroideries, glass, &c., which are sold at moderate prices, and the profits devoted to this and other charitable institutions. Though the expenses amounted this year to upwards of a million of reals, they were more than covered by the sale of the articles manufactured. Children are employed according to their abilities, and those persons who are too old or infirm to labor, are well cared for and attended to. This establishment is under the charge of the provincial junta, with a director, chaplain, directress, and various other *employés*. We visited their chapel, where there is a fine painting by Giordano, representing the taking of Seville, by San Fernando.

The college of the *Desamparados* (unprotected) was founded in the year 1600, for the education of poor children; more particularly for those who, at the age of seven, are sent there from the foundling hospital. Here they receive instruction in the doctrines of the Christian religion; they are taught reading, writing, arithmetic, and grammar; their moral education is carefully attended to, and when they leave the college, they are put to some trade, or placed in a situation to gain an honest livelihood.

The foundling hospital, or *Inclusa*, as it is called, because it contains a miraculous image of Our Lady, brought by a Spanish soldier from the Dutch town of *Enkuissen*, the word having been gradually corrupted into *Inclusa*—is under the direction of the provincial junta, and served by the Sisters of Charity. Its object is to provide for the support of all infants exposed at the doors of the various hospitals, which are said to amount to upwards of four thousand annually. These children are intrusted to nurses, either within the house or in the country, and as the expenses are great, every imaginable method is put in practice by the principal ladies in Madrid, for obtaining sufficient funds for its maintenance—public subscriptions, concerts, raffles, and so on.

Then there is the college of Our Lady of Peace, for the education of these children, where they are taught to make gloves, straw hats, to embroider, sew, &c.; their work producing upwards of fifty thousand reals annually. They are sent there from the Inclusa, at the age of seven.

Another excellent establishment is the Asylum of Mendicity of St. Bernardino, whose object is to collect all the beggars who formerly swarmed in the streets of the capital. These were all collected together in the old convent of San Bernardino, through the energy and intelligence of the Marquis of Pontejos, then *corregidor* of the city. They are divided into bands, some employed in cultivating the garden, others in washing, cooking, or cleaning the house; some in manufacturing shoes, in printing, or in making clothes; while others work during the day out of the establishment, and are employed in carrying the sick to the hospitals, in taking care of the benches in the churches, &c. They wear a clean uniform, a gray blouse with a belt, and on their hats the number which corresponds to each member of the asylum. It is impossible to see an institution of the kind better regulated. We visited the dormitories, workshops, large kitchen, and refectories; all was clean and spacious; the food plain and plentiful; and abundance of water throughout the whole establishment. It is under the care of the municipal junta.

There is another college for orphan girls, founded by the Viscountess of Forbalein, who devoted her whole fortune to this object. Here there are about sixty girls, brought up strictly and religiously, and instructed in all kinds of useful works, for which they have female teachers. They remain in this establishment from the age of seven to that of fifteen. This college is under the immediate direction of the general junta.

One of the most interesting visits we paid was to the Deaf, Dumb, and Blind Asylum, of which it is impossible to speak too highly. It is directed by Don Juan Ballesteros, who has devoted the principal part of a long life in endeavoring to ameliorate the condition of these unfortunate beings. All that the most enlightened charity and enlarged benevolence could do, has been brought to bear upon this subject, and with astonishing success. He has lately obtained from the government a large garden for the establishment, which he told us had been for years the object of his ambition. I was astonished at the proficiency of the blind girls in music. One, especially, sung a variety of airs from the last operas, accompanying herself with a degree of skill and correctness which would have been remarkable in a girl possessing all the advantages of eye-sight and a good musical education. Her voice was fine and powerful, and the intense pleasure which she herself took in the performance, might be seen even in spite of her sightless orbs, in her happy smile, and in a look of enthusiasm which I could not have believed compatible with the entire absence of expression in the eye. The pupils are taught reading, writing, arithmetic, music, singing, every kind of needlework, geography and geometry, the whole based upon a thoroughly religious education. A printing-press and an office for bookbinding is attached to the college; and the ingenious mechanism for teaching the pupils to read and write, the beauty and fineness of the embroideries and needlework, the correctness of the printing, the excellence of the binding, all the work of the pupils; prove the zeal and intelligence with which this establishment is conducted. We went there one morning, by invitation, to be present at the inauguration of their pretty little chapel, when mass was performed by the pope's nuncio. The music, entirely executed by the blind pupils, was surprisingly good.

As we were walking home, my friend Don ——, who had so kindly accompanied me in all these expeditions, gave me various particulars concerning the duties of the "Holy Confraternity of Refuge and Pity," to which he belongs, and which I already mentioned to you as having the charge of the Hospital of St. Antonio *de los Portugueses*. The brothers, who all belong to a distinguished class of society, and many of whom I constantly meet in the gay world, take turns in visiting and assisting the poor and dying in their houses, pay for their medicines and baths, give an asylum to all poor strangers, maintain a college of orphans, and employ themselves in other beneficent works. No poor traveller is refused admittance at their hospital—he is sure of a good supper, and a comfortable bed, at least for one night.

He also gave me an account of the various asylums established here for unfortunate women; that of St. Nicholas de Bari, founded in 1691, for women of a better class, who for misconduct are banished from the houses of their husbands or fathers; that of the *Arrepentidas*, for penitent women; that of the *Recogidas*, founded in 1637, for the correction of women who are sent there by their families, in order that they may be induced to return to the paths of virtue; it is under the direction of the "Sisters of St. Mary Magdalene."

A hospital for the insane has, he tells me, been recently established in the village of Leganés, near Madrid. Formerly this department belonged to the general hospital. There are innumerable schools for poor children, of both sexes; amongst others, that of the *Niños Doctrinos*, founded in time immemorial; that of the *Leganés*, for girls, founded in 1630, and in whose church the beauty of the female voices in the choir has become very celebrated; that of the *Niñas de Loreto*, founded in 1581; the royal college of the "Niñas de Santa Isabel," in 1595; and that of the "Niñas del Refugio," founded in 1651. Besides all the establishments of public beneficence, there are many others in Madrid, such as the Royal Association of Domiciliary Beneficence; that of ladies for the support of nuns, which owes its origin to the Marquesa de Malpica; that of charity, called the Good Shepherd, for poor prisoners; that of mutual assistance of various corporations; besides numerous gratuitous establishments of public instruction; such as the Lancastrian School, School of Piety, &c., &c. It may be remarked that the greater part of these public charitable institutions were founded in the 15th, 16th, and 17th centuries, when the population of Madrid was much less than it now is.

Don —— was anxious that I should visit the *Mont de Piété* with him; but as it was past the hour of admission, we deferred it to another opportunity. It is a large establishment, founded in the time of Philip V., at the suggestion of his chaplain, Don Francisco Piquer, with the intention of suppressing usury, where money is lent gratuitously upon clothes and jewels, and connected with which is a savings' bank, inaugurated in 1839. It is remarkable, on account of the liberal and philanthropic manner in which it is conducted, the perfect fairness with which each article is valued by the *tasadores* or appraisers, and the fact that when, at the end of a year, the property is sold at public auction, if the owner has not claimed it, whatever is paid over and above its value, is made over to him.

CHAPTER XVI.

All Souls' Day—Prayers for the Dead—A Jesuit Priest—M—— declares his Scepticism.

November 3d.

In spite of political discussions, vehement disputes, party spirit, opposition clubs, and prognostics of the fall of the cabinet, Madrid presented yesterday a striking spectacle, proving the influence of religion on an occasion when all the sympathies and sorrows of the human heart are called into action. Yesterday was All Souls' Day, rigorously observed throughout this country; when the whole population of Madrid repair to the cemeteries in the environs of the capital, to offer up their prayers for the repose of the dead. This immense crowd, on foot or in carriages, inundated the churches and *Campos Santos;* quiet, orderly, and for the most part, with an expression of seriousness on their faces rarely observable in Spaniards. Every street leading to the cemeteries was almost entirely blocked up by the pilgrims; families of men, women, and children proceeding in the direction of the various *necropolis;* a whole city of the living visiting the city of the dead. In fact the town was nearly deserted, whilst thousands of carriages filled up the avenues outside the gates. The tombs were ornamented with flowers, garlands of *immortelles*, and wreaths of perishable roses. Innumerable wax-candles burned before each monument, and strains of solemn music and of funereal hymns issued from the interior of the churches. I met Father ——, a learned and excellent Jesuit priest, coming out of San Ysidro, and joined him as he stood wrapped in meditation before the tombs. "Here," said he, "is the invisible chain connecting this world with the other, the known with the unknown, the world of Time with the world of Eternity. No human being is forgotten this day. The church remembers them all in her prayers. No soul so humble or hidden on whom the dew of her compassion does not descend. Look at that poor old woman, herself tottering on the brink of the grave, her little grandchildren supporting her feeble steps. I heard her pray just now, 'for the soul in greatest need.' This is the true communion of saints; this is pure and perfect charity."

"Yet these people," said I, "so pious, so devout, so filled with sad remembrances of their departed friends, will forget to-morrow the lesson they have had to-day." "Many will, no doubt, though surely not all; and it is much to be regretted that their faith is not more practical. Yet still they have *Faith*, undoubting, unwavering; and as long as they retain it we need never despair of our people."

"Padre mío," said a poor man with a wooden leg, making his way through the crowd; "my daughter is worse to-day, and would see your reverence. The fever has come back, and the doctor thinks she may not live through the night." At this intimation the good padre hastily touched his hat, and followed the lame man.

The bells tolled mournfully all day and night, and only glimpses of blue peeped through the dark curtain which covered the sky like a funeral pall. "Like a widow smiling through her weeds," said M——, who had followed the multitude on horseback, and was now on his way out to the country, to get rid, as he said, of the saddest day in the year. "Superstition in some, habit in others, hypocrisy in many," said he. "Not in those beautiful children in deep mourning," said I, "crying so bitterly as they lay that wreath on their mother's tomb." "Not in them, of course," said M——, "but an unnecessary cruelty on the part of their old nurse. She had much better have kept them home, to have a game of romps in their nursery! No need to look shocked, my dear count. I confess that all this is very affecting, and very right on the part of those who believe in what to me seems an idle superstition, if not an interested invention of the priesthood. Seriously speaking," added M——, "if I believed in the efficacy of prayers for the dead, I should acknowledge this to be a sublime and touching spectacle, and therefore I am far from blaming those who do, for devoting one day in the year to a special commemoration of the 'faithful departed;' but being an unbeliever in this, and other Catholic doctrines, all I now see produces no other effect upon me but utter weariness, and an oppressive feeling of gloom, from which I trust to be delivered by a hard trot to B——s, a good dinner, and a few glasses of *amontillado.* So *adios.*" And M—— took his leave with a very forced smile, and the air of one who would gladly get rid of his own thoughts.

CHAPTER XVII.

Opening of the Cortes, Election of President, and Description of the House—The Senate Chamber—Voting and Debating—Debate on the Concession of Railroads—General Armero and the Marquis of Molins, their Speeches—Ball at the French Embassy—M. Soulé—London and Madrid Ladies—The Duke of Alva's Remark on Madame Soulé—Extravagant Costume—Young Soulé Challenges the Duke—A Raffle.

November 19th.

THE session of the Cortes was opened this morning. This is the one grand event of the year. I accompanied Count A—— to the Hall of Congress of the Deputies, where they were busy electing the new president. Every thing looked bright, within and without, for the fine weather has returned, and Madrid, with its blue sky *privilégié*, looks like itself again. The votes were carried in favor of Martinez de la Rosa, which seemed to give great satisfaction in general. He appeared very indifferent to the result, and chiefly employed in reconnoitring his friends in the gallery through his eye-glass, while the voting was going on. There were not many persons in the gallery, and only a few ladies in the diplomatic tribune. The chief interest during this session is expected to be in the Senate. The house is large and commodious, and without being remarkable for architectural beauty, forms a sufficiently imposing object in the Carrera de San Gerónimo, where it stands at the lower end, where that beautiful street of palaces opens out into the *Plaza de Cervantes*, or *de las*

Cortes. It stands upon the site formerly occupied by the old convent and church of the *Espiritu Santo*, and in 1843 Queen Ysabel laid the first stone of the building with her own hand. It occupies a large space of ground, upwards of forty-two thousand feet, with eight sides, built at right angles, the principal entrance fronting the *plaza.*

The hall of session is semicircular, the seats of the deputies disposed in the form of an amphitheatre, the throne and president's table fronting the public gallery. The mahogany benches of the deputies are covered with red velvet, with a desk in front of each member. The bench reserved for the ministers is distinguished from the others by being covered with blue velvet. The throne is very richly carved and ornamented, and the royal arms, embroidered in gold and velvet, are said to be a wonder of art—the performance of some celebrated *brodeuses* from Mayorca. On the white and gold pillars which adorn the hall, are the arms of the nineteen provinces represented in Congress, in alphabetical order. A gallery is reserved for the royal family, the diplomatic corps, and other persons of distinction. The whole of the hall is covered with *escayola*, which is an imitation of white Carrara marble, has a good effect, and must look well at night when the immense lustre and candelabra are lighted.

The roof is beautifully painted by Ribera, and represents the chief personages of four great periods of the Greek and Roman dominion, the Gothic, Arragonese, and the Restoration of Spain. In the centre is represented the present queen, with the fundamental code of the state, surrounded by those who have illustrated the monarchy at different epochs—the Cid, Christopher Columbus, Mariana, Cervantes, &c. There are also four noble historical paintings by Madrazo.

The Senate chamber, to which we adjourned upon leaving that of the Deputies, is a fine hall of an elliptic form, adorned with Ionic pillars, and the very perfection of comfort, well carpeted and well heated. The throne has a rich canopy of crimson velvet, and fronts the great *tribuna* or gallery destined for the public. There are various other tribunas for the diplomatic corps, for the newspaper reporters, for ex-ministers and others. The seats for the ministers of the crown are on the floor, to the right of the throne. The queen, however, did not open the session, on account of her situation; neither did she hold a drawing-room, as usual on her birthday, this 19th of November, though she received the congratulations of her ministers and household.

When we arrived, the president had not yet taken his seat, but the galleries were crowded. Gradually the senators arrived and took their places. The ministers of the crown came in full uniform. The president, the Marquis of Viluma, entered with an air of great dignity, bowing to several ladies whom he recognized in the tribuna, took his place, and rang a little bell to announce that the business of the day was about to begin. We were in the diplomatic tribune, which is on a level with the floor. The French and Austrian ambassadors were there, and as there were no ladies, I had every opportunity of seeing and hearing. But being the first day, nothing of interest took place. The president of the council read the royal decree announcing the opening of the Cortes; the president announced that, in consequence of this decree, the sessions had commenced, and requested the committee destined to felicitate her majesty on the return of her birthday, to hold themselves in readiness until the hour in which her majesty was to receive them should be made known by the *mayor-domo mayor*.

Meanwhile the national flag waved on all the public buildings; and a brilliant review had already been held in the Prado by the captain-general. The streets were crowded, the weather perfect. In the evening the theatres were illuminated, together with all the principal public buildings and several private houses. The queen celebrated the day in a worthy manner, by sending a large sum of money to the governor, to be distributed amongst the different charitable establishments and juntas. Went in the evening with the R——ses to the *Teatro del Instituto*, to see the French company, which is tolerably good. They played one or two amusing vaudevilles. I left them at the end of "Riché d'amour," and arrived in time for the last act of Rigoletto at the Royal Theatre. The queen-mother arrived yesterday, accompanied from Somosierra by the governor of the province. She was received, they say, with enthusiasm as she passed, although it is generally supposed that she has become very unpopular. The queen waited for her in the plaza of the Senate, and the authorities presented themselves to offer their respects, while the beautiful band of the guard of honor played the Royal March.

24th.—Nothing very interesting as yet has taken place in the Senate. The voting in of secretaries, the division of the Senate into sections. In the House, a list of *expedientes* for railroads, which, if carried through, will make Spain a less poetical, but certainly a more prosperous country than it now is; a royal decree on the subject of debtors, which appears to be very good. On the 22d, four senators were sworn in and took their seats—Calderon de la Barca, Estevañez y Calderon, Espeleta, the Marquis of Castillo, and the Count Nagaez. The ceremony is short but solemn. The oath is taken kneeling.

I pass my time in the Senate, but I fear the debates will prove very uninteresting to you. To me no theatre is half so amusing; but besides the animation of the speakers, I am acquainted with many of the senators, whom I have met in society, and the determined opposition to the government throws great vehemence into the discussions of subjects which to me, at least, do not appear to possess any vital importance. Fronting the diplomatic tribune, sit the Marquis of Duero and General José Concha, who, having obtained every honor in the gift of the crown, are said to feel like Alexander, when he wept at finding no more worlds to conquer, and even to covet some honors higher than subjects can claim; General O'Donnell, immensely tall, a fine-looking man, and, like the Conchas, violently opposed to the government from the same motives; General Ros de Olano, a fiery, wiry, spare, white-headed veteran, more than suspected of republican principles. Then there is the Marquis of C——, with his quick, penetrating eye, and a sharp, active, lawyer look; the Marquis of M——s, an old statesman, who is said to believe himself to be the only man capable of saving the country; the Duke of R——s, with a fashionable, rather roué air, very busy, very important, going about from one senator to another, and talking in whispers to his neighbor, the venerable Archbishop of Toledo, who, with his tall, thin, dignified figure, enveloped in his cardinal's robes, and his mild, handsome countenance, forms the most striking feature in the assemblage.

On the 25th, the war-signal was given by what appeared a very peaceable communication from the government to the Senate, in which they requested that body to be pleased to suspend the discussion upon the decision of the commission of railroads, because the government had presented a project for a law relative to the concessions of railroads to the Congress of Deputies. The president added that this communication would be passed to the sections, that they might name the commission which was to give its opinion. Then Señor Calderon Collantes rose, and made several remarks, which appeared to occasion a great sensation in the Senate. He observed that this communication was of the most transcendent importance, since its object was to request the Senate to abdicate its prerogative on a subject of such immense moment; and that it would be natural, logical, and suitable, that it should pass to the commission which then existed upon that affair, since no other could offer so many guaranties of success.

Nevertheless he protested that he desired a pacific discussion of the question, and would throw no difficulties in the way of the president's proposition, thus giving a proof of the moderation of himself and his party, and of the falsehood of those accusations of impatience which had been thrown out against them.

Shortly after, the railroad commission was named, consisting of the Duke of Sotomayor, General Concha, Señores Lopez, Olivan, and Moreno, the Count of Torre Marin, and General Ynfante. As we were leaving the Senate, I observed much apparent cordiality between the two parties; much cordial hand-shaking between ministerialists and oppositionists, and much friendly recognition between the ministers themselves and those whom they expect to be their most violent opponents. Nothing is talked of throughout Madrid but the expected defeat of the ministry upon the railroad question. As M—— says, it is as pretty a cause for a quarrel as any other.

News has arrived of the death of the Queen of Portugal. On account of her majesty's situation, a great deal of *ménagement* was used in telling her the news, but it was found that she was the first person informed of it. They say walls have ears, but that the palace walls have tongues. An order is issued for three months' mourning.

25th.—A long speech from General Armero, ex-minister

of the navy, a large, portly, good-natured looking commodore, though he spoke with great indignation. His complaint is the union, in the person of the Captain-general of Cuba, of the command of the army, with that of the navy. He gave a long list of naval engagements, and of incidents which had occurred in the maritime history of Cuba, going to prove the necessity of the existence of two separate authorities in those two important commands. He speaks in a familiar tone, and with the air of an honest admiral treading the quarter-deck, and making remarks to his lieutenants. His speech was replied to by the Marquis of Molins, minister of the navy, with the most exquisite courtesy. He limited himself chiefly to prove that the crown possessed the prerogative of disposing of its armed forces, and of distributing them in the manner which it deemed most suitable, and its perfect right to confide the command of the navy to one not belonging to the navy, the same principle holding good with regard to the army. And then the speaker, who is a true orator, launched forth into examples justifying this system, beginning with Hernan Cortez, and proving how navies had been commanded by military men, and with what glorious results. He spoke of Trafalgar, where army men had commanded the navy along with the admirals; of the hero of Lepanto, Don John of Austria, and brought his examples up to modern days, showing equal eloquence and knowledge of history. The lateness of the hour stopped his speech, which is to be resumed to-morrow.

26th.—Molins concluded his brilliant discourse. Of the merit of the question I cannot pretend to judge. Of the merit of the orator there can be no doubt. Armero answered with great modesty and candor, denied all intention of attacking the prerogative of the crown, and ended by withdrawing his proposition. Molins returned thanks in a few expressive words, in which, amongst other remarks, he declared, in answer to some expression which had fallen from General Armero, and which he retracted, that the most important mission of the government was to act as a shield, as a wall of defence to the sovereign; that when the queen did well, it was due to herself alone; when ill, to her ministers only. Hereupon, this question terminated amicably.

I have been so much engrossed with these matters, that I have forgotten to give you an account of the great ball given at the French Embassy on the day of St. Eugénie, in honor of the empress, a few days before the opening of the Cortes. The Countess de Montijo, who had prepared her beautiful salons to celebrate the same event, waived her right to the representatives of France. On that evening, at least, diamonds were taken from their cases and saw the light, and it would have been difficult to find a greater combination of beauty and magnificence in any ball-room. Of course, all that was most distinguished in Madrid composed the assembly, and as the rooms were crowded, I was amused to hear the complaints of the old Condesa de ——, that many had been omitted who should have been invited. "Better for them and for us," said I. "By no means," said the old lady. "Better that we should all stifle, than that any one should be offended." Between the intervals of a quadrille and a waltz, I observed the American minister, Mr. Soulé, standing alone, and apparently in rather an isolated position, and it struck me, that though the most polite attention was shown to him and his family by the host and hostess, there was not much anxiety manifested to make his acquaintance. "He has only himself to thank," said M——. "If you were informed that a man had been urging his neighbors to rob your house, you would not feel very cordially disposed towards him. But the Spaniards are a good-natured people, and I have no doubt they will soon forget their motives of complaint against him, if he is prudent and conciliating. There are some very good-looking people here to-night," continued M——, who as usual had taken up his post of observation in a corner, with his back against the wall. "That little Countess S—o—i is a nice little independent-looking thing, a good rider, a good shot, and yet no *lionne;* besides caring no more how she looks than I do." "Fortunately she is extremely handsome, and some one dresses her remarkably well. Then she dances like a zephyr." "But after all," said M——, "one does not see that high-bred air amongst the women, which we find in a London party of the same standing." "They are *so* much prettier here," said I, "so much more graceful, so much more *piquante.* When did you ever see such feet in London?" "Possibly never, but there are very few such *grandes dames* here as we have in London." "I disagree with you. There are none who have so much pretension, and they are not *fenced off* as these ladies are in London. But they are quite as *grandes dames,* and perhaps in reality quite as proud of their old names and families, as your London duchesses."

"I am not to be convinced. There is not the air of high-breeding that the English women have, not that look of *race* which we see amongst the daughters of our aristocracy. In fact there is no very marked difference here between the wives of the bankers and merchants, and the señoras of the *sangre azul.*" "I think M—— is right in the latter remark," said C——s, "but I draw a different inference from this circumstance. I think it proceeds from the fact, that those of a secondary class here are always ladylike, and in England this is not invariably the case; especially when they happen to meet with the higher class in society, and look as if they felt themselves out of place. On these occasions, your great ladies are apt to look high and condescending, and the others fluttered and embarrassed, from an exceeding desire to appear quite at their ease." "Two against one," said M——; "nevertheless, I hold to my opinion."

A few minutes afterwards, I happened to form one of a group of *pollos*, amongst whom was the Duke of Alva. They were very merry, and making remarks, critical or laudatory, upon all the world as they passed,—upon the beauty, the toilettes, &c., especially of the girls and young married women. Amongst others who passed us, was the lady of the American minister, dressed, I think, in dark green velvet, and leaning on her son's arm. "Here," said the duke in French, "comes Marie de Bourgogne." Some one whispered to him that the lady was French, and he turned away and changed the conversation.

Alas! what mighty ills from little causes flow! As it turned out, the young man had heard the remark, and treasured it up as a matter of grave offence. Want of knowledge of the world—for he seems very young—and the idea of an intentional offence to his mother, may plead his excuse. Be that as it may, it seems that he left the assembly, boiling with rage, and determined to make it a matter of life and death between himself and the duke. Fortunately, some cooler head than his own prevented him from making an *esclandre* in the ball-room. It seemed a night famous for indiscreet remarks; for a little while after, as the handsome young Duke of F——a was leading his partner to a chair, she exclaimed—"I want you to look at the most ridiculous dress! Observe that lady with rubies and diamonds, and such a *baroque*-looking gown, of every color under the rainbow." "So it is," said the young duke; "I told my mother it was frightful, but she insisted upon wearing it." The young lady was shocked; but her partner, laughing heartily, went up to his mother. "Mamma," said he, "everybody thinks your gown a fright." "I am sorry for everybody's taste," said the marquesa, good-humoredly, "for I think it a beauty."

Notwithstanding these *lapsus linguæ*, the ball continued with great animation, and was kept up till four in the morning. As for the brilliancy of the toilettes, it would require a fairer hand than mine to do them justice. "We particularly remarked," as the English newspapers say, the magnificent dress of the Countess of Montijo, although, except her being in one blaze of diamonds, and wearing on one arm a bracelet of large gray pearls—a gift, I was told, of the emperor—I cannot pretend to give any description of her costume. The corps diplomatique and cabinet ministers were, of course, in full uniform. All the remarkable generals and statesmen were present, and if politics were discussed in corners, which no doubt they were, there was at least no outward demonstration of any thing but careless enjoyment. Busts and pictures of the heroine of the fête were dispersed through the rooms. "*That* is an aristocratic head, you will allow," said I to M——, as he was leaving the supper-room. "Because she has Anglo-Saxon, or at least Scotch blood in her veins," replied he triumphantly.

Even the debates, even the ministers, even politics seemed forgotten, swallowed up in the excitement caused by two duels, following each other, and all proceeding from a velvet gown! It appears that the supposed intentional insult of the Duke of Alva to Madame S——, rankled in the mind of her son, and both father and son agreed that an apology must be demanded. All remembrance of the remark had, no doubt, passed away from the duke's mind, and he was preparing to set out with a party, consisting of various members of his family, to church, to assist at the baptism of his baby, of which, I believe, her majesty was to be the godmother, when he received a note from young Soulé, which, after hastily reading, he immediately answered, disclaiming all intention of giving offence to Madame S——é, all recollection even of having remarked upon her toilette, and a total ignorance of having even seen her; regretting, however, that he should inconsiderately have said any thing which could give the slightest offence to a lady. It was supposed, therefore, that the matter was satisfactorily adjusted; but somehow or another, it was whispered about, and repeated by good-natured friends, that the young man was crowing over his having forced an apology from the Duke of Alva, and that imputations were thrown out against the courage of the latter; and so, from less to more, the matter grew serious, and a challenge was sent by the duke and accepted.

Every one had gone that day to the *rifa* or raffle, an affair got up upon a great scale for the benefit of the poor, under the direction of a society composed of the principal ladies of Madrid. It was held in La Trinidad, formerly a convent, now belonging to the department of *Fomento;* and for months preparations had been making for it. One could not enter a house where the young ladies were not embroidering, or pasting, or drawing, or manufacturing something for the *rifa.* It was somewhat in the style of the fancy fairs which I have seen in London, only every thing was drawn by lot. Of course the blanks bore a most disproportionate majority to the prizes; but as it was for the poor, to provide them with coals and clothing during the winter, no one was allowed to complain.

The first ladies in Madrid presided at the various tables. The Duchess of Gor, Countess of Montijo, Marquesa de Malpica, and others, were the presidents, and distinguished by a lilac ribbon tied round their arm. It was their office to receive the tickets that had been drawn, and to have them compared with a book in the charge of a clerk, where the corresponding numbers were marked. If it was a prize, they directed the lucky individual to the table where the article was marked with the same number. I admired the indefatigable patience of these ladies, who sat in this great hall day after day, from morning till night, unrolling tickets, answering questions, and attending with unwearied politeness to every individual who came up to them.

All classes were there, from the highest to the lowest. One table was especially dedicated to beautiful gifts, sent by the Queen, the King, the Ynfante Duchess of Montpensier, and the little Princess of the Asturias. Of course every one was desirous to gain something from this table; the watch and chain of the queen, the opal bracelet of the Ynfante, and so on. I had taken tickets for at least a dozen young ladies, and neither they nor I had won any thing excepting a remarkably ugly yellow pincushion, which I insisted upon transferring to E—— C—— V——, one of the handsomest girls in Madrid, when C——s came up, and whispered to me that a duel was to take place that day between young Soulé and the Duke of Alva, and that they had gone out to the country; the duke's seconds being Gen. Concha and the Count of Piñon-Rostro, and those of his antagonist, Mr. Perry, Secretary of Legation, and the fiery Milaus del Bosch.

I looked towards the Duchess of Alva, who, with her exquisitely beautiful little boy beside her, was unconcernedly unrolling a number of tickets which she had taken; and at the Countess of Montijo, who was opening papers for a young countryman with a pretty girl by his side; and felt certain that the report had not reached them.

We went to the Casino in the evening to hear the result. Neither were wounded. They fought with swords, which were found too heavy, and exchanged for lighter ones. Of course there were a thousand versions of the particulars, but the important fact was, that the duel, a foolish quarrel for a foolish cause, was well over.

Although some very important political events have occurred, I shall give you an account of them afterwards, and so fill up a long gap in my journal. But now I must leave you to imagine the astonishment of the Madrid world, when it was announced, that not satisfied with the reparation to his wounded honor which had already been given, Mr. Soulé had challenged the French ambassador! This was a more serious business than the first. That two young men should have a rencontre, did not excite much surprise, absurd as it was, the cause considered; but that two men of advanced age, the one a minister plenipotentiary, the other ambassador and doyen of the diplomatic corps, should fight upon the same subject, was rather out of the usual way. The letter from Mr. Soulé, which appeared in the *Illustrated London News* some days afterwards, I copy for your edification.

Monsieur le Marquis:—

The difference which has arisen between the Duke of Alva and my son, took place in your *salons.* It was at your house, where I and my family were invited guests, and on the occasion of a fête of which the Duke of Alva might consider himself in some measure the hero, that the latter insulted Madame Soulé, without any thing having hitherto happened to exonerate us from the bond of good fellowship, which that circumstance causes to weigh upon you. It is even positively asserted that the insulting expression afterwards made use of by the Duke of Alva, and so nobly taken up by my son, first proceeded from your mouth. That being the case, Monsieur le Marquis, I have a right to go to the true source which placed swords in the hands of the Duke of Alva and of my son, to make it mine as far as you are concerned, and to demand personally a satisfaction which you cannot refuse me. Mr. Perry, an American citizen, and my friend, is charged to receive your reply. I have the honor to be, Monsieur le Marquis,

Your very humble servant,

PIERRE SOULÉ,

Citizen of the United States.

December 17*th*, 1853.

As might be expected, the answer from the marquis, *un vieux militaire*, was not conciliatory. A challenge was returned by the emissary, and Lord H——n agreed to act as second. The duel was fixed for a certain day. The project got wind. The government was resolved to do all in their power to prevent its taking place. Lord H——n being informed of this, considered it a point of honor to hasten the affair, and the combatants accordingly stole a march upon the authorities. The result was that a ball was lodged in the ambassador's knee, and as it has not yet been extracted, considerable uneasiness is felt by his friends as to the result. The Soulés have flown at high game; but that this will advance their social position, or render Mr. Soulé's diplomatic duties more easy, remains to be proved.

In almost all cases of this nature, sympathy is felt for the sufferer, but more especially where, as in this latter instance, his opponent is the aggressor. This is actually the one topic of conversation in Madrid, and various are the motives attributed to Mr. Soulé for having sought this meeting. The whole of Madrid, without exaggeration, have made inquiries at the Embassy, the diplomatic corps of course amongst the first. The reception-room of the Marquise was crowded this morning. She seems very courageous, and thankful that it is no worse, though likely to be very lingering; and it is probable that, in the way of entertainments, their hospitable house is shut for the season. I was told by M——, who had it from an American gentleman, that Mr. Soulé, who was as cool as if going out to breakfast, remarked just before the duel began, "I shall not kill M. Turgot; I shall merely put a ball in his knee."

I must now return to the Cortes, in which I have spent nearly my whole time. Passions ran very high, yet much decorum was preserved, though the president had some difficulty in moderating or preventing the noisy demonstrations from the galleries. "Order! gentlemen, order!" was the frequent cry from the presidential chair. The ministers maintained a very grave and composed attitude. San-Luis spoke upon various occasions, and I have rarely listened to a better orator. He has a remarkably fine-toned and mellow voice, which does him good service, and that flow of language which seems an inherent gift in the Spanish race. The language itself is so grand and sonorous, that it no doubt assists their fluency. They have besides perfect self-possession, unless, as happened in the case of General Concha, where there is too much anger and vehemence to permit any choice of expression. His words seemed to come tumbling over each other, and formed a contrast to the cool energy of the discourse delivered by the president of the council. The Marquis of Molins, as I have already mentioned, Domenech, Collantes, and the Marquis of Girona, all spoke. All are orators. Molins has perhaps most elegance and choice of words. Domenech and Girona were remarkable for the plain and practical good sense of their speeches. Collantes was more energetic and ardent. Every one spoke with an ease and fluency which is not often met with in other assemblies. The earnest and brilliant oratory of the

Spanish Senate forms a curious contrast with the rather *nonchalante* and conversational tone adopted in the House of Lords. Shortly after the beginning of the session, the Duke of Rivas delivered a flowery discourse, eloquent, but frequently wandering away from his subject. The Marquis of Miraflores made rather a long speech, which was listened to most irreverently, amidst several peals of laughter from the galleries, instantly reproved by the president; but which seemed to have no power to annoy him, as he continued quietly and slowly, with the most perfect ease and self-possession, to the conclusion. His object was to prove that the question under discussion, was neither a question of opposition, nor one concerning railroads; that its importance consisted solely in its being a question of prerogative. He considered the prerogative of the Senate offended, by the transfer of the discussion to the lower house. I confess it appeared to me rather a splitting of straws, and that when the important point was to carry through these great improvements with all convenient speed, it would have been wiser to leave etiquette out of the question. The marquis recommended the ministers to withdraw their proposition, observing that to err was human—that he had frequently erred himself, and had never been ashamed to confess it.

Then up sprung my friend the Marquis of C——s, and logically defended the conduct of the ministry, and proved at least to my satisfaction, that the government not only had the right, but were in duty bound to have carried this question in the first instance to the Chamber of Deputies. He proved it by the Article 36 of the Constitution. He referred to the examples of France, Belgium, and England, "from whence," said he, "we have taken our parliamentarianism, but not our representative system; our parliamentary forms, but not our liberty, for that is more ancient in our nation than either *parlamentarisimo* or parliamentary forms." The Duke of Rivas replied to him in the speech to which I have already referred. He considered the question under discussion as being "lofty, grave, most important, transcendental." When the Duke of Rivas speaks, one is apt to regret that the Spanish language has so many words to express the same idea. His opinion being in substance the same as that of the Marquis of Miraflores, I shall spare you a detail of his arguments, but the poetical conclusion is worthy of record: "Some," said he, "have spoken of restoring a pure monarchy, because they dislike publicity in carrying on their private objects; others, loyal gentlemen, because they are wearied of that crowd of locusts, which, springing from the sands, have covered the whole surface of Spain. It is not the system, gentlemen, but its observance which produces these evils. Give me back absolute monarchy with all its conditions, with a good government, and I shall be the first to raise its standard throughout the whole monarchy.

"Make time roll backwards. Place upon the throne of the great Charles III. our adored queen. Place by her side, the wise Count of Floridablanca, and the honorable Count of Aranda with his point lace and collar; surround that throne with a rich aristocracy, exercising an immense jurisdiction over the whole territory of Spain, with its illustrious and influential clergy, and add to all that the Council of Constable, jealous of all that belongs not to ancient manners and customs. Give me all this, and let the Spaniards preserve the same faith, let them say the rosary daily, let them hear mass every Sunday, and confess every month, and I accept the absolute system.

"But," continued the duke, "has it now any conditions of vitality amongst us? No, gentlemen, I cannot raise that standard—for on my march I should be detained by History, which would show me in its pages the termination of the in digenous dynasty, and of that monarchy, which, created by the Catholic kings, was reduced in the time of the imbecile Charles II. to nine millions of inhabitants, and which possessed five vessels rotting in the arsenal of Carthagena, and a few ragged Germans, as his majesty's body-guard."

Here the president begged to remind the duke that he was wandering from the question, a fact not to be disputed. He concluded shortly after, pleading fatigue. This was on the 2d of December, and was answered the following day by Collantes, in a very able speech. He was particularly happy in alluding to some of the "arguments" of his adversary. Amongst other mythological allusions, the duke had exclaimed in one part of his speech, "I know not what there is in this question of railroads so ugly, so disgusting, that we cannot look at it. What Pandora's box is this, which, when opened, is going to cover the whole world with disasters?—This question is a singular question, it is a Proteus which takes all forms. It puts on the mask of economy, it appears under the aspect of a *coup d'état;* it causes the suspension of the Cortes; and now that at length we have succeeded in seizing this Proteus, do not let us loose our hold of him, until we have examined him on all sides."

"This," said Collantes, "is precisely what the government desires to do. The Senate has not got hold of this Proteus, the government holds him fast, and has nailed him tight to the table of Congress. There he is, with his 22 faces, with the 22 expedients which accompany this question. Neither will the Proteus escape, nor will any evils issue from this Pandora's box. The arguments of the Duke of Rivas would be terrible, if the government desired that the question should not be discussed; but the contrary being the fact, his arguments fall to the ground."

I do not pretend to give you the various arguments used on both sides of this question, so unimportant in itself, nor to give you even a *résumé* of the speech of Collantes, which appeared to me conclusive. He was answered by the Count de Velle, one of the opposition. The speech most worthy of note after that of Collantes, was that of the minister of grace and justice—calm, sensible, dispassionate and conciliatory.

General Ros de Olano answered him like a man in a state of intense nervous excitement. His object, however, seemed chiefly to attack the Bravo Murillo cabinet. His speech was vehemently applauded in the gallery, which called forth the wrath of the president, and a threat of clearing the tribune. The Marquis of C——, with whom I dined that day, assured me that the opposition is merely personal, directed against men, not measures; and that thus they are losing their time in discussing a question of no real moment. "It is to be regretted," said he, "that a man of talent, at least of literary acquirement, like the Duke of R——, should indulge in this frothy style of discussion. I am the more surprised at the sneering tone in which he spoke of faith in Spain as of an old-world superstition, now out of date; that one of his family is about to be united to a young nobleman, of whose alliance any house might be proud; one as distinguished for his piety as for his talents and high rank. I can answer for it that young —— not only goes to mass every Sunday, but every day of his life; not only confesses once a month, but once a week; and, thank Heaven! he is no rare example. A few fashionable freethinkers, and but very few, float on the surface of society. We have sins enough to answer for, but so far, want of faith is not amongst their number."

On the fifth of December continued the discussion of the same vexed question. The Marquis of Miraflores made a speech of some length, for the purpose of rectifying some remarks of Ros de Olano, concerning the Bravo Murillo cabinet. He asserted that that cabinet, of which for some weeks he formed a part, had zealously attended to the material interests of the country. He gave an account of the fever for railroads which prevailed in Spain at that period, when every individual solicited one for his province, for his village, for his very house. He asserted that the ministry might have gone too far in their zeal, but were to be pardoned in favor of their motives. The public, he said, could judge of the conduct of political men who had arrived at his age. It was unnecessary, said he, that one should declare, 'I am virtuous, I am honest or pure,' &c. My principle is, that all may be *improvisé* in this world, such as rank, position, riches, but respectability never."

He then passed on to rectify some remarks which had fallen from his friend to the Duke of Rivas, with a kind of reproachful tenderness; complimented the government on their good intentions, and hoped they would fulfil them, and positively refused *not* to identify himself with the Bravo Murillo cabinet.

A long speech from Ros de Olano. He read several articles of the constitution, in order to prove that the government had acted unconstitutionally; that they had destroyed one project of a law concerning railroads to insert another. He read the articles of the first plan of the Senate, then of the government plan; his chief charge being, that as the project of a law was pending in the upper house since the last session, the government had no right to present another analogous to it in the House of Deputies. He ended by saying: "If we lose, it is death to the Senate; if we gain, it is death to the ministers."

Then came a short speech from the Marquis of Cerceres,

followed by an excellent speech from Molins, one of the best that I have heard during the session. He wished to show that the law proposed to Congress by the government was infinitely better than that which had been presented in the Senate; that this law would be discussed in both houses; that the privilege of the Senate had not been attacked, but recognized; and he observed, that whilst these painful discussions were continuing, they were losing time, advancing nothing, and remaining, after all, at the very point from whence they had started.

On the sixth, the Marquis of Armandariz spoke at great length in favor of the government, followed by speeches from the Marquis of Miraflores, the Count de Mirasol, General Ynfante, and Señor Collantes. But, perhaps, the most remarkable speech of the session was that of the Count of San-Luis, against whose person there is no doubt that this violent opposition is chiefly directed. It was rather remarkable to see this self-made man president of the council at the age of thirty-eight, with a battery of unfriendly eyes directed against him, self-possessed, and in appearance calm, perfectly aware, in all probability, what the result of this question would be, confronting his opponents with quiet energy, arguing as if in a cause in which he had no personal concern, and making his opponents wince under his powerful and polished sarcasm—laying bare their hidden motives, and, by a great moral effort, keeping down the indignation to which, I have no doubt, he would gladly have given vent.

He remarked, that it might have been supposed that, on addressing the Senate for the first time from his present position, when the Cortes had been so recently opened by orders of her majesty, and in accordance with her majesty's government, he was unprepared for having to defend himself against unjust attacks, grave accusations, and injurious calumnies;

in short, to reply to a formidable opposition. Nevertheless, he had expected all this; gratitude not being the distinctive quality of parties, still less of the opposition.

He was aware that opposition was not to be disarmed by flattery; nevertheless, that the welfare of the country had required that the government should adopt the plan which they had pursued, and that the results had been precisely what they had expected. The opposition had not been disarmed, but continued as violent as ever, and had conjured up a tempest over their heads, which he trusted would soon pass, and that the rainbow would again appear in the blue sky, in the bright and calm light of justice. He denounced the opposition to the present government as systematic, gratuitous, and unfounded; and appealed for the truth of his assertion to the public conscience, to facts, to the debates which had recently occupied the attention of the Senate.

He had observed tranquilly the progress of the debates. The Senate had heard the reasons adduced against the conduct of the government of Spain, and Europe would shortly hear them. The more trifling the cause, said he, which has been the pretext for commencing hostilities against the government, the greater, in all future cases, would be the Senate's responsibility.

He complained that the question had not been examined, without which the truth could not be made manifest. He stated his intention of giving a *résumé* of facts which might be considered in the light of an accusation on his part; but that, if so, the fault lay in the facts themselves. Before this government existed, the opposition, he said, had formed, or rather accepted, a programme, for it had gone without one until a minister, who could not agree with his colleagues on a certain question, drew out one which was accepted. This programme was reduced to certain points: that the question of senatorial immunity should be resolved by the return of the Duke of Valencia—that the railroad question should be decided—that the effect of the decree ordering that the property of the Duke of Alcudra should be restored, was to be suspended—that the Cortes should be opened, that the project of constitutional reform presented before it should be withdrawn, together with a petition that important men of all political parties should enter into public offices, as corresponded to them by right.

"This ministry," added he, "was inaugurated under this programme; and this ministry, in the chronological order of the opposition, occupies the fifth place."

The nucleus of the actual opposition in the moderate party was formed, he observed, during the administration of the Duke of Valencia; and though, with some intermission, grew stronger during the succeeding administrations, and had continued opposing the cabinet of Bravo Murillo, the cabinet of Alcoy, the cabinet of Lersundi, and that act which had the honor of occupying the ministerial benches at the present time. And if all these cabinets had acted alike, it was clear, he said, that the opposition would have been logical, because it might have said, "all represent the same principles, consequently it is our duty to oppose them." Therefore he considered the opposition of the *progressista* party as natural, legitimate, respectable, and that it need not wait one single act of the Moderado party to combat it, because differing essentially from that party in political principles they could only agree upon secondary questions; "but here," said he, "are five cabinets, all opposed by the conservative party, a circumstance which I cannot forget, in speaking from this seat, where we have much more to fear from our own friends, from those professing the same political opinions as ourselves, than from those who differ from us essentially in principles and doctrines."

Hardly, he said, had this cabinet been sworn in, before even the ministry were reunited, when there had fallen upon their heads such a storm of attacks, charges, and prognostics of evil, that he would have been curious to see some of the members of the opposition in the same circumstances, and to have observed their conduct. Patriotism," he added, "had made them resolve upon prudence, resignation, and calmness; had made them determine to bear injustice, without being irritated by it; and to keep all passions out of the ministry. They resolved to embrace as brothers those who received them as implacable adversaries—they had done so—and hardly was the cabinet formed, when the Duke of Valencia was recalled, and the most important offices, those of most trust and weight, were bestowed on their most bitter adversaries.

And this was done without fear; for should these conciliatory measures be one day construed into a proof of debility, they would then show that they might break like the oak, but would never bend like the reed.

He observed how public applause had greeted these measures, even that of the opposition; but how, immediately after, the manner of the Duke of Valencia's recall had been criticised. The ministry had been called upon to open the Cortes—as an arena where all public interests might be discussed. Doubts had been thrown upon their intention of taking this step; nevertheless it was taken, and the public again applauded, but the opposition was silent. He went on to prove that all conciliatory measures had failed to disarm the opposition, and that the pretext now employed for opposing the ministry upon this question of prerogative, was a mere pretext, since, before the opening of the Cortes, meetings had been held by a considerable number of senators, and plans concerted against the ministry, the result of these meetings having been published the following day—meetings at which many respectable persons had assisted, and presented their adhesion, to prove that a formidable opposition existed against this cabinet. The question of prerogative did not then exist. He contrasted the conduct of these senators with that of the deputies, who had patiently awaited the opening of the Cortes and the acts of the government, before taking part for or against it.

The orator then gave a most luminous exposition of the true state of the present question. But it is impossible to do justice to this speech in a few words, or to give any idea of the bursts of eloquent indignation into which he occasionally broke forth, as if in spite of himself. I am convinced that not one candid mind among his listeners in the opposition but felt condemned as a mere personal opponent, whose vote was to be given against the ministry, either because it was headed by the Count of San-Luis, or because he himself did not form part of the government. Hatred or ambition was probably the mainspring in nearly each individual; and each one, no doubt, winced in his heart as his true motives were publicly unveiled.

He concluded by a hope that the senators would meditate well upon the vote which they were about to give. "Let them reflect calmly," said he. "The government could not have been clearer, franker, or more explicit in the explanation of their conduct, than they have been. Afterwards, gentlemen, *fiat justitia, ruat cœlum.*"

General Concha rose to answer, he said, a personal allusion. He was evidently irritated beyond all bounds of patience by the speech of the president of the council. He denied all project of a conspiracy to overthrow the actual ministry; he denied the assertions of the president that the cabinet had resolved all the questions that were pending before the opening of the Cortes, that they were governing constitutionally, or that they had adopted a conciliatory system of policy. He declared that he himself had accepted the office of director-general of the cavalry against his inclination, but as a soldier accustomed to obey; that his opposition to the present government arose from the fact that this cabinet had the same vice in its formation as those which had preceded it—that Señor Domenech, the minister of the treasury, had belonged to the Progressista party, and yet formed part of the San-Luis cabinet—that Señor Collantes had belonged to the anterior ministry, yet, in a few days after giving in his resignation, also formed part of the new cabinet—that he and his party were disposed to support whatever ministry should be formed, according to certain conditions, which they considered necessary to assure to the country respect for the constitution and the strictest morality in the administration—not that he accused the present ministry of want of morality; but that it frequently happened that the pressure exercised upon a cabinet, formed as this had been, necessarily influenced its actions—that certain honorable and virtuous men had been deprived of their places, and had been replaced by certain others, who might be as good, but had not the character or representation of the others; that he himself had no other ambition but to serve his country and his queen—nor had he any desire for high places or for great riches; but that he would oppose, not only five cabinets, but fifty cabinets, until he found one which should fulfil all the conditions which he considered necessary under a constitutional form of government.

He was answered by San-Luis, and some rather sharp

skirmishing took place between the two senators. Collantes replied to the accusation brought against him by Concha; remarking, that his political opinions had undergone no change, since his entrance into the present cabinet, as would be proved when the decree signed by him in the anterior ministry came to be discussed, as he trusted it soon would be. It was evident that the discussion was beginning to assume a more personal and more bitter character than at first. The galleries, towards the end of this day's session, gave symptoms of intense agitation, and when the president of the Senate gave out that the discussion was suspended till the following day, loud murmurs of disapprobation were heard from the public tribune. The president angrily rang the bell—declared the session to be raised, and abruptly left the house. That the ministers would be in the minority was then a matter of little doubt. As the crowds were pouring out, and groups formed in the vestibule waiting for their carriages, still was observable the same amenity, the same outward cordiality, between the members of each party. I observed General Concha shaking hands with the minister of state, and the Count of San-Luis in polite conversation with one of his most violent opponents. As the venerable cardinal Archbishop of Toledo came out, every one near him—ministers, generals, and statesmen—stopped to kiss his ring.

The next day, the 9th of December, the question was decided. A long speech from the Marquis of Miraflores, various explanations from different senators, as to the motives which would induce them to vote against the ministers—an excellent speech from Domenech—several others not particularly worthy of note—and the president announced that they would proceed to call for the votes. Then, indeed, a breathless silence reigned throughout the house, as each individual answered *si* or *no*. I could not help admiring the outward calmness of the ministers, especially of San-Luis, who had most at stake. I had left the diplomatic tribune, and got in upon the floor. In the upper tribune I saw several of the ladies of the ministers, listening anxiously to each *si* and *no*, and certainly not concealing their anxiety as well as their lords and masters. In a very short time it was evident that the ministers were to be defeated, for which they were probably prepared. The president sat grave and impassive, only raising his voice to enforce silence, when, towards the end, an occasional demonstration of applause was heard from the public gallery. As several high names—such as Medina-Cœli, Oñate, &c.—were called out, and their votes given against the government, a grave, clever-looking man, who stood near me, said, in a distinct voice, as if speaking to himself, "The grandees of Spain have committed suicide this day!" ("se han suicidado.") I found afterwards he was a distinguished member of the other house.

The votes being summed up of *Señores que dijeron que si* (gentlemen who said *yes*), there were 105; of *Señores que dijeron que no*, 69; making a majority of thirty-six against the government. Immediately a round of applause proceeded from the galleries, which the president had no power to check. The Senate poured forth its multitudes, the defeated party endeavoring to conceal their chagrin, and the conquerors their triumph, each as usual saluting the other with the most well-bred cordiality. C——s, whom I met in the lobby, showed me old General Tacon, supported between two servants; he had caused himself to be transported there, in spite of his age and infirmities, for the first time this session, that he might give his vote against the government. Carriages were hastily called for, and conquerors and conquered went home to dinner with what appetite they might. The queen is said to be indignant at the defeat of her ministers.

Some say they will give in their resignation; others, that nothing will induce the queen to accept it. On the 11th the following decree appeared in the Gazette:—

Using the prerogative granted to me by the twenty-sixth article of the constitution, and in conformity with the opinion of my council of ministers, I have resolved that the sessions of the Cortes shall be suspended.

Given in the palace, &c.

At the same time several of the members of the royal council (*Consejo Real*) are removed, and their places filled by friends of the government. Generals Concha and Ros de Olano are removed, the first from his office as director-general of the cavalry; and the second from that of director-general of the corps of *Sanidad Militar*.

And now, in appearance, all things go on as before. People crowd to the royal theatre to hear Marie de Rohan. The Prado is more than usually gay, now that senators and deputies have time to spare. The queen bows smilingly as usual as she drives through the crowd. The ministers are more than usually busy, and are carrying on various measures of improvement. But no doubt, there is vengeance, scarcely slumbering, in many hearts.

CHAPTER XVIII.

Duke and Duchess of Montpensier—Royal Armory—Its Treasures—Chivalrous Spain—Naval Museo—Royal Stables—Academia, Paintings of Murillo—Velasquez—The Museo—Female Education—The Confessional—Spanish Gentlemen—Countess Montijo.

December —.

I HAD the honor of a presentation to the Ynfanta Duchess of Montpensier. The diplomatic corps were invited at a certain hour, but, as I rather suspect from anxiety to avoid Mr. Soulé, went an hour earlier, and found no one to present them. The duke and duchess occupy a suite of apartments in the palace. The Marquesa de Malpica was in attendance. The duchess is thin, slender, brown, very pale, and looks in delicate health. She has fine eyes, and has a shy manner and rather a cold expression. She was dressed in mourning, on account of the queen of Portugal—a plain black silk gown and white collar—and looks even younger than she is. She is in appearance a complete contrast to the queen. Almost impossible to imagine them sisters. I saw her at the opera the same evening, when she was more animated, and looked extremely pretty.

The duke was very polite, and took the principal part in the conversation. The secretaries and attachés did not go with the diplomatic corps, but Count A—— was kind enough to present me privately, on the plea of my father's former acquaintance with Louis Philippe, when minister in Paris. The Montpensiers are very popular in Andalusia, giving largely to all public charities; and the duke has had tact enough to become as much as possible identified with his adopted country. The duchess seems to look up to him on every occasion, and —— says, does not choose a ribbon without consulting him—all very proper.

December —.

Went with M—— to visit the royal armory, one of the most curious collections in Europe; containing trophies of past glory, memorials of the golden age of Spain, recalling the noble deeds, the patriotism and grandeur of her monarchs and heroes, from Pelayo to Ysabel the Catholic, from the Cid down to the *Gran Capitan;* reminding us of the days when her banners waved over the continent of the new world, over the East Indies, the islands of the Ocean, the coasts of Africa, and the finest portion of Europe.

The building itself, situated to the south side of the royal palace, was concluded in the time of Philip II., by Gaspar de Vega. It is of considerable extent—the principal gallery about two hundred and thirty feet in length, and thirty-six in breadth, well lighted and kept in perfect order. Unfortunately, at the time of the French invasion, the people of Madrid, in a moment of blind enthusiasm, forced the doors of the armory, seized the precious objects which had been collected for ages under the reigns of successive monarchs, and used them as weapons of defence. The result, as may be imagined, was the loss or total destruction of an innumerable number of these invaluable relics. Moreover, during the government of Napoleon, the sword of Francis I. was taken from the gallery, and transferred to Paris, by way of healing the wound inflicted on the national susceptibility of the French, by the sight of this trophy of their captive monarch. An exact model of this sword is now shown in the armory, placed there by orders of the present king consort.

In the time of Ferdinand VII., the gallery was partially restored, and embellished with various new and valuable acquisitions, but it is only during the reign of the present queen that the various objects have been properly classified and arranged—and that a catalogue of the riches of this fine gallery has been formed with great labor and skill by Señor Martinez del Romero. We bought this catalogue on entering, but when I tell you that the list amounts to two thousand five hundred and thirty-eight objects, you will believe that I preferred examining those which were most curious, with M—— as my guide, to the labor of going methodically through the whole catalogue. There for example is the coat of mail of Alphonso V. of Arragon; the armor of Don John of Austria; that of Philip III.; the beautiful armor of the Emperor Charles V., both Spanish and German; that of Garcilaso de la Vega; of Juan de Padilla; of Juan de Aldana, who took Francis I. prisoner; the standard brought by Charles V. from Tunis; the Turkish bracelet of Ali-pasha, the Turkish admiral at Lepanto; the sword of Boabdil, the last monarch of Grenada; that of Pelayo; the beautiful shield of the Emperor Charles V., representing the head of Medusa; the Toledo sword of Ferdinand the Catholic; that of the Prince of Condé; that of the *Gran Capitan;* that of Ysabel the Catholic; *La Colada*, the famous sword of the Cid Campeador; that of Bernal Diaz del Castillo, presented to the queen by the Count de la Cortina; that of Philip II.; that of Charles V., brought from the Monastery of Yuste; and that of Hernan Cortés.

There are the standards of the battle of Lepanto, and

the fine equestrian armor in which Charles V. made his entry into Milan; also the equestrian armor of Hernan Cortés, and the armor of Christopher Columbus; the complete armor of Philip II. upon his barbed horse; the Chinese armor presented to that monarch by the Emperor of China; and the helmet of Francis I., which seems to have escaped the notice of his countrymen; most of these are exquisite in their workmanship, considered merely as objects of art; but how they bring back to the mind the whole history of romantic, chivalrous old Spain! I stood beside the effigy of St. Ferdinand, examined the trophies telling of the glorious engagements at Lepanto, Tunis, St. Quintins, Paira, &c., the Valencien sword of the Catholic Ysabel, the swords of the Cid and of the Great Captain, and then remembered all the petty and paltry ambition, all the envious passions brought to light in the short session I had lately witnessed in the hall of the Senate.

"*Sic transit*," said M——, laying his hand upon my shoulder. "Are you totally *désillusionné*, as the French say, my dear count? Is your Spanish day-dream rudely dispelled? Have you weighed Spain in the balance, and found it wanting?" "Not so," said I; "more than ever is Spain my admiration and my marvel. What other country would be what Spain still is, after years of civil war, torn by parties, convulsed by factions; constantly passing from one government to another—a mere plaything in the hands of selfish and ambitious men? Where would the people have remained noble and independent as in Spain? Where would not every feeling of honor and chivalry and loyalty have been extinguished except in Spain? Where even would material poverty have been so little felt as in Spain? No—I do not believe that the Spanish character has degenerated. I believe that it still retains, as in the days of its glory, the firm faith, the high sense of honor, the noble independence, the chivalrous generosity which distinguished the old Spaniard. The froth, the scum floats on the surface, and hides the generous liquor below. In spite of an indolent aristocracy, ambitious generals, and place-hunting patriots so-called, I can never despair of Spain, for in the character of her people, the elements of her future greatness still remain!"

We afterwards visited the naval *Museo*, curious to those who are learned in nautical matters, and well worth inspecting even by those who, like myself, are mere fresh-water sailors. The plan for the building, together with the arrange ment and distribution of this rich collection, are due to the zeal of the Marquis of Molins, now, for the second time, minister of the navy. It was inaugurated in November last, in the presence of their majesties. The building consists of a first and second story, the first containing three spacious halls; that of the *Arsenals*, the hall of *Columbus*, and the Cabinets of Artillery. The first contains the models of the Spanish arsenals in Cadiz, Ferrol, Carthagena, Puerto Rico, and the Philippines; and the designs of the dikes, boats, &c. of the various establishments for the manufacture of every thing destined for the navy; and the walls are ornamented with portraits of various admirals (*generales de la armada*).

The second is presided over by the bust of the great Genoese, whose name it bears. Here also are the portraits of various Spanish admirals; the model of the three-decked ship, the Santa-Ana; with flags and military trophies taken from the Moors in the Philippine Archipelago, in recent actions. In the Cabinet of Artillery is a collection of cannons and mounting of both the ancient and modern systems; the keys, projectiles, in short all that pertains to the defence of vessels of war.

In the first hall of the second story, are the portraits of

Columbus, Pizarro, Cortés, Vasco Nuñez de Balboa, Magellan, &c., with those of various celebrated navigators, and also a valuable collection of arms and other objects brought home by different navy-men from all quarters of the globe. We also found here a painting representing the three caravels which, under the orders of Columbus, first approached the unknown shores of the new world.

Then there is a hall containing the portraits of the admirals and captains, killed in naval engagements, surrounded by colors and trophies taken from the French on different occasions. To the right is the *Midshipman's Cabinet*, all the objects in which have been constructed for the use of the young midshipmen belonging to the college of St. Ferdinand. Next comes the Chinese Cabinet, with paintings of mandarins, Chinese costumes, punishments, &c.—the Hydrographical Cabinet, where there is a complete collection of instruments, ancient and modern; amongst the first, the *Astrolabe*, together with chronometers, telescopes, mariner's compasses, and all the various machines and instruments used in astronomy and navigation. There also the walls are covered with portraits of celebrated astronomers and hydrographers, such as Espinoso, Navarrete.

The next hall is called the Salon de la Reina, on account of a full-length portrait of her majesty which hangs there There is also a large painting of the battle of Lepanto, presented by the Marquis of Molins, portraits of various celebrated admirals; of *Bernardo Bonifaz*, the first who in Spain received that title, and who assisted with St. Ferdinand at the taking of Seville—that of Andrew Doria—of Don Alvaro de Bazan, first Marquis of Santa-Cruz, and many others. There are models of ships, ancient and modern, and various curiosities, such as the sabre presented by Napoleon to General Uriarte, and the ataghan presented to General Arias by the Emperor of Morocco.

The last *salon* which we entered is called the hall of the Ministers of the Navy, and contains portraits of all those who have distinguished themselves in that position, such as Patiño, Ensenada, Escaña, and others, together with fine models of steam-ships and sailing vessels. But I shall not tire you with details of the cabinets of Natural History, Mineralogy, Zoology, and Anatomy, which I have lately visited. I shall rather pass on to what I confess interested me more than these—the *Royal Stables*, to which I went the other day with M. de —— of the French Embassy.

This fine building is due to the magnificence of Charles III., under the direction of Sabatini, the famous architect of that day. The principal entrance is from the street of Bailen, by an arched porch of granite, surmounted by the royal arms. Within is a spacious court, surrounded by a portico, in the centre of which is a small chapel, dedicated to *San Antonio Abad.* The principal part of the building consists of the immense galleries supported by pillars, which constitute the stables, with all the apartments attached to them, containing the infirmaries, baths, forage and stalls for five hundred horses. At present there are three hundred and fifty horses, and mules innumerable; many of the former splendid animals, both Spanish and English. Some bright-colored chestnuts for the queen's own riding, are superb animals. Their names are affixed to their stalls—*Valoroso*, *Emperador*, *Monarca*, &c. The harness room is 160 feet long, containing 65 presses, in which are kept the magnificent harness; and the liveries of the royal coachmen and lackeys. In this room we were shown the curious old coach which belonged to *Juana la loca*, the first which ever rolled in the streets of Madrid.

In the immense coach-houses, we saw upwards of a hundred carriages, from the splendid old gala coaches down to a one-horse *traineau.* This extensive establishment is clean, and well kept, and yet there is a want of neatness and finish observable throughout; and the grooms and stable-boys have not the smart air of the same breed in England. To give you an idea of the size of the building, I need only say that besides these great stables, coach-houses, harness-rooms, &c., upwards of five hundred persons, consisting of the employés and their families, are lodged there, and that the annual cost of keeping it up amounts to nearly three millions of reals.

December —.

The weather is now dry and bright, with no prospect of rain. It is the most exhilarating sky, and certainly influences the disposition of the people. No one can look cloudy under these cloudless heavens. As we were passing, this morning, down the Calle de Alcalá, M—— proposed that we should take a look at the *Academia*, where there are still several fine paintings, though the principal number have been transferred to the *Museo.* The rooms are large, cold, and neglected-looking, and I cannot imagine why these master-pieces of Murillo and other great artists, should languish there in comparative obscurity, instead of being also sent to that magnificent gallery. Here is a superb painting, by Murillo, of St. Isabel, Queen of Hungary, Curing the Sick. But perhaps the two finest Murillos I have ever seen, hang in the second *sala.* A man of a noble countenance, a Roman patrician, his hand resting on the sacred volume, has fallen asleep, and his wife, fair and beautiful, seated at his feet, is also sunk in deep repose. Every thing seems to breathe such perfect stillness and tranquillity, that one feels afraid to disturb their slumbers. Even the little dog is sleeping at their feet. But at their right appears a radiant vision. The Blessed Virgin is pointing to the spot where she desires them to build a church dedicated to her; and in the rapt expression of their countenances, we can see that this seraphic glory gilds their slumbers.

In the next painting, which forms the pendant to this beautiful design, the pious couple are kneeling at the feet of the sovereign pontiff, and in the distance is seen the sacred edifice (*Santa Maria Maggiore*) which they have built in compliance with the mandate of the heavenly vision.

The Royal *Museo*—of which I have never written, because every visit I make there, I discover new beauties, and feel as if no description could do it justice—has one material advantage in the extreme comfort which enables the lovers of art to pass hours there without suffering, as in the gallery of the *Academia*, either from cold or weariness. The vast galleries are heated to an agreeable temperature, comfortable chairs and benches of crimson velvet are placed along the walls, and the most perfect order and stillness constantly prevail there. I have been frozen in the Louvre, excepting in the principal gallery; and in Versailles, both frozen and tired, without being repaid for the suffering.

The construction of this great building is due to Charles III., who destined it for a museum of natural sciences; but when Ferdinand VII. came to the throne, he found it totally ruined by the occupation of foreign troops. Immense sums were necessary for its reparation, and in justice to the monarch, it must be allowed that the Spaniards owe him a vast debt of gratitude for the creation of this royal gallery. Its cost is said to have exceeded seven millions of reals, of which his majesty paid twenty-four thousand monthly from his private resources. The three first *salons* were opened in 1819, and the work was zealously continued during his reign. Since the accession of the present queen, great improvements have been made in the Museo; new galleries opened, and the finest paintings transferred there from the Escurial.

The gallery of paintings may now be considered the finest in the world; the less astonishing, when we reflect that besides the encouragement given by Spanish monarchs to the artists who illustrated the three great national schools of Seville, Madrid, and Valencia, all the great artists of these kingdoms which owned the dominion of Spain in the golden age of painting, contributed to enrich her churches and palaces with the finest productions of art, and to offer the most noble efforts of their genius to the monarchs of the Austrian dynasty. Therefore this gallery is unrivalled in what the Spaniards call *conjunto*, the union of the principal productions of so many great masters; not only of Murillo, Velasquez, Zuanes, Ribera, &c., but of Raphael, Rubens, Vandyke, Titian, Leniers, Leonardo da Vinci; in short, of all the great masters of every school—Spanish, Italian, Flemish, Dutch, German, and French.

When I first visited these galleries with M——, who has a high appreciation for the fine arts, though his own talent chiefly lies in drawing the cleverest caricatures imaginable, he hurried me past the most wonderful productions of the greatest masters, to the gallery called the *Tribuna*, in imitation of that in the Pitti palace in Florence. This beautiful hall, which has been lately opened, is of an elliptic form, open in the centre, and surounded by a balustrade, giving a view at the same time of the sculpture gallery below, and containing the quintessence, the *crême de la crême* of both the Spanish and foreign schools of painting. Here the famous "Pasino de Sicilia" of Raphael hangs conspicuous, fronting the spectator as he enters. Every one knows this wonderful work of art, representing our Saviour falling under the weight of the cross. Each figure is so perfect—the godlike expression of the Redeemer, in its divine and meek agony, the tender anguish of the mother, the despairing and deprecating grief of the other women, the fierce countenances of the Roman soldiers, each feeling and passion is so forcibly represented, that it is hardly possible to tear one's self away from the contemplation. Some new beauty strikes the eye each moment. But beside it, to the left, is that almost divine painting, the Assumption of the Virgin, by Murillo. Surely no holier countenance ever breathed upon canvas. From its youthfulness and tender expression, breathing nothing but the expectation of the fulness of joy, without a trace of past grief, or of the bitter anguish of the heart through which a sword had pierced; we may see that the artist intended to portray the rising of the glorified body, serene in immortal youth and unfading beauty.

Then to the right is the triumphant master-piece of Velasquez, the picture of "The Lances," as it is called, representing the surrender of Breda, where each figure stands out clear and distinctly defined in the bright atmosphere, under the blue sky with its fleecy clouds.* "You must take a bird's-eye view of the galleries the first day," said M——, "and if you have any spare hours, they will never be wasted here. Look at that Velasquez!—'*Las Meurinas*—the ladies of Doña Maria of Austria presenting her with a vase of water. How he brings the little whale-boned archduchess and her attendants to life before us! And that bedizened dwarf, prime favorite and diversion of his royal mistress! If women had these pleasant indoor recreations nowadays, they would gad about less. Observe how the whole light is produced from behind, in the centre of the picture.' No man

* Grand old Dons are the Spaniards of Velasquez! men who never danced the polka, or whirled round in the waltz *à deux temps*. They may have trode a stately measure with their courtly partners, but these men never gossipped about their lady-loves, or abused their queen. "*Mon Dieu, mon Roi, ma Dame*," is the device written on their grave, calm brows.

ever painted light and air like Velasquez!" "He is wonderful; but I even prefer Murillo." "Because you are young and romantic, and, for female beauty, Murillo is unrivalled. But for life, there is no one like Velasquez. We must come here to see him in his glory. In England we have no idea of him. Look at these drunken, laughing revellers! One feels inclined to join them and have a share in their fun."

The Museo is divided into different galleries, according to the schools; Spanish, Italian, Dutch, Flemish, German, and French, with the exception of this *Tribuna*, where, as I have already mentioned, the chief productions of the great masters are put together, side by side, in noble rivalship. Two great *salons* are occupied by the ancient Spanish schools, and contain the noble works of Murillo, Velasquez, Juan de Juanes, Alonzo Cano, Zurbaran, &c. In another we see the principal works of the artists of the modern Spanish schools; paintings by Goya, Bayeu, Lopez, Madrazo, and others.

The great gallery which contains the chief productions of the Italian masters, is a truly wonderful collection of master-pieces. There are the San Sebastian of Guido Reni; Leonardo da Vinci's Mona Liza; the famous Holy Family of Raphael, surnamed *La Perla;* his Virgin of the Fish; the Visitation of Our Lady, certainly one of his most perfect works; Michael Angelos, Titians, Saso-Ferratos, &c., &c. The eye wanders over a profusion of riches, hardly knowing where to fix, and never resting upon one painting unworthy of examination.

For the first few days that I visited the Museo, I hardly left the Tribuna, the ancient Spanish, and the Italian gallery. It was only by degrees that I went through the French, German, Spanish, and Dutch galleries, and gradually appreciated the Poussins, Albert Durers, Claude Lorraines, and Holbeins; the Rembrandts, Wouvermans, Van Dykes, and Terniers; the numerous works by Rubens; the Snaders, Brueghels, &c. A number of young artists are generally to be seen there, copying the works of the great masters, and I frequently observed several young girls similarly engaged, whose mothers sat sewing beside them. There is a great deal of taste in this respect amongst the girls here. The water-color daubs which, in England, fond mothers call upon their visitors to admire, are fortunately not to be seen here. You would be astonished at the masterly oil-paintings of the Spanish young ladies, whose education it is the fashion to cry down. They make it a serious matter, and work in their blouses *con amore.* Their accomplishments are certainly not intended for show. The first day we went to the Museo, the Marquesa de B——, formerly a Grecian princess, was engaged in copying a Rubens, and her work was clever enough to lose very little even by the side of the original. "You are sure to see a pale, thin, black-eyed woman," said M——, "giving the preference to the golden-haired, snowy-skinned beauties of Titian, or to the glowing, unideal women of Rubens. An English or German girl, on the contrary, would be sure to search out some dark-visaged, gloomy saint of Ribera's."

And this reminds me that I have not yet given a categorical answer to the numerous inquiries of my sisters, as to what kind of an education the Spanish girls have. They pretend that I am so carried away by their beauty and grace that I inquire no further. Since I am convinced that being possessed with this idea, they would set little store by my opinion, I shall give them instead the *synopsis* of a discourse delivered to me by Madame —— upon that subject; certainly a good judge, both as being a foreigner, as having resided fifteen years in Madrid, and as being a remarkably clever and well-informed woman herself: "You want to know my opinion of the education of Spanish girls?" said she. "You will not suspect me of being impartial, for unjustly suspected as I am of being a little *blue* myself, I am at least not likely to commend ignorance in others. As to what it was in former days, concerning which so much has been written by foreigners, who I believe knew nothing about it, I know as little; but unless we consider the works of Santa Teresa and other holy women as inspired, we know that they have had female writers unequalled in the classic eloquence of their style. As to education in the present day, we must always keep in view that large fortunes are very uncommon in this country; I mean fortunes in keeping with the rank of the individual; and that there is almost invariably a position to be maintained, to which the means are unequal. Therefore, generally speaking, the daughters of a grandee of Spain must be made useful before they are made accomplished. But first as to the most important point, their religious education, nothing can be more strictly or earnestly attended to. Whether a girl is brought up within the walls of a convent, or under her father's roof, her first communion is the great event to which she looks forward with feelings of awe and joy. The most dissipated mother will never neglect having her child prepared for this holy solemnity, generally by the time she has completed her tenth year, whilst the generality of mothers devote their chief time and attention to prepare their children for receiving this great sacrament. The child who is accustomed to confession from its earliest years, who is taught habitually to examine its own heart, rarely falls into any very grave error; and the childish sins which children sometimes hesitate to disclose, even to their own parents, are confided to the priest of God, and by his pious counsel eradicated." "I must say," interrupted Mrs. ——, an English lady, who was present at what she called this morning lecture, "that I quite disagree with you here, my dear friend. I should wish my children to have no other confidants but me, and should feel very much mortified if they were to tell any priest what they would conceal from their own mother. Confession alone, had I no other reason, would prevent me from becoming a Catholic." "Your opinion would be different if you were one," said Madame gently. "To me there is not a more touching sight than a little boy kneeling before the priest, with a grave and earnest face, and eyes glistening with tears, whispering his faults and errors; while the good priest, with his hand on the child's head, gently and gravely chides and consoles him; or to see a mother bringing her little girls to the confessional, and to observe their grave and innocent expression, as they kneel beside the grating, and receive the fatherly advice and blessing of their spiritual teacher. Depend upon it, that in after days they rarely forget these lessons learned in their childhood. And what can be more striking than the sight of young girls at their first communion, dressed in pure white, the emblem of their own pure hearts, as with faces expressive of mingled fear and happiness, they approach the altar!"

"Nothing would *induce* me," said Mrs. —— vehemently, "to allow my girls to go to confession. I am told," added she, lowering her voice, "that the *questions* girls are asked, are enough to put bad notions into their heads." "I will give you my little girls' catechism, and preparation for confession," said Madame ——, smiling, "and you shall judge for yourself." "That would make no difference," said Mrs. ——; "the priests may say what they like. They are not obliged to keep to the words that are printed. I allow that your little girls are as innocent as—as white moss rose-buds;

but no matter, the idea is revolting. I would not confess my sins to a *man*, if you were to make me queen of England!" "Well," said Madame ——, laughing, "we shall leave the religious part of the education; only you will allow me to say, that their religious duties as *Catholics* are strictly attended to.

"Next to religious instruction, the greatest care is taken to make them perfect *ménagères*, so that whatever position they may fill in after life, they are perfectly capable of directing their households; and I know no girl in Madrid, however high her rank, who is not fitted either to become the wife of a poor man, or to direct her household with perfect order, and if necessary, with strict economy. They are taught to make their own dresses, to mend their own clothes, to keep accounts, to regulate the expenditure, to attend personally to the most minute details of housekeeping; and whatever their future condition may be, this knowledge certainly does them no harm." "I quite agree with you there," said Mrs. ——, "and think that education on these points is sadly neglected in England. Our girls are elegant, accomplished creatures, but if they make a poor marriage, it is a bad thing both for them and their husbands." "Whereas here," continued Madame ——, "I know many families with an income so small, that in England they could not keep their places in society, whose houses are specimens of order and good taste, whose children are well educated and well dressed, who move in the best society, though they go out but seldom; but who, when they do appear in the world, are distinguished by the elegance of their appearance and manners. All this is effected by order and economy.

"Were this all, of course their education would be very incomplete; but I assure you that, generally speaking, they receive a good solid education, though they neither study

Latin nor metaphysics. As for accomplishments, music and painting are with them almost a second nature, and were they to devote one half of the time to their acquirement that girls do in England, they would be artists." "Certainly," said Mrs. ——, "fine voices are as common here as fine eyes. No one can pretend to sing, who is at all *médiocre.*" "Then," added Madame ——, "French they all speak—English is becoming nearly as common. In short, a young Spanish girl of the present day,—pious, modest, useful, sufficiently accomplished, and thoroughly ladylike, appears to me all that can be desired in a woman. It is true that their acquaintance with general literature is not so extensive as that of their contemporaries in England, but what they read is good, and thoroughly understood. Eugene Sue and George Sands are unknown to them, except by reputation." "Dear, clever, wicked creatures!" ejaculated Mrs. ——. "In natural talent," added Madame ——, "I consider Spanish women superior to those of all other countries. I will not deny that a more learned education might make them more brilliant, but I am not sure that it would improve them. You know how charming they are in conversation, how full of wit and vivacity. Give them a knowledge of general literature, and with their quick perceptions and lively imaginations, they will become the most remarkable women in Europe. In the mean time, their education fits them to be good wives and mothers and judicious mistresses of their families, and their natural talent supplies the want of knowledge, where this want exists. In short, my dear count," said Mrs. ——, laughing, "you must take a Spanish wife back with you to that chateau of yours, with its unpronounceable name; make her go through a course of literature, and she will become a formidable blue." "And the men, my dear Madame ——, what do you say of them?"

"Oh! I leave them to the judgment of Europe. Their good looks, good manners, and good education, need no comment. But there is one trait in their character not so generally known; I mean their devotion to their families; especially to their mothers and sisters. That devotion and almost chivalrous respect with which the young Spaniard treats his mother—the sacrifice of every pleasure to her comfort—the *obedience* even towards her, from which he never emancipates himself—is undoubtedly carried to a much greater extent here than elsewhere. Numerous are the instances in which the son, left in charge of his widowed mother and sisters, sacrifices every inclination to marry, lest he should not have sufficient means to perform the sacred duty of providing for them.

"The intimate friendship and confidence existing between the son and the mother is never dissolved. As long as she lives, she is his first thought, his first care, and attention to her his chief occupation. Neither politics nor pleasure, nor love nor ambition, can distract his thoughts from her. It is her advice that he seeks—it is with reference to her that he forms his plans, and nothing but death can ever dissolve that sacred union of heart and feeling. I never feel the loss of my own poor boy so vividly as when I go to see my friends, the Señoras de P—— and F——, each a widow with an only son, handsome young men as they both are, and rapidly advancing in their professions, forming the pride and consolation of what would otherwise be their lonely and unprotected old age."

"Take it with a reservation," said M——, as we were discussing the subject after dinner, "and all that Madame —— says, is true enough. The Spanish girls are extremely clever, but they get none of their cleverness from books, depend upon it. So much the better—give me any thing but a woman who reads that she may talk, and talks to show her learning." "*J'adore leurs yeux noirs*," said M. de T——. "*Et moi leurs petits pieds*," said M. de E—— "They have wonderful hair!" said Count G——. "They are good-natured, unaffected, clever, and have no nonsense about them," said M——. "They never try to show off, and no one but a rich bachelor, or one reputed rich, knows what a relief that is," added he, pathetically. "You are taking a leaf out of our friend Don Juan's book," said I, laughing. "Not a bit of it," said M——, "for not one of them would marry an Irish protestant, were he as rich as Crœsus."

Madrid is all alive now with balls and dinners, operas and suppers. A beautiful ball was given the other night at the Countess Montijo's. She certainly possesses the social talent more than any one I ever met with, and without the least apparent effort seems to have a kind of omnipresence in her *salons*, so that each one of her guests receives a due share of attention. The principal drawing-room, all white and gold, is a noble room. The toilettes were more than usually elegant, the jewels universal. The finest diamonds were perhaps those of the Countess of Toreno, widow of the celebrated minister. The Duchess of Ternan-Nuñez and the Princess Pio (an Italian lady), wore tiaras of emeralds and brilliants of a size and beauty that I have never seen surpassed. The Duchess of Alva was as usual dressed in perfect taste, but alas! I am not able to describe. It was something white and vapory, and covered with flowers, with a few diamond pins fastening in the flowers in her hair.

I observed that whenever a young girl was without a partner, there was the hostess introducing one to her—or if an awkward-looking youth stood neglected in a corner, she took his arm, brought him forward, presented him to some one and made him dance. Or if some scientific man, invited for his merits—for her parties are much less carefully *winnowed* than those of the aristocracy in general—stood with his spectacles on, looking a little like a fish out of water, there was the countess beside him, making him take her to the buffet, conversing with him, as she does well upon every subject, and putting him so much at his ease, that in a few minutes he evidently felt quite at home.

The chief ornament of the supper-room is a full-sized painting, representing the Empress Eugénie in a *maja* dress, mounted on a beautiful Andalusian horse. This dress, which she introduced the fashion of wearing in the country, is rich and becoming. An embroidered dark velvet jacket, with silver buttons, a dark colored merino skirt, shorter than the usual *amazone*, trimmed with bands of velvet the same color as the jacket, a silk sash, and a *calañes* hat, such as the men wear, make a very pretty and picturesque costume de fantaisie. A little dagger or knife in an ornamented sheath ought to be stuck in the belt, to make the dress complete. I saw one the other day, sent from Seville to a young lady, with an inscription on it in pure Andalusian, saying, "You do not need me—your eyes do execution enough."

CHAPTER XIX.

The Rifa—Rigoletto and Trovatore—Christmas morning—Duke of Alva knighted.

December —.

The *Rifa* concluded very brilliantly. The Condesa de —— tells me they have cleared ten thousand dollars. The Count of San-Luis has been seriously ill, from which his enemies have conceived great hopes, at least of his *démission*. All sorts of absurd rumors as to the cause; amongst others, that immediately after the suspension of the Cortes, he fought a duel with General Concha, and was wounded in the head. As duelling, like murder, sometimes becomes a kind of epidemic, it was reported and believed that Lord H—— and Count E—— were to fight, owing to some dispute arising out of the Turgot affair. In consequence of this, police officers were stationed before their doors for several days, until it was ascertained that they were both pacifically inclined.

The delay of her majesty's *accouchement* seems to give serious offence, and to be considered as in a great measure the fault of the ministry. If she is fortunate enough to have a prince, they will doubtless become very popular, and many honors will be showered upon them. Their ladies will receive the order of Maria Louisa, and crosses and grades will probably be distributed with an unsparing hand. I have heard it made a subject of complaint, that so few crosses have been given during this administration; an extraordinary circumstance, as they have hitherto been so lavishly bestowed as to lose nearly all their value.

The Marquis Turgot remains in a precarious state. The ball has not been extracted. The marquise remains entirely confined to his apartments, and receives no one. Rigoletto continues to attract all the world to the opera. The Royal Theatre has now one great fault. It is insufferably cold. All the Señoras have to wrap up in shawls and cloaks, which greatly injures the brilliancy of the general effect. Why it is not heated, I have not discovered. Christmas passed off without any remarkable festivities amongst the higher classes. Each family has its own circle, and social meetings. But as for the people, they have enjoyed themselves to their hearts' content. The whole world has been dancing, singing, eating *besugo*, *mazapan*, almond soup and turkey. The Plaza Mayor has been a show for fish, vegetables, and myriads of fat turkeys—wonderful *dulces*, and cakes of every variety, sold in temporary booths—amidst such a din of talking, laughing, singing, beating of rustic drums called *zambombas*, strumming of guitars and three-stringed instruments called *rabeles*, that it was positively deafening. On the *Noche Buena* (Christmas Eve) the animation and noise of the whole city was something indescribable. The theatre that night was unusually brilliant, and the quantity of light made some amends for the want of heat. The Trovatore, the great triumph of la Gazzaniga, was performed, and she was encored vociferously, deluged with bouquets, and enveloped in flights of white pigeons, carrying sonnets and wreaths. One flew into the minister's box, and was caught by the president of the council, who threw it on the stage—a pacific omen.

The dying scene in the Trovatore is really a triumph of genius in la Gazzaniga. The agonies of death seem to steal gradually over the face, and her reappearance before the curtain, when she was enthusiastically called for, seemed like a wonderful resuscitation.

On Christmas morning every church was of course crowded. We went to the Chapel Royal within the palace, and got in with difficulty. The chapel, which is of an oval form, is not spacious, but beautiful in its architecture and adornment. The *tribuna* of her majesty fronts the high altar, above which is a painting representing the Archangel St. Michael, to whom the chapel is dedicated. There is a fine Annunciation, by Mengs, and the vaulted roof and cupola are covered with paintings *al fresco*, by Giaguinto, representing the Holy Trinity, Our Lady, various choirs of saints, the battle of Clavigo, where Santiago fights for the Spaniards, &c. The whole is adorned with pillars of black and white marble and marble statues. The music was very fine, the band led by Señor Valdemosa. The queen was not present, but the king and Ynfantas occupied the royal *tribunas.* The Archbishop of Toledo celebrated mass. The sermon was deliverd by Father Arenal, a celebrated preacher. Prayers were offered up for the safe delivery of the queen.

Count A—— has received an invitation to be present at the investiture of the Duke of Alva with the order of knighthood of Calatrava. The invitation is as follows:—

Don Juan Pedro Sanches Pleytes, Marquis of Sotomayor, Grandee of Spain of the first class, Senator of the Kingdom, Knight Commander of Almagro in the Order and Knighthood of Calatrava, &c. &c., requests your Excellency to be pleased to assist at the chapter which will be held in the church of the *Señoras Comendadoras* (the female Superiors of a military order), on the 28th of this month, at one in the afternoon; in order to arm as knight, and to invest with the habit of the same, his Excellency Don James Stewart and Ventimiglia, Alvarez of Toledo, Duke of Berwick and Alva, &c. &c. &c.

The ceremony was very fine. The church is spacious and handsome. Its lofty dome forms a fine object in the street of Alcalá. The principal seats were reserved for the knights, and for the members of the Alva family and their friends. It has a strange effect, in this practical century, to witness this pale reflection of the middle ages. The knights wore their white mantles, with the red cross on the shoulder, and black velvet caps, with lofty white plumes. High mass was performed before the ceremony of the investiture began. The duke, according to ancient custom, had passed the night in the church, beside his armor. Mr. de —— assured me that it was with difficulty he obtained absolution, in consequence of having fought a duel, an offence which, in the church, belongs to the *reserved cases*, which can only be pardoned by the sovereign pontiff; and that it was at last given him by the pope's nuncio, to whom the right, in certain cases, is occasionally transferred.

The vows were taken kneeling by the duke, in a clear and distinct voice. It is, after all, little more now than a vain ceremony, but the Spanish grandees cling to it as to an embalmed corpse when the soul is departed. In Spain it is still an imposing sight. In any other country it would seem ridiculous. The Marquises of Viluma and Molins would, in their appearance, have done credit to the knights of former days. When the ceremony was concluded, we were invited to visit the convent of the Comendadoras, all noble ladies of the order, dressed like the knights in white mantles and red crosses, though with the nun's hood and veil.

CHAPTER XX.

The New Year—Ball—Birth of the young Princess—Preparations for Baptism—Death of the Ynfanta—Lying in State—Opposition to Government—A Proclamation.

January 2.

WE brought in the new year with a gay supper at Countess M——o's, but both Christmas and New Year make me feel like an unhappy schoolboy. I miss our social gatherings. I miss our Christmas fire. I miss the roaring log-fires in our great hall. I am very near having a fit of *hain-weh*, and yet there is no part of the world, where kindness and cordiality so soon make the stranger feel at home. I *felt* that my health was drunk that night at Castle ——, by more than a hundred familiar voices; and I pledged them silently in steaming punches, under the fire of a whole artillery of dark eyes, and with the cordial sounds of "*felicespascuas*," from a chorus of kindly voices; although Mr. —— told me I looked lugubrious and sentimental, and even like a pelican in the wilderness! To-day the cabinet and diplomats have gone to pay their respects to the queen, who at present can have no public reception. There is a party to-night at the Countess de Montijo's and a ball at the Marquis de Gavria's, a rich banker, one of that class which is beginning to take a conspicuous part in Madrid society, in this golden age.

Many are the ancient palaces now overshadowed by the handsome modern edifices belonging to the aristocracy of wealth.

January 3d.—The ball was very fine, very crowded, and as magnificent as immense wealth could make it. The house standing in the Calle de Arenal is a palace, the fine court and noble staircase leading to suites of spacious rooms, the roofs painted *al fresco*, and furnished with all that modern luxury can devise of rich and splendid. The supper was a banquet, where more money was probably expended than in half a dozen of the flimsy *buffets* which are considered quite satisfactory at entertainments in other houses. There is no people less *gourmand*, more temperate in eating and drinking than the Spaniards. Here, however, was collected every delicacy in and out of season, and if the tables did not groan under the weight of gold plate, and vases filled with exquisite flowers, *I* did, on finding myself wedged in, in the midst of the immense crowd, and struggling violently to obtain an ice for my partner, who was no less than a daughter of her Majesty Queen Christina, who, with her family, honored the ball with her presence. Few of the aristocracy were there. The society consisted chiefly of the banking or mercantile class, the corps diplomatique, and ministers of the crown; and though there were quite as many fine diamonds and rich toilettes as usual, there was perhaps somewhat less elegance and distinction in the wearers. But it was an entertainment well worth seeing. At three in the morning I adjourned to the Countess Montijo's in time to have a famous polka with the Countess S——i.

January 5th.—This morning very sleepy, after a supper at S——'s. I was wakened about three in the morning by an ominous and thundering knock, and by the voice of the porter at Count A——'s door. "Her majesty the queen *está de parto.* Your excellency is requested to go immediately to the palace." I went to my chief's room, and found him making a hasty toilette, while a halberdier with a long cloak stood sentinel in the ante-chamber. When he was equipped in full uniform, and had driven off, I returned to finish my interrupted slumbers. About eight o'clock I was aroused by the booming of cannon, announcing that a prince or princess was ushered into the world. But the ringing of all the bells in the city, and the tremendous noise made by the people, who were pouring along the Plaza del Oriente, on their way to the palace, made it impossible to count correctly the number of *coups.* Some said they had counted five-and-twenty, others nineteen. The heart of the city was beating tumultuously. Shortly, however, a lugubrious silence reigned throughout Madrid. Her majesty had given birth to a princess!

Impossible to describe the disappointment legible on every countenance. Soldiers passed by, muttering and swearing in a low voice. The queen and the ministers had sunk below par. My chief returned early. The queen was doing well. The new-born babe was brought in by the king on a golden *plateau* to be presented to the corps diplomatique. It seemed, he said, to be a fine child, but the day was bitter cold, and the apartment in which they were assembled not heated. It is to be hoped that the baby inherits the royal peculiarity of never feeling cold. Sorrow, anger, or consternation appears upon the generality of countenances. It is evidently regarded as another ministerial blunder.

The baptism is to take place to-morrow. A dead calm has succeeded to this morning's uproar. Many are, no doubt, bidding a mental adieu to crosses, grades, and promotions. The poor little Ynfanta does not see the light under happy auspices. The opposition press washes its hands of the whole affair, by keeping the most contemptuous silence concerning the event. The bulletins of the physicians, though inserted, are put in, not at the head of the newspaper, where all interesting and important events are recorded, but amongst the indifferent news, without remark or commentary.

January 6th.—The bulletin of the *Gaceta* this morning is favorable.

"Her Majesty the Queen, Our Lady (whom God preserve) has passed a tranquil night, and continues to recover. Her Serene Highness, the Ynfanta, continues well."

Nevertheless, there were certain rumors to-day that the little Ynfanta had taken cold, and was not well. Notwithstanding which, preparations continue for the baptism in the Chapel Royal, where *tribunas* are prepared for the diplomatic corps, the royal household, and the ministers of the crown. I translate the invitation received yesterday for your benefit.

EXMO. SENOR

Camarera Mayor of the Palace.

Her Majesty, the Queen Our Lady (Q. D. G.), has been pleased to appoint the hour of three in the afternoon of to-morrow, sixth of this month, for the holy ceremony of Baptism, which is to be administered to Her Serene Highness, the Ynfanta, to whom Her Majesty has happily given birth, and to which act H. M. has desired that your Excellency be invited, which invitation I accordingly send, that your Excellency may assist at the ceremony, in your *Tribuna.*

Which I communicate to your Excellency by Royal Order, and with the information that those who assist at this act are to appear *de gala*, and the ladies with train and white veil. Dios guarde à V. E. many years.

Palace, 5th January.

Signed by the Countess de Valloria, Duchess of Gor.'

His excellency went at the hour appointed, and desired me to accompany him, though it was not probable that we subs. would find room in the diplomatic *tribuna*. An immense number of carriages blocked up the side entrance of the palace, the front entrance being prohibited, in order not to disturb the queen. The day was cold and gloomy. To our surprise, we met many ladies in court dresses coming away, and the count inferred that the report of the Ynfanta's illness was true, and that the baptism had been delayed. On the staircase we met Countess —— coming down, and she told us that the baby was dangerously ill; that the queen had not yet been informed of it, and was merely told that on account of the coldness of the day, it was considered advisable that the Ynfanta should not be taken to the chapel; that the ministers had been sent for to the queen's ante-chamber, and that the patriarch of the Indies was now administering private baptism to the Ynfanta in the presence of the king, the cabinet, and the principal members of the royal household. "Fortunate now that it was not a prince!" said Count A——, as we re-entered the carriage. We met a number of ladies of our acquaintance driving by, in trains and feathers, some looking sad and some looking cold; amongst those who looked both, were the ladies of the cabinet.

8*th*.—The Ynfanta died yesterday. Went to the weekly *tertulia* at the house of Madame Calderon de la Barca; very pleasant, rather crowded; but, on account of the Ynfanta's death, no music as there usually is.

Followed the crowd into the chapel to-day to see it lying in state, under a gorgeous canopy, dressed in lace cap and robes, with the crown of Spain at its feet. Connoisseurs say it is a fine-looking baby, and very large. The chapel was crowded, chiefly by the lower class of people, who walked round, surveying rather gloomily the small atom of royalty reposing in the majesty of death—guards standing sentinel at the head and feet.

Count A—— went to inscribe his name for the queen. A number of people were in the ante-room. The queen has not yet been informed of her child's death. She was visited to-day by her ministers, and is said to be looking very well. The privileges of royalty are sometimes not agreeable, I should think. It is said the baby died of cold from being kept up all night—it being against etiquette to put it in bed with its nurse. The poor nurse is no doubt a sincere mourner. Had the child been a prince, I believe there would have been a mob in Madrid this night.

The little princess is to occupy her niche in the Escorial. Certain persons are named to accompany the body, and Count A—— has got permission for me from ——, to accompany the procession in one of the carriages.

The opposition newspapers have not even mentioned the death of the Ynfanta, certainly a public mark of disrespect to the queen, upon which the *Heraldo* and other government papers have not failed to comment. The anger of the opposition party at the continuance of San Luis in power, knows no bounds. Meetings are held in the *cafés*, and at the houses of the principal malcontents. The president of the council is seriously abused, because, in publishing the act announcing the birth of the Ynfanta, he added the surname of *Tapia* to that of Don Luis Sartorius, and it is said that as a crowning piece of vanity, the Marquis of Molins, Don Mariano Roca de Togores, has signed himself Don Mariano Rocamora! It is reported that San Luis will be raised to a dukedom, will be made a grandee of Spain, &c. The queen, meanwhile, continues to repose perfect confidence in her ministers. Papers are circulated throughout Madrid, of the most inflammatory description. I will give you one as a sample.

"SPANIARDS!

"We have endured long enough. The degradation of power has arrived at its height. The laws are broken. The constitution does not exist. The ministry of the queen is the ministry of an imbecile, absurd and ridiculous favorite; of a man without reputation, without glory, without talent, without courage, without other titles to the supreme favor but those which can be found by licentious feebleness.

"A new Godoy, he pretends to put his foot upon the neck of this heroic nation, immortal mother of the victims of the 2d of May, of the heroes of Saragossa and Gerona, of the wars of Arlaban, Mendigorria and Luchana. Are we to suffer so much ignominy with impunity? Are there no swords in the land of the Cid? Are there no pikes? Are there no stones? Up, up, Spaniards! To arms every one! Death to the favorite! Long live the Constitution! Long live Liberty!"

Absurd as this is, it is greedily devoured by those who are discontented with the government, and who hope to profit by any change, no matter at what expense it may be effected.

CHAPTER XXI.

Burial of the Ynfanta—A singular document—Funeral procession—The Escorial —Religious ceremonies—Internal grandeur of the Escorial—The return.

January 18th.

THREE days have elapsed since my visit to the Escorial, and I have not yet thawed. All was on a gigantic scale; the ceremonies, the building, the cold. The coldness of the day, one of the most severe we have had in Madrid, was almost unbearable within the precincts of the Escorial, but it was a scene which I can never forget. All my day-dreams of old Spain were realized, or rather surpassed. I was about to write you a description of all the pomp and circumstance with which the poor little scion of royalty was conveyed to the tombs of her fathers; but an official statement published this day in the *Gaceta*, is so characteristic and so accurate in its details, that I think you will find it more curious to read a translation of it, than were I to give you a less circumstantial and less accurate account of what I saw.

"Act of the delivery and conveyance of the dead body of her serene highness the Ynfanta of Spain, to the Royal Pantheon of the Escorial." "I, Don Raphael Ramirez de Arellano, secretary of her majesty, subsecretary of the ministry of grace and justice, appointed by royal order of the 9th of this month, to execute as delegate of the minister of that department, the office of chief notary of these kingdoms, and consequently to assist at the delivery of the royal body of her serene highness the Ynfanta of Spain (now in glory), daughter of the most illustrious sovereigns of Spain, Doña Ysabel II, and Don Francis of Assissium Maria, born in the royal palace of Madrid on the 5th day of the present month, and baptised on the following day, the 6th, by the hands of his excellency, Senor Don Thomas Yglesias y Barones, patriarch of the Indies, without any pomp or solemnity, but in the manner usual in cases of necessity:

"Do certify and bear witness: that her royal highness, having died by a natural illness in the said royal palace, at ten minutes past eleven, on the morning of the 8th, I repaired in fulfilment of the duties of my office, on the morning of the 9th, to the said royal palace, and saw with respect in one of the saloons, upon a table, the face entirely exposed, the dead body of her royal highness, dressed in a robe of white cambric, richly embroidered and trimmed with lace, and placed upon a plateau of silver.

"Her excellency Doña Maria de 'Carmen Alvarez, de las Asturias Bohorgues, widowed Marchioness of Povar, grandee of Spain, lady of honor to the queen our lady, and governess of her serene highness the Princess of the Asturias, who stood at the head of the royal body, accompanied by the ladies of the royal household, addressed herself in a clear voice to his excellency Señor Don Antonio Agüera y Mollinado, Marquis de los Llanos, mayordomo of the week to her majesty, named by her order, to transport the body to the Pantheon of the Royal Chapel of St. Lorenzo of the Escorial, formerly the monastery of that name, saying to him:

"I deliver over to your excellency, in compliance with the orders of their majesties, the royal body of her serene highness the Ynfanta of Spain, their august daughter. Does your excellency undertake the charge of it?"

"And the mayordomo of the week, Marquis de los Llanos replied: 'I do undertake the charge of it.'

"Then the aforesaid marquis addressed the royal body of monteros (*chasseurs*), then and there represented by Don Matthew Madrazo, Don Maximus Merino, Don James Fernandez Gil, and Don Sandalio Villasante, and said:

"'Monteros of the royal chamber and guard; do you recognize the royal body of her serene highness, the Ynfanta of Spain?'

"The monteros replied: 'Yes, we do recognize it.'

"'Do you take charge of the body of her royal highness?'

"'Yes, we do take charge of it.'

"Then the mayordomos of the week, his excellency the Count of Casa Flores, his excellency Don Manuel Rosales, Don Fernando Trujillos, and Don Luis Garcini y Castilla, took up the plateau on which the body of her royal highness was placed, and preceded by the other mayordomos of the week and by the *Gentilhombres de Casa y Boca*, Don Pedro José de Mendoza, Don Francisco Aguirre y Mollinedo, Don José Paspati y Bracho, and Don Pedro Juan Cuenca, the procession continued through the principal gallery to the royal chapel.

"At the door was his excellency the patriarch of the Indies, clad in his semi-pontifical robes, with the chaplains of honor" (whose names are here enumerated), "and the other individuals belonging to the said chapel royal.

"The royal body was placed in the centre of the chapel on an imperial bed, hung and covered with rich stuffs of yellow satin, embroidered in colors, with raised work of silver.

"Two monteros of the royal chamber and guard watched at the head and at the sides, and at the foot of the imperial bed two guards of the queen.

"At the right of the head was placed the standard of the royal brotherhood of the servants of their majesties and highnesses, with two individuals of the same, and in the enclosure of the chapel the corresponding lights.

"The procession surrounding the royal body entoned the hymn *Laudate pueri Dominum*, all holding the lights usual in these ceremonies.

"At half-past eleven the royal chapel was opened for the public, until six in the evening, and remained open the two following days, during which three days an extraordinary concourse of persons assembled to see the royal body, giving unequivocal proofs of sorrow and regret. On the 11th, a solemn mass of the angels was sung in the royal chapel, at which his eminence the Cardinal Archbishop of Toledo officiated in his pontifical vestments, and at which assisted his excellency the patriarch and the chaplains of honor.

"Amongst the numerous concourse of persons who had the entry into the said chapel, were his excellency the *Mayordomo Mayor*, the chiefs of the palace, and the grandees of Spain, lords in waiting on her majesty.

"At eight in the evening, with all necessary precautions and security, the Marquis de los Llanos ordered that the royal body should be placed, and it was placed, in an inner case of lead, covered on the upper part by a glass, the act being performed in the presence of the aforesaid monteros of the royal chamber and guard of various individuals of the royal household, and of the royal corps of the queen's guards.

"The leaden case being placed in an exterior one, lined with silver tissue and golden lace, and the coffin containing the royal body being guarded from that hour as it had hitherto been, the Marquis de los Llanos arrived at the royal chapel at seven, on the morning of the 12th, accompanied by me, and we proceeded to verify, and did verify, the identity of the royal body through the crystal.

"His excellency, the patriarch of the Indies, then presented himself in semi-pontifical robes, preceded by the cross of the royal chapel, with the chaplains of honor (here enumerated), and with the corresponding chaplains of the altar, the psalmists, singers, and musicians of the said chapel royal.

"The usual prayers being chanted, the coffin was raised from its imperial bed. After being locked, and covered with a cloth and cushion of golden tissue, by the mayordomos de Semana (their names enumerated), and carried by them through the midst of all the assistants to the head of the staircase, where it was received by the lords of the bedchamber of her majesty, Señores, &c. &c.) who delivered it over to the equerries, Don Francisco Villavicencia and Don Gabriel Sanchez del Cid, in order to have it placed in a beautiful *estufa* (a kind of carriage), belonging to the *Caballerizas Reales*, of massive mahogany, all adorned with branches and garlands of artificial flowers, and hangings of white satin, with embroidery and borders, arrows, cords and tassels of gold.

"The coffin being placed there in my presence, in that of the Marquis de los Llanos, and of the individuals belonging to the royal corps of the noble Monteros de Espinosa, above mentioned, the funeral procession set off at eight in the morning, preceded in front by a picquet of cavalry, two trumpeters, the officers riding in two lines, two horses with rich housings, the standards and members of the royal confraternity, the cross of the royal chapel, the clerk, psalmists and singers of the same, the chaplains of honor, lords of the bedchamber and household, mayordomos of the week, two life guards, the carriage containing the body of her royal highness, by the side of which rode four lords of the chamber and household, and two masters of the horse with torches, two monteros of the royal chamber by the coach-steps, and two footmen behind. Behind the carriage followed the Marquis de los Llanos, who, with my assistance, presided over the procession, having on his left his excellency Don Nicholas Louis de Lega, archbishop of Seleucia, abbot of San Ildefonso, the march being closed by a picquet of the queen's guards, under the command of Colonel Don Felix Ortega, with an escort of cavalry, commanded by an officer of equal rank, Don José Maria Colarte; bodies of all the regiments in Madrid being drawn out on parade, under the orders of the military governor of the city.

"In this order the funeral procession arrived at San Antonia de la Florida, amidst a numerous assemblage of people collected in spite of the inclemency of the weather, to witness the funeral ceremony. Here, those persons for whom carriages were prepared, got in, and the procession continued in the same order as before, &c."

Here I shall take leave of the veracious chronicler, whom I have followed so far, because my account could not vie in accuracy with that of the royal secretary, and also because the manners and customs of Spain are so unchanged in certain ceremonials, that it might form a pendant to an old MS. shown me by ——, describing the nuptials of Philip II. with Mary of England. But having arrived at San Antonio, where, though I cannot say that a carriage was *prepared* for me, a place in one was permitted, I found myself forming part of the procession, in a comfortable coach, drawn by four sleek mules, with three other young men, who accompanied the cortege in an official capacity. The morning being bitterly cold, we drew up the windows, wrapped ourselves in our cloaks, ventured to light our cigars, and proceeded, of course at a very slow pace, behind the magnificent car containing the remains of the little Ynfanta.

In the villages of Las Rozas, Galapagar, and what is called the *Escorial de Abajo*, long delays were made. The clergy of the parish churches came out to meet the procession, and again the beautiful psalm, *Laudate pueri Dominum*, was entoned in solemn accents, under the clear blue cold sky. It was dusk long before we arrived at the Escorial, at nearly half-past six. I strained my eyes in the darkness to distinguish this wonderful monument of the stern Catholic monarch, into whose domains we thus entered in the darkness of the night, to deliver up, as it were, to his guardianship an innocent little descendant of his race. It loomed out in the darkness, immense, mysterious, lonely. The snowy crowns of the Guadaramas were distinctly visible. The wind blew fiercely, and sounded like a sad and moaning requiem, proceeding from the everlasting hills. The stars shone out clearly and coldly, through the dark clouds that were blown across their silvery disks. The procession halted.

The Brigadier Purrind, chief of brigade; Moral, commander of the infantry; Velasquez de Velasco, commander of the artillery; and the constituent corporation, came out to meet and receive the body of the princess. The procession moved slowly towards tho monastery, aud drew up in front of the royal chapel. The two masters of the horse descended the coffin from the hearse, and delivered it to the lords of the royal household, who placed it upon a kind of *estrade*, prepared for its reception under the portico leading to the great entrance of the Spanish monarchs.

Here the scene was most striking; a long procession of chaplains and churchmen, headed by the abbot in his cope, the crucifix borne in front, advanced to meet the body.

Then the chaplain, *Prosecretario*, read in a loud and distinct voice an order from their majesties, transmitted to the abbot by the patriarch of the Indies, in which they communicated to him the death of her serene highness the Ynfanta, desiring that her royal body, now transported to the Escorial, should be deposited with the usual solemnities. The abbot, president of the royal chapel, then demanded of the Marquis de los Llanos whether he were charged to bring the royal body there, which he answered in the affirmative, at the same time delivering to the abbot the order which he had received from the *Mayordomo Mayor* to that effect.

Another schedule was then read by the *Archivero* (keeper of the records), in which King Philip IV. had decided a controversy existing between the chapel of the royal palace at Madrid and that of the monastery of San Lorenzo. A new and solemn recognition of the body was then made, and being identified, the abbot, deacon, and subdeacon threw holy water on the corpse, and the solemn music of the church resounded through the lofty vaults: *Sit nomen Domine benedictum*, *Laudate pueri Dominum*, songs of praise and thanksgiving, suitable to the obsequies of the royal infant, who has exchanged her chance of an earthly crown for the certainty of one of eternal glory. Meanwhile it seemed as if all the winds of heaven were unchained that night, their hoarse voices howling round the massive building, blowing through the vaults, extinguishing the great torches, and moaning in tones that sounded like the wailing of infernal spirits, or of souls in agony.

The procession entered the church, and it required little imagination to believe the whole scene a vision of by-gone ages. " A hut for myself, a palace for God," said the monarch who designed this glorious pile. I cannot pretend to describe it, for all was indistinct in gloom and grandeur. The blazing lights which yet but faintly illuminated the immense cathedral—the echo of the music, *Beati immaculati in via*—the abbot and priests—grandees and officers in uniform—all this preparation for receiving the remains of an infant who had scarcely opened her eyes on the light, but who was the descendant of a long line of princes—the immense magnitude of every thing in this gigantic temple, making the tallest men dwindle into pigmies by comparison—the whole produced an effect which no time can efface from my memory.

The procession proceeded, bearing the coffin, with all its rich adornings, and placed it upon a monument prepared for its reception in the centre of the church, upon the golden cushion, at the head of which was a royal crown; at each side numerous vases of flowers, and to the right and left eight tapers of white wax. On the high altar burned a huge bronze candelabra, destined exclusively for royal interments, with nine lighted torches. Though the whole edifice was illuminated, it still looked gloomy. When the prayers were concluded, the royal corps of monteros and the queen's guards received the body into their custody, and remained to keep watch over it during the night. I could not with propriety remain, as I would willingly have done, to examine the wonders of the church, so I took one glance at the little upturned waxen face of the Ynfanta, lying in her calm sleep, all unconscious of the royal honors paid her, left the guards to their cold and solemn night-watch, and followed the procession into the palace.

I must confess that the sight of a spacious tapestried hall, well lighted, at the further end of which was a roaring fire, of huge logs of wood, and of a long table covered with smoking dishes, brought me down to real life, and made me forget for a while every consideration but that of the intense cold and hunger from which I was suffering; feelings which had until then been kept in abeyance, probably from the philosophical conclusion that they could not be appeased

The abbot, archbishop, lords of the bed-chamber, officers of the household, and other dignitaries, took their places with all due etiquette, and I found myself seated between two of my travelling companions, young Z. del V—— and F——, with a smoking turkey as a vis-à-vis. We did all justice to the feast, even while giving an occasional thought to the little princess with her monteros in the cold church. The repast was royal in its profusion, the guests quiet and decorous. The robes of the priests and the brilliant uniforms did not appear out of keeping with the ancient Flemish tapestries, marvellously preserved in their coloring. I felt as if we should hardly have been startled had Philip II., with high ruff, black hat and plumes, glided in and assumed his chair of state at the head of the table.

It was late when the numerous party retired to the various apartments assigned to them. I was roused from a deep sleep by the increased fierceness of the wind, and by the tolling of the bells for the dead. The sun was already high in the heavens when all the persons composing the royal cortège were again assembled in the church of San Lorenzo, and together with the city corporation, had taken their seats on the long benches placed on either side of the monument. The Marquis de los Llanos, and the notary occupied two ancient velvet chairs at the head of the coffin—the monteros, royal guards and officers, stood in their respective places.

The snow had hardened in the night, and the sunbeams struggled through the lofty windows, the faint rays nearly extinguished by the blaze of the numerous tapers and torches. Even more wonderful the mighty temple appeared to me than it did on the preceding night. The great organ pealed forth a strain of solemn and triumphant psalmody, accompanying the voices of the choir. The pontifical mass *de los Angeles* was celebrated by the Archbishop of Seleucia, assisted by the royal chaplains. At its conclusion they left the high altar and surrounded the sepulchral monument, chanting the antiphon *Juvenes et Virgines*, followed by the psalm *Laudate pueri Dominum de Cœlis*, during which the coffin was raised from its temporary resting-place by the four mayordomos, and carried to the entrance of the Pantheon, where it was received by the *Gentilhombres*, who carried it down to the second landing-place of the stair. There it was delivered to the monteros, and by them placed before the altar, on a tomb erected in the centre of the Pantheon.

Then the exterior case was opened, and the Marquis de los Llanos, followed by the royal notary, advanced to identify the corpse, declaring it to be that of her royal highness the Ynfanta of Spain, daughter of the illustrious sovereigns of Spain, Doña Ysabel Segunda and Don Francisco de Assis Maria. The same ceremony was performed by all the guards and noblemen, by the archbishop, chaplains, corporation, and in succession by all who were present. After which the Marquis de los Llanos asked aloud:

"Monteros of the royal chamber and guard, do you recognize in this corpse that of her royal highness the Ynfanta of Spain, which was delivered to you by me in the royal palace of Madrid on the ninth day of this month?"

And the monteros replied, "Si Señor; this is the body of her royal highness the Ynfanta of Spain, which was delivered to us by your excellency, and as such we recognize it."

The same question was put by the notary, and the same answer given.

The exterior case of the coffin was then locked, and the key delivered by the Marquis de los Llanos to the abbot president of the royal chapel, with an order from their majesties that the royal corpse should remain in the Pantheon, the iron door being locked until their majesties should dispose otherwise. The abbot received the key, and promised to obey faithfully the orders of their majesties. At the same moment a discharge of musketry was fired by the garrison. We reascended the gloomy staircase leading from the sepulchre. The iron doors were closed, and the little princess was left to moulder into dust amongst her royal ancestors. The absurd fancy that she must suffer from the coldness and gloom to which she was abandoned haunted me for hours afterwards.

Unfortunately, it was in vain for me to attempt gaining a sight of the library, the frescos, the paintings, the palace, or the monastery that day. I lingered behind the others a few moments, while one of the chaplains showed me the narrow chamber where Philip II. passed several years, and where from his hard couch he could see mass performed in the church, and the cushion worn by his daily prayers. He called on me to remark the eleven great arches behind the high altar, with their gigantic crucifixes worked in blood-red jasper upon pure white marble, the beautiful tabernacle composed of the finest jasper and gilded bronze—the *Capilla Mayor*, a wonder of art, the whole ornaments of which are also entirely composed of fine jasper and precious metals. He told me that the height of the cupola was three hundred and thirty feet from the floor of the temple to the pinnacle of the cross; that the principal *façade*, where is the public entry, is seven hundred and forty-four feet wide, and sixty-two high, up to the cornice which surrounds the whole edifice; and that the front facing the south is five hundred and eighty feet from tower to tower. I followed him into the vast, deserted cloisters, and took a hasty glance of the magnificent paintings *al fresco*, as fresh in their coloring as if the hands that executed them, instead of having mouldered in the dust for centuries, had but completed their work. One tantalizing look at the principal staircase, gigantic in its proportions; at the vaulted roofs covered with wonderful paintings, which seem lavishly strewn, like bright flowers of the field, over every corner, and wall, and crevice, and vault of this marvellous creation of genius, and then I was obliged to hurry through the solitary court-yards, and arrived just as the guards were mounting their horses, and the carriages drawing up.

As we drove off, I took one last look of the Escorial, now brilliantly illuminated by the morning sun! Alone in a desert, it can be compared with no surrounding object, unless with the lofty mountains behind it. The embodiment of a grand idea, a great and gloomy mind could alone have accomplished it. I promise myself to return hither in spring, yet it seems to me that winter is the most appropriate time for seeing the Escorial in all its stern gloom and grandeur.

Our return, though less tedious than our journey there, was sufficiently slow and tiresome, and when I presented myself at the dinner-table of the Legation, I was greeted by an exclamation of amused surprise from M——, who was dining there. "You look as white as a sheet, my dear count; one may easily see you have returned from a pilgrimage to the tombs of the kings." "He looks frozen," said his excellency, "and no wonder." "I plead guilty to cold and hunger, sir," said I. "You have no idea how comfortable you look here." But neither a good dinner, a good fire, nor pleasant talk could banish the mighty Escorial from my mind. In sleep I distinctly saw the ancient kings arising to welcome their descendant. They passed like the kings in Macbeth, crowned and shadowy and colossal, like the bronze statues in the Plaza. The little Ynfanta, with her waxen face, sat up in her coffin and bowed to them as they formed a circle round her. It was a real nightmare, and I was quite relieved to be awakened by a blind woman, who was shrieking aloud: "Horrible legend of a young female who killed seventy children, and was carried away by an evil spirit." I thought it was high time.

CHAPTER XXII.

The Prince of Parma—Balls and Reunions—The good policy of keeping quiet—Coup d'état—Gen. O'Donnell.

January —.

Reports of a change of ministry—an expected crisis—a coup d'état predicted. It is known that private meetings are held at various houses of the opposition party. The queen was informed of her child's death the day of its removal to the Escorial. She had already begun to suspect the truth, and was naturally in very low spirits. She has, however, had a rapid recovery, and has already held a council of ministers. The Prince of Parma is expected. The palace of the Casino is prepared for his reception. Hernani at the royal theatre. The house may vie in coldness with the Escorial. The ladies sit muffled in cloaks and shawls.

Met the Prince of Parma at a party at the Countess Montijo's. Had the honor of an introduction to his royal highness. He spoke to me in German like a native. He seems to have a wonderful gift of tongues. In French, English, and even in various *patois* he is perfectly at home. He looks younger than his age, which is about thirty; and though very amusing, has a kind of reckless gayety in his manners, which, while it provokes laughter, has something sad in it at the same time. He has a good, slight figure, and a clever face, but is not handsome, and certainly not princely, either in appearance or manners. He waltzed furiously, yet never seemed to grow tired, and while he made his partners laugh, always looked grave himself. There is a certain dignity in his air when he pleases to adopt it, which is seldom. When going up to lead out Countess S—— for a waltz, finding a table in the way, he vaulted over it! He is undeniably good-natured, and has plenty of talent, with no judgment to direct it. He lives for amusement, yet never looks amused. It was a strange lot for poor "Mademoiselle" to be taken from her convent in order to be mated with this royal harlequin.

As the court mourning for the Queen of Portugal is over, the balls look more animated now. A beautiful one was given, some days ago, by the young Duchess of Fernan-Nuñez —one of the best I have been at this winter; but very few of the grandees of Spain open their houses. They have generally their own nightly *tertulias*, where half a dozen of their *habitués* pass an hour or two without ceremony, but they give neither balls, dinners, nor parties. The Marquesa de M——a receives once a week; but it is a very clannish affair, consisting almost entirely of the relations of the family, with the addition of some of the most distinguished *pollos*. The embassy, of course, is closed. Some of the diplomatic ladies showed faint symptoms of an intention to give weekly receptions, but the duels seem to have damped their ardor. The Marquis de Molins gives literary suppers, where only men are invited. The Duke of Rivas has also reunions of men, literary, political, and poetical, at which the duchess and her daughters occasionally appear. Mme. Calderon de la Barca has weekly musical soirées, and the Countess de Montijo is indefatigable in her hospitalities.

Many reasons are given as to the motives of the grandees in keeping their houses hermetically closed. Some say it is solely from indolence; others, that it is because their fortunes cannot compete with those of the banking class; and others, that it arises from the necessity now existing of asking every one or of offending many; and that they prefer having no entertainments rather than open their doors to mixed society. None of these reasons seem to me very satisfactory. I should think it was at least as troublesome to dress to go out, as to receive friends at home. Great expense is not necessary here in giving a *soirée dansante.* Except at regular balls, chocolate or tea is considered sufficient in the way of refreshments; and the houses of the nobility, if not so splendidly furnished, are in my opinion much more noble-looking and in better taste than those of the *nouveaux riches.* As for the last reason, I cannot imagine why they should not choose their own society, or set so much stress upon popularity, when, with a very few exceptions, they avoid as much as possible taking any part in political affairs.

C——l says there is another cause much more potent than any of the former, viz: that in Madrid it is unsafe to be distinguished for any thing—for wealth, talent, or even for beauty—and that the only way to get on well here is to *keep quiet.* He says that those who have passed any length of time in this country of revolutions, never fail to find this out; and that here it is always wise for every one, especially for a public man, to appear poorer than he really is. "If the wife of a cabinet minister," said he, "has fine diamonds, they are pointed out as proofs of the scandalous robberies of her husband. If he gives good dinners, they are remarked upon as another strong proof of his criminality. If he builds a fine house, his reputation is blasted. If a pretty woman, whose husband is not rich, appears with a new bracelet, she has received it from her lover. The fine jewels of the aristocracy excite no comment, because they are supposed to have inherited them; but if they made a certain display of wealth in their own houses, it is more than likely that they would be accused of having enriched themselves by some nefarious transaction." If this be true, even with some exaggeration, it is a melancholy state of things.

January 17.

Severe measures have been adopted by the ministry, differently judged of course, by each party. The oppositionists are furious. The advocates of the ministry say that they are not severe enough. The Marquis of Duero has received orders to proceed to his quarters at the Canary Islands; General Ynfanta to Majorca; also General José Concha to the same place; General O'Donnell is sent to Santa Cruz de Teneriffe. If the discoveries said to have been made by the government are certain, these measures are no doubt very mild. Great agitation and excitement in the *Casino* this evening. The *Café Suisse* was crowded, and political discussions carried on to a late hour.

The Marquis of Duero has obeyed orders, and embarked for the Canaries. General José Concha has escaped from Barcelona, and is said to have embarked for France. When the orders arrived at the house of General O'Donnell, his servants informed the agents of the government, that the general had gone to a hunting party in the country, and since then he has not appeared. A circular is sent to the governors of the provinces with orders to arrest him should he be found in any one of their respective districts. The general belief is that he is concealed in Madrid; some say, in his own house —others, that he is hidden in the English Embassy.

January 22d.

The momentary excitement caused by these measures seems to have died away, and it is certain that there are now fewer political meetings, that a stop has been put to the circulation of inflammatory papers throughout the city, and that the enemies of the government begin to fear that the cabinet is more firmly rooted than they had supposed. All this, however, produces some restraint in general society. At a small party the other evening, where were present several friends and relations of the Conchas, and various ladies of the palace, and of the ministers, it seemed to me that there was more politeness and less cordiality than usual, lower curtseys, and cooler greetings.

—— says that the conduct of certain military men in this country is, in his opinion, greatly owing to the rapidity of their career, which leaves them, while still young, with no legitimate objects of ambition. General O'Donnell for example, who is now forty-five, and whose family were devoted to Ferdinand VII. and absolutism, received, when a mere boy, a brevet of sub-lieutenant. At nineteen years old, he was a captain, and at twenty-four a colonel; at thirty, a lieutenant-general, and immediately after, he received his present rank and title of Count de Lucena, in consequence of having caused Cabrera to raise the siege of that place. At one time he was attached to the army of Espartero, and was afterwards made commander-in-chief of the forces directed against that general. When in 1840 Espartero aimed a blow at Queen Christina's regency, O'Donnell gave in his resignation, which the queen-mother refused, bestowing on him at the same time the grand *cordon* of Charles III. Under the regency of Espartero, O'Donnell headed an insurrection at Pamplona, to re-establish the authority of Queen Christina. From that time till the year 1848 he remained as an emigré in France, till he was appointed Governor of Cuba, where he remained several years. In 1849, he was named by General Narvaez director-general of the infantry, which post he occupied till the year 1851, when he became, as he has since continued, one of the most ardent members of the opposition in the Senate.

"When a man is a general at thirty," said ——, "without having performed any very distinguished services, he has a long career before him. He has the highest rank in the army, an immense fortune, he is (at least in this instance) married and a *père de famille*. If all legitimate sources of love, wealth and ambition are exhausted for him, what more does he aspire to? *Power*. He must have authority. It is easy to find motives of dissatisfaction with any government, and even to persuade ourselves that the country would be happier and more prosperous under our direction. Self-love and patriotism, far asunder as the poles, are yet constantly mistaken for each other, in a man's own heart. General O'Donnell pretends to consider himself a victim of tyranny. Because he is resolved to leave nothing undone to crush this cabinet, and because the government, having discovered his designs, take measures to prevent their own ruin, and what they, with at least equal sincerity, believe would be the ruin of their country; he begins by setting an example of insubordination, ruinous in its effects upon the *morale* of the army. I foresee a storm coming, though the cloud is now little bigger than a man's hand. From what quarter it will come, or where it will burst, I cannot say, but all portends it. The Cortes dissolved, I am of no further use here, and to-morrow I start for Valencia, to wait for the dénouements of the dreamer, amongst fields of roses and carnations. We shall not meet again till——" "Not," said M——

"Till the hurly-burly's done,
Till the battle's lost or won."

I regret ——'s departure. Besides having found him very friendly, he is one of the cleverest men in Madrid.

The death of the little Ynfanta has made the court rather dull this winter. No balls have been given in the palace, and, as yet, no *besamanos*. Queen Christina is about to open her palace for a series of entertainments, which will probably be very agreeable; but I hear that in these *réunions de famille*, as they are called, the diplomatic corps will not be included. I have some hopes, however, of being considered as an exceptional case, in consequence of my mother's relationship to the Neapolitan Prince ——.

CHAPTER XXIII.

Reunions at the Queen-Mother's—Fashionable life—Queen Christina—Her second ball—Review of the troops—Proclamation against General O'Donnell—Madrid gay.

January 24.

THROUGH the good-nature of the Prince of Parma, I received an invitation to the queen-mother's *réunions*, which promise to be the best parties that have yet been given in Madrid.

The soirée begins at ten, unnaturally early for Madrid, where the system prevails of turning night into day. I know one very distinguished family, where the young ladies never rise till two in the afternoon, and hardly ever go out, even to mass, as they have a chapel in their own house. From that time till the evening, they read, write, play, &c., each one having her own apartment, beautifully fitted up, and containing a small library of choice volumes. In the evening, the family meet in the common drawing-room, and receive their habitual visitors, never retiring to rest till four or five o'clock. This strange system is not generally carried to such an extent, but prevails more or less from the queen downwards.

The fashionable world of Madrid never appear in the Prado till the sun is setting, and the air begins to be cold and disagreeable. About the same hour the queen drives through with the little princess and her suite. The doctors attribute half the *pulmonias* in Madrid to this absurd fashion. Very few balls begin to be crowded till one o'clock. Queen Christina's, however, are an exception.

Ten is the hour at which her majesty enters, followed by her three daughters, with their governess. Few persons, however, except the cabinet ministers and their families, arrived before eleven. The company consisted exclusively of them, the ladies and gentilhombres of the palace, and a certain number of the grandees, who, I believe, are invited alternately. There might be about one hundred and fifty in all.

The queen-mother has, like the Countess of Montijo, the art of putting her guests at their ease. She sat on one side of the room, very richly and tastefully dressed. The two Ynfantas, Amalia and Christina, with their governess, sat on her right —the Ynfante Don Francisco, and his son, on her left. Her three daughters, who are charming girls, were of course the principal personages in the assembly. The Duke of Riansenes, still a handsome man, though very bald, remained in the ante-room, and received the guests very cordially.

The ball began with quadrilles, and was at first rather stiff and courtly. The salon was beautifully lighted, the music in the ante-room very good. The queen's daughters, who live in a kind of semi-royalty, which must be sufficiently tiresome—with much of its state and few of its privileges—seemed to enjoy with their whole hearts this occasion of amusing themselves. They were dressed very simply and tastefully in white, with colored flowers.

To all who came up to pay their respects to Christina, she had something kind and agreeable to say. Whenever she rose, every one, in spite of her earnest request to the contrary, rose also. "I am going into the next room—I beg no one will rise," upon which the whole room rose simultaneously. The ball began with quadrilles, and at first was rather stiff, but by one o'clock, gayety was at its height, waltzes and polkas were danced with great spirit, and all courtly etiquette seemed forgotten. Nearly all the beautiful young married women of Madrid were collected in one nucleus. I must confess they carried the day over the unmarried girls, perhaps owing to their advantages of dress, in the way of jewels and lace, which were superb.

The only exception to the exclusion of the diplomatic corps, was in the presence of the Neapolitan minister and his daughters, who are invited on account of Queen Christina's Neapolitan origin. About two o'clock she and her daughters, with the Ynfanta and princesses, their governesses and ladies in waiting, passed into the refreshment room, which was afterwards thrown open to all.

The ball ended with the interminable German cotillion, in which flounces were torn, flowers dropped, fans broken, handkerchiefs lost, and during all which the queen sat till four o'clock, with exemplary patience, apparently enjoying the spirit with which it was carried on. A little after four, she rose and wished good-night to every one, saying a few words to each as she passed, and retired followed by her daughters, and the other members of the royal family. For a few minutes the guests remained, taking refreshments or talking. Then came the shawling and cloaking, and calling of carriages, and a descent down the very steep and inconvenient great staircase, affording to those below an opportunity of judging of the beauty of Spanish feet and ankles. The morning was dawning bright and cold, and the sky glimmering with half-extinguished stars, when we who live in the Plaza del Oriente rushed on foot to our houses, like muffled conspirators.

Dined in company with the Prince of Parma. He was as usual in reckless spirits. The dinner was at the house of the Duke of M——, whose son is connected by marriage with the royal family, and whose daughters are very handsome. Neither the presence of ladies nor of the servants, prevented his royal highness from saying every thing that came into his head. He tells a story capitally, and is a first-rate mimic. He went away early with the intention of paying a visit to his royal cousin at the palace, and made his exit by sliding down the banisters, to the great wonderment of the powdered servants. M—— made a bad pun, which I record for your benefit. "Why is the government of Parma likely to be *stable?*" "Because there is a groom at the head of affairs!"

January —.

Another ball at Queen Christina's, still more brilliant than the last, and even gayer, owing to the presence of the Prince of Parma. He set off in a polka with the youngest Ynfanta, in a furious style, which seemed both to frighten and amuse his partner, a modest, well-educated and intelligent young princess. He led off the German cotillion, inventing various new and extraordinary figures, danced with Queen Christina's youngest daughter, a serious-looking child of twelve years old, and thanked her with mock gravity for her extreme condescension in honoring him with her hand. When the cotillion was first proposed, he observed with much dignity that he scarcely thought it was a dance fitted for a royal assembly, but his scruples seemed to melt into thin air when once engaged in it.

A review of the troops got up for the Prince. M—— and I rode down early to the Prado to see it. His royal highness looked extremely well on horseback, in a superb Hungarian uniform. He rode along the lines *at full gallop* on a beautiful bay from the royal stables. For the first time I felt a certain interest in him this evening. We dined at the Marquis of ——'s, a man's party. The spirits of the prince had risen to more than their usual height. After dinner, he kept the party in a roar, with anecdotes of his numerous adventures. He mimicked the various characters in his stories to perfection, talked slang, showed how he could leap over the table, without breaking more than half-a-dozen glasses, and then, as he was taking leave of his host, suddenly said in a tone of perfect conviction, "I shall not live out this year. It is a presentiment. I leave Madrid to-morrow, and you will never see me again."

I am told also that when he took leave of the queen, and she expressed her hopes that he would return next year, he replied: "I shall certainly accept your Majesty's invitation, unless I receive an *estocada* (a stab) before then."

Before his departure, he received the Torson d'or and crosses for himself and his children.

A proclamation has come out against General O'Donnell, depriving him of his rank, honors, and dignities. He is said by some to be hidden in a foreign legation, but it is more probable that he is concealed in some private house. Many of the opposition party appear to be perfectly aware of his whereabouts. It does not say much for the police of Madrid that they cannot discover the hiding-place of a man of his remarkable appearance, known to the whole of Spain. Every now and then it is reported that he has been seen in the Prado very late at night, or towards morning. I am inclined to infer that the government wink at the affair, and are disinclined to drive matters to extremities, fearing the odium that might result from the punishment which they must necessarily inflict upon the general for military disobedience should he fall into their hands. In my humble opinion, they are wrong. All history has shown us that half-measures never succeed. With regard to the police, they decidedly "manage these things better in France."

January 30th.

Madrid is now very gay. Another great ball at the Countess de Montijo's last evening, to celebrate the "*dias*" of the Duchess of Alva, and the anniversary of the empress's marriage. The tea-table is always presided over, on these occasions, by a respectable old English governess who brought up the empress and duchess, and is treated by the countess as one of the family. Under the plea of being a great amateur of tea, I always have a long talk in English with good Miss F——, and like to see her devoted attachment to the countess and to her former pupils.

Robert le Diable is now the great attraction at the Royal Theatre. The scenery is wonderfully got up. I have seen nothing to compare with it in any theatre in Europe. But the opera is too long. A masked ball is announced for next week at the Teatro Real, to which people go by invitation, consequently it is infinitely more select than those in Paris.

CHAPTER XXIV.

Masked Ball—An Adventure—A Mysterious Beauty—May have been a Ghost—Grows feverish—Convalescent—The Mystery heightened—My Doctor's Opinion.

February —.

I WENT to the masked ball. Four or five young men, Spaniards and *pollos*, joined M—— and me. We went late, after a noisy supper at S——'s. I had an adventure which will satisfy me for the season. I have only revealed it to one person, as of course were it known I should only be laughed at, for having been made the dupe of some horrid mystification, some carnival trick. I see the eyes of Caroline and Julia sparkling with curiosity, and have a great mind to defer my story to some winter night, when the wind is roaring round the castle, and making the lofty fir-trees bend their stubborn heads, and the fire is blazing in the great hall, and all minds are wound up to drink in a tale of the marvellous. But to say the truth, I feel a selfish desire for sympathy, and, therefore, shall no longer keep you in suspense.

We went to the ball about one o'clock. I amused myself tolerably for an hour or so, trying to find out one after another of the masks, who amused themselves by saying witty things at my expense, and some I must confess were very witty, and their repartees very amusing, one especially whose accent betrayed her to be an Andalusian. Tired at length of the squeaking voices, the eternal "Me conoces? Te conozco,"—for nothing is more monotonous than a masked ball, when one has no particular object in view,—I went into S——'s box, and sat down in an arm-chair near the door.

I might have been there about half an hour, when the door was slowly opened, and a masked figure appeared, with a mysterious air, half shaded by the curtain. She was dressed in mourning, even her mask fringed with black lace. Her gloves, however, were white, and she held in one hand a remarkably beautiful large white rose. She beckoned me with a quiet but very imperious gesture, and I got up, expecting the usual "*te conozco.*" These words she certainly said, but in a whisper, and added, "Follow me."

I obeyed her orders, and she glided on before me, till we reached the ball-room. There she took my arm, and for some time walked on in perfect silence. I guessed her to be the marquesa of this, the duchess of that, but she gave no answer, merely shaking her head as a negative. Her hands were small and beautifully formed, her feet remarkable even for Spanish feet. Of her face nothing was seen but two remarkably bright eyes, which flashed from out of her black mask. After walking round and round the room for some time, she stopped near the door, and in a sepulchral whisper said, "Have you courage enough to come with me?" Of course my answer was in the affirmative. My curiosity was excited, my vanity flattered, for there was an elegance and languor about my mysterious companion, that convinced me she was no common person. Her figure was that of a young girl, tall and slight. Her dress was of the richest materials, a kind of cloud of black lace and jet. Many people had observed her, but no one knew who she was. M—— and several other men standing near the stove in the lobby, made a hundred jesting remarks as we passed.

"Have you a carriage?" said I. She shook her head and whispered: "To-morrow I shall have the finest one in Madrid. To-night I go on foot." "The night is cold," said I. "Not for me—I am colder than the night," she answered. As we hurried along, I began to feel a kind of absurd, vague uneasiness. It seemed to me that I was following the footsteps of a phantom, a kind of *Lurelei*, and her hand, which rested on my arm, was so deadly cold, that it made me shudder.

As I observed the thinness of her dress, I lamented that I had left my cloak at the opera. "I might have induced you to accept it, mysterious mask," said I. "I shall find my cloak at home," was the not very satisfactory reply. "The house where I live is colder than this." Once I stopped short, and insisted upon knowing who she was, but she grasped my arm tightly, and a kind of fascination seemed to impel me forward. Through the most round about and least frequented streets she threaded her way, and at last emerged into the Calle de Alcalá, stopped before the old church of San José, and to my consternation mounted the steps. "What mockery is this?" said I. "You are not going into a church, in that dress, at this hour?" The front doors were closed. She descended the steps, pulled me after her, went swiftly round the corner of the street, and entered by a side door. "One moment!" she said earnestly. "I shall not detain you long."

We passed through the sacristy, then along a dark passage which led into the church. In the centre of the middle aisle, faintly lighted, was a *Catafalque*, covered with black cloth, towards which she directed her steps, whilst I watched her movements in consternation. Suddenly it occurred to me that my mysterious companion was mad, and I forcibly unclasped her hand from my arm, the white rose remaining in mine. She turned round, and put her finger to her lips. "Hush!" she whispered. "Tell no one. I was buried there this morning. Adieu." It was nearly dark where we stood. All at once I perceived that I was alone. Where she had flitted to, I am unable to say. My eyes were riveted upon the black monument, and it seemed to me that I saw the hangings move, it might be from the air which blew in at the open door leading into the passage. I looked round in vain. No human being was visible. I groped my way out of the church with great difficulty, shuddering with cold and horror.

I could not go home, but wandered about distractedly. Carriages were driving by full of masks, and shrieks of laughter and mocking voices resounded through the streets. Masks in quaint costumes, peasants, pierrots, dominoes, sprang past me, shrieking in their falsetto voices, and laughing at my air of bewilderment. I felt as if oppressed by a nightmare, which I could not shake off. In vain I said to myself that it was a carnival trick, a mystification, got up by some young men, to try my nerves, and the extent of my northern belief in the marvellous. The air was piercing cold, and I did not feel it.

How long I wandered through the streets, trying to collect my scattered senses, I hardly know, but at last I found myself again in front of San José. The doors were now open. The bells were ringing for the first early mass. A few poor men and women of the working class were going in—women with little children and baskets. The sun had risen, but in the church the light was still faint, and a few candles were burning at a side altar. There, however, was the coffin with its black hangings, and at the head, a crown of large white roses, similar to the one which I still held in my hand!

I asked a woman who was kneeling near me, if she knew whose funeral service was to be celebrated that morning, but she could give me no information. I went out by the side door, which led into the sacristy, and put the same question to one of the boys of the choir, and he told me it was the young Countess of ——, who had died two days before. I knew this young girl, had often danced with her, and had not heard a word of her death. She had long been in delicate health, yet continued going to balls, and would not be persuaded that dancing and late hours were injurious to her.

I felt more than ever like one in a dream, and hastily left the church. I now observed for the first time that I was trembling with cold. I went over to the Café Suisse, asked for some hot coffee, and then taking a *berlina*, went home and to bed, hoping that a few hours of sleep would make me feel more rational. I put the rose in water, so that when I wakened I might be sure that my night's adventure was not a dream.

But I soon found that I was going to be seriously ill, and had every symptom of a high fever. I called one of the servants, and sent him for Doctor ——. Before the doctor could come, Count A—— was by my bedside, giving orders for hot *tisane*, warm blankets, a good fire, &c. To his precautions I owe my escape from an attack of *pulmonia*. The doctor approved of all that had been done—attributed the attack to cold, and checked perspiration, made several sapient remarks upon the imprudence of foreigners, ordered me to remain in bed, and promised to return in the evening.

"For," said he, "I am now going upon a melancholy duty, to the *Honras* of the poor young Condesa de ——, who died suddenly the day before yesterday. Her father is inconsolable." "I never heard of her death!" said Count A——. "It is only a few days since I met her at Countess M——'s ball. Poor young girl! so gay, and so fond of society!" "She was very imprudent," said the doctor, "and her father never could resist her wishes. I tried in vain to dissuade her from going to that very ball, but she assured me that she never felt better, and that she was looking forward with delight to the masked balls at the Royal Theatre. Her father, who was always too indulgent, tried to remonstrate with her, and appealed to me for my opinion if it were not very imprudent to go to these public balls, especially on account of the drafts of air in the entry—but she showed him a beautiful dress of black lace and jet which she had procured for the occasion, and ——. You are very feverish," said the doctor, stopping short, and returning to feel my pulse. "You must keep perfectly quiet, and take my prescriptions regularly. I shall look in early," and away he went, leaving my head in a complete *maze*.

When the doctor returned I was in a high fever, and for three days and nights was, I believe, occasionally delirious. I was watched by turns by L—— and C——, and others of my friends, for it is considered a matter of course here, if any one falls ill, that his friends should attend him day and night. On the fourth day the fever left me, and I was pronounced convalescent.

"You have paid dear for a masked ball," said the doctor, who was feeling my pulse with an air of satisfaction that morning when we were alone. "You have escaped very narrowly a terrible *pulmonia*. I am told that you went out on foot after the ball, very much heated, without your cloak! It was very imprudent, my dear sir. Foreigners here have constantly to pay dear for their experience in this particular." "Doctor," said I, suddenly, "can you keep a secret?"

"Many are the secrets we have to keep," said the doctor. "We are a kind of physical confessors," added he, laughing. Now this doctor, with his ugly, honest physiognomy, had always inspired me with confidence. He is besides an old friend of Count A——'s, and is well known in Madrid for his charities to the poor.

I took my resolution, and recounted to him my adventure, enjoining the strictest secrecy.

The doctor's large round eyes distended preternaturally, and he felt my pulse again to convince himself that I had not got a fresh attack of fever.

"Quite calm and regular—rather feeble—all right," said he.

"What was the Condesa de —— buried in?" said I, after a pause.

"In the identical black dress destined for the masquerade," said the doctor. "But that's all nonsense," added he quickly. "She may have had fifty black lace dresses."

"Do you see that white rose, doctor? An uncommon kind at this season; and do you remember the crown of white roses in the head of her coffin?" "Very odd," said the doctor. "She always had her flowers sent from Valencia, where her father has some property. These roses don't grow here, at least don't bloom at this season. *Caramba!*"

I saw the worthy doctor was nonplussed.

"I must get to the bottom of this," said the doctor, after a pause. "Of course it's a trick, an infernal trick, and such a trick as I should have thought no countryman or countrywoman of mine would have played. Respect for the dead—respect for the church—I never heard of such a thing—and she so much beloved, so much regretted, poor thing! But you must shake off all idea of the supernatural, my dear young friend. It has been a bad joke, got up to try your moral courage. I should have thought the mysterious mask must have been a man, but you lay so much stress upon the small hands."

"And the small feet, doctor, and the beautiful figure; and stay—I recollect noticing a long tress of dark brown hair that had escaped from beneath her mask, the very color of the condesa's."

"Let me see," continued the doctor, without noticing my interruption. "She had a German *doncella* (lady's maid). Perhaps *she* borrowed her mistress's dress for one night, set on by some foolish young men."

"And spoke in pure Spanish, doctor?"

"Pshaw! I shall find it out. Keep your own counsel, and trust to me."

So the old doctor departed, and I write you a true and faithful account of my carnival adventure. I have no doubt that the fresh air and a hard trot on Boabdil, my black Andalusian, will banish all my sinister ideas.

I have had visits the whole day. Every one is full of curiosity concerning the mysterious black mask, and I am obliged to assume as important an air as my friend Don Juan, in declining to answer their inquiries. He, by the way, has been here amongst others, and has spent nearly an hour in relating his own experiences of a lovely creature who made him go up stairs with her to the refreshment-room, insinuating that she was no other than the Duchess of ——, and of another, who, through jealousy, broke her fan upon his arm. I found his absurdity rather a relief, though he bored me with questions as to who the black mask was who had pursued me with her attentions; and guessed her to be a certain Spanish *danseuse* of his acquaintance—and perhaps he is right. She was active enough to have been a dancer on the tight-rope.

The doctor has been indefatigable in his endeavoring to fathom the mystery, and thinks he has succeeded. It appears that the poor little Condesa de —— had a sister, who for some years has been insane, and who resides in a separate apartment in the house, under the surveillance of a confidential nurse. The doctor is of opinion that during the distress and confusion of the family consequent upon the sudden death of the young daughter, this girl may have made her escape, dressed in her sister's clothes, and gone to the masked ball. He is the more inclined to believe this, because he was called in this morning to see her, and found her seriously ill with a feverish cold. He did not venture to make any direct inquiries, but fancied that the nurse who takes her out occasionally, made some mysterious allusions to her having insisted on going out very late, when she ought to have been in bed. I joyfully accept this solution, without positively believing or discrediting it. I did not even remark to the good doctor, that when the condesa was lying dead-arrayed in her black robes, her sister could not have dressed herself in them. He would probably have remarked that black dresses here are very common, that the condesa may have had several exactly alike, &c. Be it so—henceforward I shall endeavor to dismiss the subject from my thoughts.

CHAPTER XXV.

Another ball at Queen Christina's—King and Queen—Revolt and Death of Flore—Flight of the Rebels—Fate of Latorre—Another ball—Spanish Aristocracy—Masks on the Prado—M—— masked—Bal Costumé—Conservatorio—Don Juan "sold."

February —.

ANOTHER party at Queen Christina's, at which the queen made her appearance for the first time. Their majesties arrived at half-past one. The queen looked very well, and in good spirits. Her mother, with the duke and their daughters, went out to receive her. She wore a blue ball-dress, trimmed with blonde and flowers, and a few diamonds in her hair. I greatly admired two superb round brooches of the same, one on each shoulder. She had also a necklace of enormous pearls.

She spoke to every body, in her usual easy and good-humored manner.

She danced in the first place with the Count of San Luis, then with the Marquis of Molins, and afterwards with the Marquis of Viluma, quadrilles. She also waltzed with the Viscount de Pouthon, son of the Count of Casa-Valencia, and danced several polkas with the Count of Villa-Darias. Notwithstanding her size, she waltzes well and lightly, and is certainly a fine-looking woman, though older looking than her age, which is only twenty-three.

In the course of the evening, she and the rest of the royal family went into the refreshment room, and on coming out, and passing through the rows of ladies who were ranged standing, she stopped to say a few words to each, and then returned to the dance, which she seemed to enjoy like a young girl.

I was desired by the Countess de V—— to observe Queen Christina's dress of red *broché* satin covered with lace *en tablier* (I repeat her words hoping that you will understand them better than I did), and her head-dress of red feathers and diamonds. The queen herself dresses with great taste —nothing overloaded. In fact her dress was one of the simplest in the room. The king does not dance. He walked about, and engaged in animated conversation with various people, and in different languages, in which he seemed quite at home.

Her majesty went off about half-past four, and after this came a long German cotillion. I heard Queen Christina say she was *rendida* (worn out), which was not wonderful. I saw several of the ministers in the ante-chamber, looking very sleepy, and no doubt feeling rejoiced when the music stopped, and the queen rose.

February 28.

Yesterday morning I was summoned to the Chancellerie a good deal earlier than was agreeable, having returned home about six; with orders to copy a dispatch with all convenient speed. News had been received of the revolt of the regiment of Córdova in Saragossa, under their brigadier Flore. The revolt is put down, and the rebel colonel shot; but this is probably only the beginning of troubles, and unfortunately renders the late severity of the government only too justifiable. It is said that when Concha left Madrid, under pretence of obeying the orders of the government, he had a private interview with Colonel Flore, in which plans for a revolt of the troops were concerted; that the brigadier endeavored to persuade Concha to put himself at the head of the movement, to which the latter replied that affairs were not yet ripe for the projected revolution; and that it was wiser to wait until the ministry had given their expected *coup d'état*, when he would second the *pronunciamiento* with the whole of the army.

That the brigadier who has paid so dearly for his treason had counted on the assistance of other regiments, and especially had relied on the tumultuary spirit of the inhabitants of Saragossa, there can be no doubt. General Dulce, now director-general of the cavalry in Madrid, is said to have been one of the members of this conspiracy! Enjoying as he does the entire confidence of the government, we must hope, for the honor of Spanish loyalty, that this accusation is false; but my authority is the editor of an opposition newspaper, and he seems only too well informed upon the subject. It is from him also that I received the information of the Parthian dart levelled by Concha during his flight.

A few peasants united themselves to the revolted regiment, but the city preserved an attitude of the most complete indifference. A company of grenadiers, headed by the Marquis of Santiago, went out against the rebels—Flore was summoned to capitulate, but refused to obey—and fought and fell with a courage worthy of a better cause. An unsuccessful traitor meets with no sympathy, but he was at least less base than those who excited him to revolt, and abandoned him in the hour of need.

The failure of this rebellion is hailed by the friends of the government as a proof of the little *prestige* which the banished generals have with the army, and so far are they from participating in the belief of my *opposition* friend as to the treachery of General Dulce, that they lament his absence from Saragossa, at a moment when his loyalty would have prevented even this insignificant mutiny. It is a curious study of human nature, for one who has no personal interest in these affairs, to listen to the opinions of each party, so diametrically opposite, and above all to observe how ill the enemies of the government succeed in concealing their chagrin. Crosses and grades have been given to the governor and captain-general of Saragossa. The lieutenant-colonel of the regiment of Córdova, Don Salvador Latorre, followed by the revolted soldiers, and by several peasants, left Saragossa in the middle of the night, in the hopes of effecting their escape to the French frontier. After a long and painful march, escaping with difficulty from the queen's troops who were sent out to cut off their retreat, hiding themselves in the fastnesses of the rocks, fording rivers, climbing mountains covered with snow, in the most rigorous month of winter, almost entirely destitute of provisions, and worn out by fatigue, they at length crossed the frontier, and escorted by gendarmes, arrived at Pau, where their miserable condition excited the sympathy of the inhabitants. These poor soldiers, accustomed to blind obedience, victims of the passions of their chiefs, may well be regarded with compassion.

The fate of Latorre is attended with some mysterious circumstances, which as yet remain unexplained. He marched behind the column, and was accompanied by several officers, amongst whom was his brother. Arrived near the *Venta de la Mina*, about five leagues distant from the French frontier, he desired them to walk on and prepare a lodging. Whatever may have been his motives, instead of following them, he entered an uninhabited shepherd's hut, where he passed the night, paying no attention to the voices of the soldiers, although, as he afterwards confessed, he heard them distinctly, while they were traversing the mountain in all directions, searching for their colonel, whom they supposed to have lost his footing, and to be buried beneath some snow-covered precipice. It is probable that, worn out by cold, hunger, and fatigue, he had grown utterly desperate; or that, as some think, his intention was to take some repose, and then to seek the frontier by a less dangerous and difficult route. While making the attempt he fell into the hands of the queen's troops, was led back to Saragossa, and suffered death as a traitor.

The *Honras* (funeral honors) of Colonel Flore were celebrated in Madrid with great pomp, and invitations to them sent out in printed cards by his mother and widow, from the latter of whom he has been entirely separated for years. On every account this may be at least considered a mark of bad taste. It is generally looked upon as a kind of *bravado* on the part of the opposition.

February 25th.

A great ball, to which the invitations were general, was given at the queen-mother's, last evening, in the large apartments on the first floor. The entrance, enclosed with colored glass, and leading into a court, with a fountain in the centre, surrounded by large aquatic plants, and brilliantly lighted, had a good effect. All the diplomatic corps were there; amongst others, Mr. Soulé and his family—and excepting, of course, the Marquis and Madame Turgot. The queen arrived about one o'clock, dressed very simply, in white tulle, with flounces, and wreaths of different colored flowers. It was only observable, on standing near her, that each rose had a diamond heart, and that on each shoulder she had a bouquet of large emeralds and diamonds, and the same in front.

She danced quadrilles with General Blaser and the Marquis de Reario Sforza, and waltzed with young Casa-Valencia and Villa-Darias.

The ball was very animated, but too crowded. The *salle de bal* is immensely long, but too narrow in proportion. The other parties are more select and prettier, but the coup d'œil of the fountain and flowers, and beautiful women walking round the pillared court, looked pretty and Moorish. The queen seems very kind to the young Ynfantas, and to her half-sisters, and I was told that their beautiful dresses were presented by her.

She is said to be of a truly royal generosity, amounting sometimes to profuseness, and greatly annoying to her *Intendente.* She presented the nurse of the little princess, on her departure for her native mountains, with twelve thousand dollars, a set of diamond buttons, unopened cases of fine linen, rich stuffs for dresses, &c. But before the woman had been two days on her journey, she was recalled by royal order, on account of the melancholy into which the poor little princess had fallen, in consequence of her departure, and which, it was feared, would injure her health. At the same time her husband was sent for, and a comfortable apartment assigned them in the palace.

It struck me yesterday, more forcibly than usual, how mistaken is the prevailing idea that the aristocracy of this country are a mean-looking race. It seems to me that I have seldom seen handsomer men any where. There were, for example, the young Duke of Frias, the Duke of Fernandina, the Marquis de l'Aunion, the Marquis of Santa Cruz, and his brother, the young men of the Foreign Office, numbers of young officers,—in short, thirty or forty of the handsomest men I ever saw in my life, and nearly all of them above the middle size, though certainly, on an average, the race is shorter than the German or English; but all with good figures and handsome faces.

February —.

Went for the first time, this afternoon, to see the masks in the Prado, a kind of horror of all masked beings having hitherto prevented me from going there; but to-day I could no longer resist following the multitude. The Prado was crowded with carriages, extending in two apparently interminable lines, from the Fuente Castellana down to Atocha. It is at once the gayest, maddest, and yet most orderly scene that can be imagined. Not the slightest disorder amongst these myriads of masks. They jumped upon the carriages, clung to the coach boxes, leaped up beside the footmen, often sprung into the carriages, apparently to the great amusement of the inmates, the people and the better classes evidently keeping up a separation, even in this apparent mingling of all ranks.

The queen drove down towards Atocha with the king and princess, who was fancifully dressed in a little *maja* costume. Queen Christina and her daughters were also there. The people, some masked and some in their ordinary jackets, seemed in a state of intense amusement. I observed the family of the minister of state in an open carriage, surrounded by masks, on the door steps, beside the coachman, beside the footman, in the carriage. I have no doubt many witty political remarks were made to them, criticisms of places given, or crosses withheld, but all seemed to be passing in good-humor.

The next day I went out with a number of *pollos*, all of us masked. Finding it more amusing to victimize than to be victimized, M—— and I rode; and, to my surprise, M——, usually so reserved and taciturn, got so completely into the carnival spirit, that I am certain the sharpest and most absurd things said that day were uttered by him. I have remarked before, that those who are afflicted by *mauvaise honte* are sure to go to the opposite extreme when their features are covered; whilst those who have the most perfect self-possession in their own proper persons, become embarrassed and tongue-tied when disguised.

There was no absurdity that M—— did not indulge in. He rode by the side of the carriages, paying compliments, keeping up a war of wit with all the prettiest girls, whose repartees were quite equal to his Irish jokes, spoken in the purest Spanish. They guessed him to be an Andalusian, for, owing to his long residence in Seville, he has the true *Majo* accent. He encountered a group of peasants, eating their dinner beside the fountain, got off his horse, and accepted their invitation to partake of their *gaspacho*, very coolly tossed his bridle to me to hold, and in a little while men, women, and children were shaking their sides with laughter. When we returned home, and taking off his disguise, he reassumed his usual frigid air and English reserve of manner, I could hardly believe him to be the same individual.

A great *bal costumé* is to close the receptions of Queen Christina for the season.

February —.

The ball was really magnificent. The court and fountain, with the groups of figures in every variety of fancy dress, walking about in a blaze of light, had a charming effect. The dresses, generally speaking, were good, not only of the Señoras, but what is less common on these occasions, of the men. No one looks well in a fancy dress who is embarrassed, consequently it rarely suits an Englishman to appear in any *travestissement*. As Spaniards are always at their ease, they are quite at home in a fancy costume, and therefore look to great advantage. This evening

I thought them fully better dressed than the women. The young Dukes of Fernandina and Rivas were eminently handsome in old Spanish costumes. There were many who looked as if they had stepped down from a canvas of Velasquez, the dress exactly suiting the Spanish style of feature and countenance.

The Duchess of Medina-Cœli wore the dress of a *gitana*, and looked the character as if she had been born to it. The Duchess of Alva, the German Countess of ——, and many others, wore court-dresses à la Louis XVI., with powder. The queen-mother wore a ball-dress, blue, covered with lace and fine diamonds. The daughter of the Countess of Casa-Valencia looked extremely handsome as a peasant of the Pyrenees. A sister-in-law of the minister of state was dressed as a shepherdess of the time of Louis XIV., a pretty and becoming costume. A niece of Madame Buschartal's, as a Jewess, was one of the prettiest persons there. Our diplomatic ladies, and those of the cabinet, wore ball-dresses. *I* appeared in my Hungarian uniform. Generally speaking, the costumes were confined to the dancers, but the immense number of handsome uniforms, and the court-dresses of the grandees, lords of the bedchamber, diplomats, and ministers, made the scene very brilliant.

The queen came so late that her arrival was almost despaired of; but when she did make her appearance, her dress excited a murmur of admiration throughout the assembly, especially amongst the foreigners. It was certainly superb. It was said to be the costume of a Roman lady of the *siècle de Louis XVI.* I examined it very particularly for your benefit. It was, I think, of very dark green velvet, covered with embroidered gold stars and a deep embroidered gold border, very long behind, with a demi-train. A long white and gold veil, fastened behind, fell down to her feet, and she wore a velvet crown, covered with jewels. Her hair, which she generally wears plain, was curled. Her pearls were the largest and finest I have ever seen, and the diamonds which seemed to sparkle all over her dress, were a complete show.

One of her ladies told me that her majesty had been detained to that late hour, owing to the diamonds not having been sewed upon her dress in time. I am sure that I have not described correctly, but you must take the will for the deed. She looked very regal, but her dress was too long and heavy to permit her to dance much. She walked through a quadrille with the Marquis of Molins, and then sat down between her mother and the king, seeming to enjoy the sight of the fanciful costumes of her liege subjects. The music was excellent, the supper unimpeachable, the crowd immense.

After the royal family had supped, the German cotillion began, and the dancers continued indefatigable till six o'clock.

Went a few evenings ago to the *Conservatorio de Maria Cristina*, nursery for youthful musicians. The queen, usually famous for that want of punctuality in which her loyal subjects faithfully follow her example, arrived at ten precisely, when the *salon* was nearly empty. In this *conservatorio*, founded by Queen Christina, above three hundred young pupils of both sexes receive instruction gratuitously, in music, both vocal and instrumental. There was, no doubt, a great deal of youthful talent, but I confess that I found the whole affair very tiresome.

The queen and royal family sat on velvet chairs, to the right, fronting the stage, where the performances took place—their ladies behind them; the cabinet ministers to the left, and behind them the diplomatic corps. In the *entr'actes*, royalty rose, and of course the house also, and their majesties conversed for some time with the ministers, ladies, and diplomats. They then passed into another room, to take refreshments, followed only by the ladies of the palace and the cabinet ministers. The queen was dressed in crimson satin, with lace flounces. The performances, with which their majesties expressed themselves highly gratified, were not over till two o'clock.

Another masked ball at the theatre; a joyful adieu to the carnival. I went there, resolved, should my mysterious mask appear, that she should not escape me as before, but no adventure occurred to me worthy of record. A trick was played upon poor Don Juan, from which he will not recover for some time. Young S—— dressed himself as a woman, and turned his head completely; but as no adventure of this kind is of any value in his eyes, unless participated in by all the world, he put about forty people in his confidence. He walked round the room with the *fair* mask leaning heavily on his arm, fanning her with an air of tender solicitude—he waltzed with her, which she insisted upon his doing, and not being accustomed to that style of exercise, he became quite giddy, and would have fallen, but for her powerful support. He took her to the buffet, and to us who were in the secret, it was sufficiently amusing to see the quantities of *pâté de foie* which the charming creature contrived to devour under the shadow of her black silk curtain, and the bumpers of champagne which the unsuspecting Don Juan poured out for her, accompanied by expressive glances, fanning her, as she leant back with the most languishing air, after eating a supper fit for one of her majesty's guards.

M—— thought they were carrying the joke too far, when he gave her his arm to escort her home, looking round at us with a triumphant air. It seems that S—— himself was of the same opinion—for when the carriage had arrived at the Plazuela de Cervantes, he begged Don Juan to order it to stop, pretending that he felt faint, and that the air would revive him; and while Don Juan, after carefully handing him out, was paying the coachman, S—— suddenly started off at full speed, and darted round the corner of the street, leaving the unlucky Caballero alone in his glory. I rather think he suspects the trick, as he was very stiff and dignified when we met him this morning, and, contrary to custom, quite silent upon the subject of his nocturnal adventure.

CHAPTER XXVI.

Burial of the Sardine—Spanish Dance—Country and City Life in Spain—Duke Ossuna's Palace—An old Story-teller—Residence and Grounds of the Duke—Politics—Cuadros Santos.

March 1.

A STRANGE usage marks the first day of Lent. After mass, and the blessing of the ashes, the whole populace of Madrid proceed towards the canal, to perform the ceremony which is called "*the burial of the sardine.*" Thousands of people, some masked, proceed in crowds to the canal, carrying in solemn procession a *sardine* in a small coffin. Each family carries a basket of provisions, with the intention of dining *al fresco* beside the water. It is a curious sight, especially on account of the order and earnestness with which this strange ceremony is conducted, seeming as it does totally out of place, after Lent has begun.

Neither the government nor the church has been able to put it down. It is a proof among many, of the tenacity with which the people in this country cling to their ancient usages. The Marquis of Santa Cruz, when Governor of Madrid, resigned his office because having given orders that the burial of the sardine should not take place, so much discontent was produced amongst the people in consequence of this decree, that the government refused to confirm it, and the marquis gave up his office in disgust.

I have asked the origin of this absurd ceremony from

various people, none of whom have been able to give me any answer, but that it has existed from time immemorial. I bethought me of asking one of the parties interested. A handsome washerwoman who was standing by the shore of the canal with her whole family in a blazing sun, very civilly vouchsafed to satisfy my curiosity. "Formerly," she said, "in the houses of the grandees, the servants (*la familia*) were allowed daily a certain number of sardines for breakfast, and the custom arose, how I do not know, whenever the carnival was ended, to take a sardine and bury it, as a token that they were no longer to receive their daily rations, not even a sardine." I thought it would have been more appropriate to bury a piece of beef, in taking leave of *flesh*, but the washerwoman seemed quite satisfied with her own explanation, and so therefore was I.

That class of women have the prettiest, softest voices imaginable. The Manolas speak in a much sweeter tone than the higher classes. This seems inexplicable, but so it is.

If there is any moment when the gay populace of Madrid look grave, it is when they are dancing. A guitar strikes up—and they quietly form into groups, taking their places as a matter of course. They begin—the bolero, fandango, or jota. They dance on without stopping, without speaking, gracefully, monotonously, seriously. If there are not women enough, the men dance together. They never seem to tire. Their faces, though serious, wear an expression of perfect satisfaction. The crowd applauds the most skilful dancer. The most perfect decorum is observed, the utmost dignity, much more I should say than is to be seen in the polka or German cotillion in our fashionable ball-rooms.

There were some very pretty women, especially groups of handsome young girls, who were accompanying themselves upon the castanets; but on an average; the men struck me as being handsomer than they. I left them when it grew dark, many still wandering about by the light of the moon, some still dancing, others turning their steps homewards, every one in good-humor, and apparently with no occasion for the mounted guard, who ride along the roads leading to the city, to enforce order. It is hardly to be expected, however, that these immense crowds of men, women, and children, will return to their respective homes in the middle of the night, without some accident occurring, or some jealous quarrel taking place.

But though all Madrid, at least all the people of Madrid, seemed to be assisting at the burial of the sardine, *all Madrid* seemed also to be at church; for every church was crowded, and long after it grew dark the clergy were preaching in every pulpit to crowded audiences.

In spite of this strange funeral episode, Lent has come in good earnest. Balls are over—and the crowds round the confessionals, and the crowds before the altars, show that many at least have with good faith bid adieu to worldly vanities.

March —.

The weather is now like spring. The trees are in bud, and bouquets of early flowers are sold in the market, and at the corners of the streets. The country round Madrid is barren, and arid from want of water. Nature has done little. Every spot capable of cultivation has been cultivated by the country people; but no trees are planted, and few houses of any importance exist in the environs. There is no taste amongst the Spaniards for a country life. To live in the country means to lead a life of certain privations; to live in bare halls scantily furnished—with horses perhaps to kill time—guns to shoot whatever game may be found; but the comforts and luxuries of the city finish with the city itself. When the *Madrileños* say they dislike the country, it is not a matter of surprise to those who have been in their country-houses. Madrid is the focus of fashion, gayety, luxury, and ease. The nobles go to their country residences occasionally for a caprice, a party of pleasure—to hunt, to shoot, to ride, to play at billiards; but they think they have been *roughing* it, and come back embrowned and tired of hard exercise, to their comfortable houses in town.

Yet what can be done by art aiding or rather conquering nature, is clear from the few specimens of villas near Madrid. The gardens of the Countess de Montijo are the ornament of Caramanchel. The Marquis of Bedmar has a property which is an oasis in the desert, and M—— has offered to take G—— C—— and me to-morrow to the Duke of Ossuna's country palace, which he says is well worth seeing. But it is necessary to lay out immense sums to produce any result in cultivating this region of stone and rock, to bring water from a great distance, and when the result is obtained, to live in almost complete solitude—and the Spaniard is eminently a gregarious animal.

One circumstance greatly deteriorates from the general effect of the landscape. Every tree and bush has a hollow space dug round the roots, to allow the damp to penetrate, or to collect the rain, so that every tree seems to be planted in a small hollow or basin, and the ground appears unequal, and has an unfinished look.

We rode out yesterday, M—— and I, and two or three others, to the Duke of Ossuna's country palace—called the *Alameda*, or the *Capricho*. We left Madrid by the gate of Alcalà, by the broad high road, dusty and sandy, though in good repair, with the most uninteresting landscape on either side, always excepting the mountains, the view of which redeems its insipidity. Yet every patch of land is cultivated, up to the bare gray rock, which defies the skill of the laborer. Neither water nor trees enliven the dreary scene. A hard trot of one hour led us to the gates of the Capricho.

Taste, aided by wealth, has done wonders for this place, and made "the wilderness blossom like a rose." Water at an immense expense has been introduced into the grounds; a deep stream runs through the plantations, and a large tank as clear as crystal, serves as a mirror for the beautiful trees that shadow themselves in its waters. The palace itself is a light handsome edifice, the site well chosen for a fine view and good exposure.

A ruined castle in the distance attracted my attention. According to M——, a certain Duke of Ossuna in by-gone days, named by his sovereign Viceroy of Naples, was accused of aspiring to the throne, recalled and imprisoned for life in this old castle. His descendant, the Duchess of Benavente, bought all the surrounding lands, including the ruins of her ancestor's prison, and entombed his ashes with pomp on a small island in the Capricho, making him a kind of posthumous suzerain over the territory where he had languished in captivity. This same duchess of whom I have already spoken to you, and who by her beauty, wit, and magnificence reigned a despotic queen in Madrid, was pleased to expend immense sums in the embellishment of her property. It was a costly *Capricho*, and her entertainments there were attended by all that was most distinguished among the nobility of Spain.

The grounds are extensive, beautifully laid out, and kept in perfect order. The present proprietor, her grandson, the actual Duke of Ossuna, seldom visits this property, or indeed any of his vast possessions in Spain. As I observed, life in the country here must needs be lovely. To enjoy it, one must have the feelings of a hermit or a philosopher. Some one must begin by setting the example, and the man has not yet appeared. The aristocracy consider the court their proper sphere, where they live confounded with each other, and undistinguished. A century must elapse, before they could be brought to understand by experience how much greater a man is who lives on his paternal acres, a petty sovereign—how much good he can effect—how these decayed old villages would flourish by the sunshine of his presence—how the country would be beautified by the chateaus of rich proprietors, by the woods they would plant, by the gardens with which they would embellish their estates—how much nobler a man's position is as lord of the manor than as lord of the bedchamber.

Those who rail against the dryness of the climate, the want of shade and water which makes the country unendurable, put the consequence for the cause, and here is this very *Capricho* a proof of what one clever rich proprietor can do.

The interior of the house gives token of its being now a bachelor's establishment, and bears no traces of feminine supremacy. The old gray-headed servants seem to form an integral part of the family. No old Spanish family is without some of these faithful ancient retainers, who have the honor of the house as much at heart as any son or daughter of it, yet never (let me repeat it) presume upon the confidence which their masters have in them, or the familiarity with which they treat them. I have heard many anecdotes of the kindness of the queen to the old servants of her father, and of one old woman in particular whom it is her delight to send for, to make her sit down beside her, and tell her stories of the olden time. If I might, I should give you such a pretty peep into a courtly chamber, as an eye-witness described it to me, and show you a royal lady seated at the feet of this shrivelled old mummy, and with good-natured petulance begging for stories as old as the hills—telling her to give her an account of the flood, and of Noah's daughters; and of the old woman laughing herself into a fit of coughing, and of her royal mistress telling her she will let her off if she will tell her all about her father when he was a little boy; but all this gossip was not told me to be repeated, or at least to be written; I may give it you in detail *de vive voix* one of these days—but you must now follow me back to the *Capricho*.

A——, who was with us, being a cousin of the duke's, we were received with the honors due to the family of the *potentate*, and shown all over the house. There is a fine billiard-room, where bull-fights are represented carved in wood, with the figures of the principal *toreros*, executed with extraordinary skill—a beautiful ball-room, and noble dining-hall. The furniture of the drawing-room, from the windows of which is an extensive view of Madrid and its environs, is of green and gold. There are suites of airy bedrooms, prettily and tastefully furnished. Most of the rooms are hung with fine paintings, chiefly by Goya, and amongst others, in the great dining-room, is a portrait of the Duchess of Benavente, slashed across with a cut, apparently made by a knife, said to have been done by her eccentric grace, who was by no means satisfied with her likeness.

The view from the roof is magnificent. Madrid, with its lofty churches and fine buildings, lies spread out as in a map, with all its surrounding villages, and background of snow-covered mountains. The grounds are so extensive, that we were at least three hours in exploring them. In the court are some colossal bronze statues, ranged in a semicircle, representing different dukes and duchesses of the family. We visited the temple, the beehives, the fountains, the hermitage, the house of the old woman (*Casa de la Vieja*), the fort, the deer-park, the stable for the camels, the English stables with their English horses and English grooms, &c. &c. In the midst of all, a latitude has been given to the most fantastic imagination. The Hermitage for instance, an old moss-grown retreat, surrounded by cypresses, by the side of a pond filled with venerable carp, is a very temple of solitude. Upon entering, I started back, seriously believing that I had disturbed a venerable old man at his devotions, for there sat the hermit himself, with long gray robe and scapulary and rope-girdle, deeply engaged in the study of a black-letter volume. The figure is so perfectly done, that it is necessary to examine it closely in order to be persuaded that the old man is not breathing.

Then at the *Casa de la Vieja*, we went into a neat, comfortable farm-house, and entered the kitchen. There sat the farmer and his family at dinner, an honest looking hard-working man, his wife sitting in front of him, cleanly and well-dressed, their children busily engaged with their food, and the old grandmother, who had apparently just put on her spectacles to resume her spinning, seated in the chimney corner. The house is so comfortable, the kitchen so well swept, the rows of kitchen utensils so bright and well cared for, the family look so contented, that it certainly causes some disappointment to find that these also are skilfully done figures.

We rowed down the little river in a boat, with a *live* boatman. A fortress and drawbridge on a small scale, are merely intended to ornament the grounds, and as we drew near, I could distinguish that the warlike sentinel armed to the teeth, who stood at the gate, was a mimic soldier.

The deer in the park, the camels in the stables, were however living creatures, and so were the duke's well appointed stud. The horses, which are English, are under the care of a first-rate English groom, who, with his English wife, reigns there in undisputed sovereignty. When we returned to the house, it struck me that, to be in keeping, there ought to be a stuffed duke in the drawing-room.

Immense sums are annually expended in keeping these grounds in order. The trees and flowers are cultivated to the highest point of perfection. Not a withered leaf is to be seen on the rolled and gravelled walks, and the grass is as soft and green as on an English lawn.

We dined on our way home at the Marquis of Bedmar's, whom we met returning from a ride with his beautiful little step-daughter. We visited his stables before dinner; his fine horses are also under the care of an English groom. His gardens are full of roses, and brilliant with the blossoms of the pomegranate. We returned to Madrid in time for the last Act of the *Trovatore*, and the death scene of the Gazzaniga, who was buried in a shower of flowers.

March —.

Political troubles are said to be quieting down. Some say it is the calm preceding a storm.

O'Donnell has not returned from his hunting-party! In the palace he is nicknamed "*Victor el Cazador*" from a character in the little piece so popular now in the *Circo*, "the Valley of Andorre." I heard some remarks made in the Casino the other evening upon the blindness of General Blaser in having intrusted the direction of the cavalry to General Dulce, who is said to be in close correspondence with O'Donnell. I have heard remarks of this nature repeated at least a dozen times, and without any injunction to secrecy.

The Marquis Turgot still continues confined to his room, but receives a few of his friends occasionally. Went one evening to the *Teatro de la Cruz* to see the *Cuadros Santos*, living pictures of holy subjects, concerning the propriety of which representation, opinions are much divided. The theatre itself, built in 1737 by the architect Ribera, celebrated for his eccentricity and extravagance, is ill laid out, and is now disfigured by various reparations and additions. Some years ago, it was officially declared *el oprobrio del arte* (a disgrace to art), and it was proposed to have it demolished; but the Madrileños, attached to this theatre on account of its antiquity and central position, with their usual dislike to innovation, opposed the decree, and it is now in contemplation to add to and embellish it. Meanwhile it forms a convenient site for extra representations of the present nature.

The *Cuadros* are beautifully executed. The chief objection seems to me to consist in the mingling of sacred with profane subjects, also that the place where they are represented should be a theatre. Many object also to the circumstance of the performers being actors.

I feel convinced that it would not be suitable in any other country than Spain; but here the breathless silence and perfect decorum of the audience took away from any feeling of profanity. The "Descent from the Cross," was magnificent—almost too painful to look at. The "Death of Abel" was very fine, but also very terrible, and when the bolt is launched against Cain, and a glimpse is given of the Godhead, I felt that the representation was too presumptuous. Besides, as C—— remarked, there must needs be a great deal of levity beforehand in the preparations made by a set of ordinary actors for representing those holy subjects. "We see," said he, "nothing but the artistic effect—which can hardly be surpassed; but fancy these men and women, who now form so exquisite a group—that beautiful Magdalene with her long golden hair—the Blessed Virgin with her expression of concentrated agony, and the Saviour himself in the last moments of his divine Sacrifice—preparing themselves for this scene, with all the tawdry accessories of their art, the probable levity of their conversation, the commonplace jests that may pass between them; and you will allow that notwithstanding the solemn silence of the audience, who neither speak nor applaud, but upon whom the effect seems wholly of a religious nature, there is much to be objected to in these representations."

CHAPTER XXVII.

Casa de Campo—Palm Sunday—Holy Week—Royal devotion—Washing Pilgrims' Feet—The Queen's Dress—The Princess—Lavatorio—A visit to the different Churches—San Ysidro el Real—Good Friday—Church of Santiago—San Ysidro—Santo Tomas—Bull Fights—Paris—Frenchmen, their acquisitiveness—The Madeleine—French Emperor and Empress—Return to Madrid—Government Loan—Death-Chamber vs. a Ball-Room—Victimized—The Result.

March —.

Rode with a party of ladies to the *Casa de Campo.* It is a summer palace of her majesty's, which she seldom visits, and a pleasant ride, after the heat and dust of the city.

To the west of the new palace gardens, and on the right shores of the Manzanares, it is almost a continuation of the palace grounds, separated by that apology for a river, which Victor Hugo had certainly never beheld but in imagination, when in enumerating the wonders of various cities he exclaimed: "Et Madrid a son Manzanares!"

In the 16th century, the Casa de Campo with its immense extent of pleasure-grounds belonged to Don Francisco de Vargas, the celebrated counsellor of the emperor, and it was bought from his heirs by Philip II., and converted into a royal domain. We entered by the gate fronting the palace of Madrid, and leading directly to the Casa de Campo, which we passed by, intending to visit it on our return. The grounds are so extensive that we rode through them for hours, and at a good pace, for the ladies whom we accompanied are famous equestrians. The roads are shaded by noble trees, which grow in wonderful luxuriance, and seem to owe very little to art, nor indeed are the walks and drives kept in remarkably good order. Lakes, streams, tanks and fountains, account for the luxuriant richness of the vegetation. We drew up our horses beside a lake filled with myriads of gold and silver fish, which give the whole sheet of water a golden color.

We met the Ynfantas on horseback, with their servants and governess, and the daughters of Queen Christina. Shortly after the king drove along in a D'Aumont, drawn by four horses, with postillions, two of whom are English. His majesty, seated, without his hat, was pronounced by the diplomatic ladies whom we were escorting *un très joli garçon.* Carriage, horses, postillions, servants and guards, were all unimpeachable.

There are various buildings scattered about the grounds; amongst others, a wonderful cow-house and dairy, famous for its cheeses; houses for the laborers and *dependientes*—a small village, and two churches. The palace itself, which we visited on our return, looks abandoned, and the rooms are but half-furnished. The gardens on which the windows open to the back of the palace, are pretty and well kept. It is too close to the city to be a pleasant residence for the court. We started sundry rabbits and hares as we rode through the woods, and the whole possession is said to abound in game of all sorts, especially in fine partridges, while the lakes and tanks are full of fish.

April 10th.

Went on Palm Sunday to San Antonio. The crowd was immense—the service very impressive. An eloquent sermon preached by a Jesuit Father. Great procession of the *Hermandad,* amongst whose members I recognized several of the most illustrious names in Spain. The service was later than usual, on account of the crowded confessionals.

Nothing can be more solemn and impressive than the ceremonies of the holy week in Madrid. The churches are crowded from morning till night, and nothing can exceed the devotion of the people. In these crowds the men and women are separated, from the circumstance, that the men from politeness allow the latter to pass, so that generally more than half of the church, from the altar downwards, is filled with women, and the remainder, down to the doors, crowded with men. In every church, two sermons are preached daily —and besides masses from six in the morning till two, there is the Benediction of the Holy Sacrament, Novenas, and in certain churches, *Cuarenta Horas* and *reservas*, which last till after dark.

When the queen meets the *Santisimo* (the Host), she leaves her carriage, into which the priests enter, with the Viaticum, and she herself follows on foot, frequently through the worst and dirtiest streets of the city, to the house of the dying person. "I saw her," said Count A——, "on one of these occasions, go up the staircase of a miserable house to the fourth story, where, in a wretched garret-chamber, she knelt devoutly, while a poor woman received the last Sacraments; and after saying some kind words to her and the children, who were crying around the bed, she left a well-filled purse in the hands of a Sister of Charity, who was attending on the dying woman. It was curious and touching to see this wretched little room, with no furniture but the poor bed with its straw mattress, and a few wooden chairs, suddenly illuminated with heavenly and earthly grandeur, and as edifying to see the sovereign of a great country thus acknowledging her nothingness in the presence of the King of kings.

The washing of the feet of the pilgrims is to take place on Holy Thursday according to custom, in a great hall in the palace, called the *Hall of Pillars.* As there seems to be rather an absence of definitive arrangement in these affairs, the ladies of the diplomatic corps have not yet been able to discover whether they are to go *en grande tenue* or not—in full court dress, or demi-toilette. They say that the mistress of the robes has returned an ambiguous answer to their inquiries, and that the ladies of the ministers, on being consulted, profess to finding themselves in precisely the same difficulty on this important point; even the *Introductor de Embajadores*, Señor Medina, the court guide, the incarnation of etiquette, gives forth a response, which, like that of the oracles of old, may be differently interpreted, according to the result; therefore great discussions are taking place in the various Legations. Is it to be a court-dress with a train? —a ball-dress without a train?—or a black dress and mantilla? which latter is the costume worn by all who have no official position, and consequently no *tribuna.*

Count A—— has received several invitations to attend the *quêtes*, which are to be held for the benefit of the poor that day, in the different churches, chiefly, I believe, for the benefit of the *Inclusa*, the Foundling Hospital. The principal ladies of Madrid sit at the doors of the churches before a table, where they receive the alms of the charitable. Those who cannot attend in person are expected to send their contributions, and in that way large sums are generally collected. Formerly the *quêteuses* wore their richest toilettes and finest jewels on these occasions, but now they generally wear black dresses and black lace mantillas.

The great question was decided at the eleventh hour. The diplomatic ladies go to their *tribuna* in court-dresses. The ladies of the ministers to theirs, in full dress, without trains.

On Holy Thursday, Count A—— having offered me a

ticket for a solemn *funcion* at the church of the Calatravas, I went there early. No carriages are allowed in Madrid on these days, but the streets are crowded with people on foot, hurrying to the different churches. At the Calatravas was a great procession of the knights of the order, in their white cloaks and red crosses. The ceremony was very solemn, the music magnificent, and the introduction of a harp, played to perfection, had a wonderfully fine effect. At the elevation of the Host, when the knights fell prostrate on their faces, the scene was very impressive. My only objection to these ceremonies is the necessity of having chairs and places kept, which somewhat takes away from the usual solemn air of the churches in Madrid, where the masses kneel undistinguished. Here no one can be admitted without a ticket, on which is the figure of a cross, and beneath which is printed, "Parish church of the order and knighthood of Calatrava. Year 1854. On Holy Thursday the divine offices will be celebrated at ten in the morning. Personal ticket."

The costume of the Spanish women on this day is the most becoming that they can possibly adopt. The dress is almost invariably black, of some rich and heavy brocade, with a mantilla of fine black lace. No Spanish face ever looks to so much advantage in a bonnet; and as few Englishwomen wear a mantilla gracefully, so very few Spanish women look at their ease in a bonnet.

The Countess de V—— invited me to accompany her to the palace, to see the ceremony of the *Lavatorio*. She looked even more beautiful than usual, and was not left in ignorance of the fact. Many were the compliments addressed to her as we walked down the Plaza de la Villa in a burning sun, not only by the common people but by young men of the better class, a species of gallantry which is not supposed to be at all offensive. "*Caramba*, what eyes! They put out the sun! Blessed be the mother that bore you!" ("Bendita sea la madre que te parió!") The soldiers especially were loud in their remarks. I confess that it took me some time to grow accustomed to the expressive demonstrations to which the Spanish Señoras are so used, that they would rather be surprised than otherwise, and perhaps disappointed, were they to pass through the streets without receiving any compliments, especially from the lower classes.

With some difficulty we made our way through the dense mass of people surrounding the palace, and when we reached the "Sala de Columnas," it was already filled with a very distinguished crowd. The countess, however, contrived to manœuvre herself and me into excellent places, just in front of the long bench occupied by the pilgrims. Long tables are placed before these benches, which are occupied on one side by twelve poor women, on the other by twelve poor men. The queen washes the feet of the women—the king, of the men. The queen, magnificently dressed, stood with her brilliant court of ladies and *gentilhombres* on either side. To the right hand of the hall, fronting her majesty, were three *tribunas*—the middle one for the royal family, where were the Ynfante Fernando, the little Princess of the Asturias, with her governess the Marquesa de Povar, the Countess of Torreno, and Marquis of Bassecour, in waiting. To the left was the tribuna of the diplomatic corps—to the right, that of the cabinet ministers. The queen and her suite were in full court-dress; also the ladies of the diplomats—those of the ministers, in full dress without trains. All the other ladies who occupied the hall were in black, with mantillas. The king and his suite were also in full court-dress—the king in uniform.

The pilgrims are chosen from amongst the poorest and most respectable inhabitants of the neighboring villages.

The ceremony is very striking. It has a touching and impressive effect to see the queen, in her robes of state, kneeling at their feet, and washing them in imitation of the humility of our Saviour; and I saw tears falling from the eyes of many a poor old woman, who probably saw her sovereign for the first time, and who would always remember that she had not disdained to kneel before her, and to perform the most humble office for the poorest of her subjects.

When this part of the ceremony was concluded, the king and queen changed places, and the latter proceeded to serve the tables of the poor men, while the king performed the same office for the women. It seemed to me that about three hundred dishes were brought in, all cooked in the royal kitchen. The servants delivered them in succession to the lords in waiting; the one nearest to the queen handed the dish to her, sometimes so heavy, that, although she placed it on the table with the greatest ease, many of her ladies had great difficulty in carrying it. After placing the dish on the table, the queen handed it to the Duchess of Gor, who passed it on to the next lady, and so on in succession to the *mozas de retrete*, female servants of the queen's chamber. They were then carried out, and placed in immense hampers, twenty-four in number. Then great jars of wine were brought in, first placed by the queen on the table, and then handed out in the same way. After this, her majesty presented each of the men with a purse, containing half an ounce, and herself proceeded to clear the table; taking up the plates, salt-cellars, knives and forks, &c., with a dexterity and dispatch which was very amusing, and as cleverly as if she had waited upon hungry travellers all her life. The Patriarch of the Indies then pronounced a solemn blessing, and the ceremony concluded.

But I must not forget to give you a description of the

queen's dress, the most astonishing thing in the way of toilette, as to splendor, that I ever remember to have seen. Besides, I had the assistance of the Countess de V——, who, with all the ladies near us, was in admiration at its magnificence. The material was gold and red brocade, both dress and *manteau*. The *berthe*, which was very deep, was entirely composed of large brilliants. On both shoulders and in front she wore a branch of great rubies and brilliants, and a white lace veil, of gossamer texture, was fastened behind by a *cache-pagire* of the same. She wore a royal diadem also of rubies and diamonds, necklace and bracelets of the same, and the *bandeaux* of her hair were studded with diamond pins like stars. You will recognize the instructions of my preceptress.

One of these diamonds fell into the plate of a poor man, who, greatly embarrassed, took it up, not knowing to whom he ought to present it. "Keep it," said the queen, with a smile. "*Te ha caido en suerte*" (it has fallen to you by lot); not a bad windfall for the poor man. Each one also, both of the men and women, receives a comfortable dress from the queen, so that this annual pilgrimage to Madrid makes twenty-four people well off for some time.

The little princess wore a pink frock, covered with white lace flounces, and bracelets on each arm, of large single diamonds. She looked very pretty and very serious during the whole ceremony, paying no attention to the signs and smiles of the queen, who constantly tried to attract her notice. "I should like to know what royal children are made of!" said the condesa. "Nothing could have bribed my little girl to stand quiet for two long hours." I suppose that, as the little princess never plays with other children, she is "to the manner born." Every morning, in a state-coach, with her governess and attendants, her equeries riding by her side, and escorted by the beautiful troop called the Princess's Guard, she is driven out to the Retiro, or to one of the royal country houses. There she walks, with the hand of her governess, followed by her suite, who are obliged to adapt their steps to those of her little Highness; and till she herself chooses to return, no one ventures to enforce it. Later in the day, she drives out in state with the queen.

But to return to the *Lavatorio* and to the Hall of Pillars. As soon as the ceremony was concluded, the queen, her heavy train held up by her attendants, passed in front of the tribunas, courtesied to the diplomatic corps, and took her departure, followed by her suite and by the cabinet ministers. I had now time to turn my eyes to the roof of this fine hall, which is covered with allegorical paintings, representing the joy of nature at the rising of the sun, the majesty of Spain, &c. It is here that the great balls given in the palace are usually held.

The nurse of the little Princess, who was standing amongst the royal servants, was pointed out to me as we were leaving the hall, and I doubt much whether any high-born dame in the assembly could carry away the palm from her, not only in the perfection of her features, but in that high style of beauty which we imagine belongs by right to noble descent.

It had been reported that, after the Lavatorio, her majesty would perform the stations on foot, in full toilette, and accompanied by her court, according to custom; but some prudential motives induced her ministers to advise the omission of this devotion. Since the terrible attempt of Merino, it had generally been considered unadvisable for the queen to expose herself on foot in the midst of the crowd, who follow the royal cortege and throng the streets on these occasions.

I accompanied Count A—— to visit the different churches, and to add our contributions to those of the faithful, which the *quêtenses* of our acquaintance were receiving. We found the Countess de Montijo surrounded by a crowd of noble contributors, the plate before her filled with gold and silver. The Marquesa de V——, at San José, seemed also to be reaping a rich harvest. With great difficulty we made our way into the church of San Antonio, where Mme. Calderon de la Barca, accompanied by her sister, was receiving gold and silver as fast as she could take it, from grandees, bankers, and diplomats, with sealed papers from liveried servants, containing the tributes of those who could not come themselves. A nurse from the *Ynclusa*, with a model baby, was seated beside them, the nurse opening her eyes in wonder and joy at the descent of the golden shower. The heat was intense in all the churches, owing to the immense crowd and the blaze of light. The altars were magnificent, and brilliant with gold and jewels, and the solemn music of the organ and choirs more than usually impressive.

We visited seven churches, and, amongst others, that of *San Ysidro el Real*, the largest and most magnificent in Madrid, and which in some measure supplies the absence of a cathedral in this city, on all occasions of solemn public ceremonies. Here, for example, is celebrated the anniversary of the victims of the *dos de Mayo*, whose mortal remains were transferred from this church to the monument in the Prado. In October last, also, the remains of Moratin and of Donoso Cortes, Marquis of Valdegamas, were solemnly deposited here with great pomp, in the presence of an immense concourse of spectators.

In 1567 a college was founded on this site by the Jesuit fathers, which, being afterwards patronized by the Empress of Germany, Doña María of Austria, this magnificent church was constructed under the direction of the Master Francisco Bautista, one of that order, in 1651. The Jesuits being banished from Spain in the reign of Charles III., this noble temple became a royal collegiate church, and in 1769 the bodies of San Ysidro el Labrador, the patron of Madrid, and of his wife, Doña María de la Cabeza, were brought hither in solemn procession, from the royal chapel of St. Andrew, whose chaplains were transferred to this church, which took the name of *Cabildo*, or Chapter of San Ysidro. The coffins containing the bodies were placed above the high altar, and this part of the church was renewed and beautified by the celebrated architect, Don Ventura Rodriguez.

The body of the saint is said to remain entire, and is deposited in an interior case of silver filigree, presented by Queen Mariana de Neobourg, placed in an outer urn of gold, silver and bronze, a tribute from the company of goldsmiths in Madrid.

The statue of the saint upon a throne of clouds, is the work of Don Juan de Mena; the urn containing the remains of Doña María is enclosed within the pedestal, which supports the tomb of San Ysidro. The church is in the form of a Latin cross, with a noble cupola, and is profusely adorned with fine paintings; amongst others is a representation of the Holy Trinity, by Raphael Mengs; paintings by Ricci, representing Saint Francis de Borja, and Saint Luis Gonzaga; several by Giordani, and one of our Saviour fastened to the pillar by *el divino* Morales, as he is called.

Many celebrated men are buried within these walls, and amongst others, Laynes, general of the Jesuits, the companion of St. Ignatius de Loyola, one who refused all the honors and dignities which were offered him as a just tribute to his merit and sanctity, and who even, it is said, declined the tiara itself. In my opinion there can be no doubt that San Ysidro is the most noble and majestic church in Madrid.

Our last visit was to the small church of Santa María, the most ancient in the city, dating back to the time of the Romans, and where, according to tradition, the gospel was first preached in Madrid. It was formerly celebrated on account of an image of the Blessed Virgin, Our Lady de la Almudena, said to have been concealed in a tower near the wall by the Christians, during the Saracen usurpation, and which was miraculously discovered the same year in which the country was reconquered from them. The church is now in course of reparation, and we found nothing but scaffoldings and wood-shavings, and all religious ceremonies suspended for the present. It was nine o'clock when we returned to the Legation, tired and famished.

On Good Friday the continued absence of all carriages in the streets, and the mourning dresses of all people of the better class, showed Madrid under a new and solemn aspect. We went to high mass at Santiago, a beautiful church where the knights of the order meet that day in solemn procession. I observed a fine picture, over the high altar, of the battle of Clavijo, with Santiago fighting on horseback in the air; one of the best compositions of Giordani; and various other good paintings.

As in the Calatravas, the church was filled by a select crowd, almost entirely composed of noble ladies and grandees. Amongst the knights were two handsome boys, almost children, the son of the Countess of Toreno, and that of the Duke of Soto-Mayor.

A shower of rain came on very inopportunely, when every one was obliged to return home on foot; but it is remarkable that I have never seen Spaniards of any class hurry on account of rain. They put up umbrellas occasionally, but walk as quietly as if they were receiving a certain quantity of beneficent dew.

I had heard a great deal of the beauty of the music in the chapel royal on Good Friday, and was fortunate enough to obtain, from one of the *gentilhombres* of the palace, a place in a *tribuna*. The *siete palabras*, or *seven words* as they are called—meaning the seven last sentences spoken by our Lord, before his death upon the cross—are set to music by Haydn, and are certainly among the most sublime productions of that composer. Between each sentence a discourse is delivered by the priest, who, on this occasion, was Padre Arenal, a celebrated orator.

The church was in darkness all but the high altar, and the gallery where the musicians of the chapel perform under the direction of Señor Valdemosa. The words are so divine in their agony, the music so well according with them in its expression—the discourses of the priest are so fervent—the darkness adds so much to the sadness of the whole—that when, towards the end, every light is extinguished, and nothing is distinctly seen but the image of our Saviour expiring between the two malefactors, the one penitent, the other blaspheming—the effect on the imagination is almost overwhelming. It was difficult to go back immediately afterwards to the scenes of common life; and although the evening was gloomy and rainy, I took a solitary walk, retracing my steps towards the Plazuela de Santiago, and re-entered the church by a side-door, with the intention of examining the paintings more in detail. No one was there but an old sexton, who was sweeping out the steps of the altar. Seeing I was a stranger, he offered to show me the sacristy, which is celebrated for its beautiful proportions, its fine pillars, and the statues of the kings of Spain and grand-masters of the order, from the time of Charles the Fifth down to that of Ferdinand the Sixth. The whole work, as my obliging cicerone informed me, was executed under the direction of Moradillo, the architect of the royal *Salesas*, by orders of King Ferdinand.

As I was leaving the church, I offered a piece of money to the old man, who positively refused to accept it. As I continued to press it upon him while he stood at the door, hat in hand, he pointed to a lame beggar sitting on the door-steps. "If your excellency wishes to give alms," said he, "there is one who will be glad to take it. Here, Juanito! This Caballero will give you a piece of silver, in the name of Santiago." The lame beggar hobbled up the steps. "God give your excellency a happy life! May the Blessed Virgin pray for you, and send you a happy death," said he. "Vaya V. E. con Dios!" said the old sexton, and I felt as if I had unwittingly offered money to a grandee of the first class!

On Holy Saturday I went to San Ysidro, where the combined effect of the burst of music, the blaze of light, and the pealing forth of all the bells of Madrid at the "Gloria in excelsis," was truly splendid. Again the streets are covered with carriages, and the Prado is in full force. On Easter Sunday I accompanied Don —— to the church of Santo Tomas, in the street of Atocha, an immense building, but got in with great difficulty and much perseverance. It is a noble church, large and lofty, with some fine paintings and statues in the side chapels; but in general the ornaments with which it is loaded are not in as good taste as those in San Ysidro and other religious edifices. But on that day began a *Novena* to the *Santísimo*, celebrated by the congregation, entitled "*de la Guarda y Oracion*" (of watching and prayer), and conducted on a scale of extraordinary magnificence. Each day the expenses are defrayed by one of the grandees of Spain. The splendor of the high altar, with its myriads of wax-lights and the jewels blazing on the tabernacle, surpass almost every thing of this description that I have yet seen. All Madrid, from the highest to the lowest class, attend this Novena, and consequently there is no hour in the day in which Santo Tomas is not crowded. I was surprised, during one of these great *funciones*, to hear myriads of birds singing on the roof inside the church, and take it for granted that cages full of these singing-birds must be kept in the loft, as formerly at least was the custom in the Spanish provinces. Amidst the music, incense, and flowers, the effect of this natural concert, which seems to come from some surrounding grove, has an extremely pretty effect.

I have again attended several bull-fights. Upon repetition I find them monotonous, and rarely feel much interest after the death of the third bull; but I am of the very few whose enthusiasm does not increase by habit. It is astonishing to observe the taste which foreigners have for these spectacles. An attempt has been made to introduce them into France, but I trust and believe that this will be a failure. They are indigenous to Spain, as much so as boxing is to England—the latter in my opinion a much more cruel and dangerous diversion than the former—and more demoralizing to the people, besides having none of the grandeur as a spectacle which makes a bull-fight endurable.

Nearly a fortnight has elapsed since I last wrote, having been sent by my chief with despatches to Paris. I travelled with the French courier. A curious contrast the two cities present! The perfect order and system that reign throughout Paris—the additions, changes and embellishments constantly in progress—the ever-watchful and invisible police—the cleanliness of the principal streets—the crowds of foreigners, especially of English, who throng every part of the capital—but especially the money-making, money-saving nature of the inhabitants, never, in abeyance even in their most ardent pursuit after pleasure; form a striking contrast to the love for all that is ancient, which in Madrid makes it almost dangerous for a government to attempt any innovation requiring the destruction of a building to which the people are accustomed—(witness the unpopularity of the plan formed by the present government for enlarging and beautifying the Puerta del Sol)—to the absence of order and punctuality in almost every transaction—to the indolence or bad faith of the police, who allow the author of an intended conspiracy to walk about the streets at night, without laying hands upon him—to the almost total absence of strangers, which gives Madrid so decided a *cachet* of originality—but especially to that generous, careless improvidence of the Spanish character, which certainly has a great charm, however disadvantageous to themselves.

You ask a question of a Frenchman—he asks you for a *sou*. It rains, and he calls a carriage for you—he begs you to give him five sous for his trouble. You get into a *remise*, some one has opened the door for you officiously. You are requested to remember the *garçon*. You go into a church, the Suisse points out some bad paintings for your inspection. He has a franc in his eye. He admits you to look at the Pantheon—you must give five sous at the door. Some one takes your cane from you, "*Deux sous, Monsieur.*" But what perfect order and method! The woman hands you a ticket, and on your return, from amidst three hundred canes, restores your own.

You go to high mass, and take a chair. At the most solemn moment of the service, an old woman holds out her hand. You give her two sous. "Trois sous, Monsieur—c'est un jour de fête." Then come three *gueuses*—more sous. There is a chinking of money all over the church, so that you feel as if you were buying so many sous worth of prayer.

The churches, it is true, are kept in perfect order, and order and cleanliness are no enemies to devotion. But at the Madeleine, for example, you find yourself in an atmosphere redolent of perfumes—you are surrounded by white plumes and blonde lace, richly-flounced dresses, Indian cashmeres, and roses more perfect than nature—you listen to the superb organ played by the masterly hand of Le Fébur—your attention is inevitably distracted by your elegant neighbors, and on raising your eyes to the high altar, they rest upon the apotheosis of Napoleon Bonaparte. It is true that this is the most fashionable temple in Paris, and that at St. Sulpice and other churches, there is a less select congregation—but commend me to those undistinguished crowds in black dresses and mantillas, who kneel upon the bare floor in those large dark churches—beggars, peasants and duchesses confounded together as they are in the eyes of Him with whom there is no respect of persons. Palmyre's gowns and Warenne's bonnets have a charming effect in the Champs Elysées; but as there is a time, so there is a place for every thing under the sun.

I had the honor of presentation to their majesties, and was received very graciously, especially by the charming empress, who, surrounded by her ladies, reminded me of Calypso among her nymphs. She asked me several questions about Spain. I had not seen her since her marriage. She is thinner, and her eyes have a deeper, more serious expression. Her head, royally set upon her shoulders, reminded me of some of the ancient effigies of the queens of France. She certainly looks born to be an empress. What dignity and grace in her walk! Only those small Spanish feet have such a tread, firm and light, as if walking to the sound of a Spanish band. What purity of outline in her figure, and what a complexion! The fairest Frenchwoman looks brown beside her. I saw Concha among the guests, looking injured and interesting. He "bides his time" in very pleasant quarters.

The Tuileries, the Opera and the Gymnase were all I had time for. I went to the latter to see "La joie fait peur," the theatre crowded to suffocation, the audience bathed in tears. Mme. de Girardin has won new laurels for herself by the most simple means. One third of its success is no doubt owing to the perfection of the acting, but its popularity proves that the most *blasé* and critical audience in the world are quite as much disposed to sympathize with an honest picture of domestic grief and family suffering, as with the meretricious woes of the *Dame aux Camelias y Compañia.*

I returned here this morning, and even while acknowledging and regretting the vast superiority of Paris over Madrid, I felt a thousand times more at the Calle de Alcalá than in the Boulevards—in the Prado than in the Champs Elysées, and was delighted to return to the cordiality, gossip and *laisser aller* of this *Court-village.* Completely absorbed in its own affairs, even the *question d'Orient*, which so entirely occupies the public mind in France, as may well be supposed, hardly excites any interest here, and is scarcely spoken of, except in our diplomatic circle. Their own affairs are rather more than they can manage.

In order to raise money, the government has issued a decree, desiring all the civil governors to invite the people and private individuals of their respective provinces to take part in a subscription, which is to be opened for the space of one month, engaging themselves to have the contingent ready, one half in June, and the other in July, both quantities to be repaid in four years in shares of one eighth, and with the annual interest of six per cent. payable each six months when due, adding to this advantage another six per cent. as premium on the anticipated loan. At the expiration of one month, should the necessary sum not be collected, it will take the character of a forced loan, to be repaid without the discount of six per cent. but with the exchange of the provisional receipts for notes upon the treasury with interest. Great excitement in Madrid in consequence of this decree. The opposition denounce it as a "high-handed robbery"—neither more nor less—they are not a bit more choice in their expressions than this. One of the principal bankers, discussing the question last evening at the Casino, gives the conduct of the government, in this instance, his unqualified approbation. Don Alejandro Llorente, formerly minister of the treasury, is named Director of the Bank of San Fernando—another cause for stormy discussions. As M—— says, "If San Luis had come down from heaven with the Decalogue in his hand, his enemies would have found something to censure in it!"

The Peruvian minister has opened his fine suite of rooms in the palace of the Dukes of Villa-Hermosa. The rooms are spacious and elegant—the furniture entirely from Paris, —Mr. and Madame Osma receive with the greatest amiability—the company is select—the supper *exquis*—therefore you may imagine that these weekly soirées are about the best in Madrid. The young Duchess of Feria, sister of the Duchess of Medina-Cœli, has died at the age of twenty-two, young and beautiful. She was a blonde beauty, entirely unlike her sister. She is said to have died of measles, complicated with some other complaint; and on the night of this first soirée at the Peruvian minister's, I could see from the windows the room in the Medina-Cœli palace where the body of the duchess was lying in her coffin, with lights at the head and foot. The contrast between the gay dancing of the German cotillion, in which many of her young companions were engaged, and the solitary stillness of that chamber of death, was striking.

First great rain—almost tropical. Having gone with E. of the French Legation, to call on the Dowager Duchess of San Carlos, in the Calle del Bárquillo, where she has a charming house in the French fashion, *entre cour et jardin*, we found that the street had become a rapid stream, where flat-bottomed boats might navigate—perhaps the etymology of its name *Barquillo* is owing to this circumstance. We escaped into the house of the Danish minister, oldest and most popular of diplomates. Lord Howden has been giving a series of farewell dinners, previous to his intended departure for Andalusia.

An amusing little adventure occurred at the Legation yesterday, in which I enacted the part of victim. An interesting female, in the deepest mourning, requested to see his excellency upon business. She was shown into the ante-room, but Count A—— being particularly engaged, desired me to inquire what her business might be. I found a remarkably pretty woman, apparently about eight and twenty, with a pair of languishing dark eyes, and a very fine figure. I expressed his excellency's regret at being unable to see her himself, and requested her to make me the medium of her communication. After a pause and a deep sigh, she commenced her history.

She was the widow of an officer—the orphan daughter of a distinguished colonel, who had lost his life in some battle, the name of which has escaped my memory. She was left to the tender mercies of the world, penniless, and with five children, daughters, the eldest eight years old. Through some neglect her widow's pension had not been paid. She had come to Madrid to solicit an audience of the queen. She had heard of Count A——'s generosity and charity. She came to entreat him to speak in her favor. I did not see how his solicitation was precisely what she required. I recommended an appeal to the Minister of War. She thanked me very much, and cast down her eyes, fringed with a dark curtain of eyelashes—then raising them again, she said, while a large tear trembled in each (I will swear to the tears)—"It is hard for the daughter and widow of two brave officers to be reduced to solicit aid—but what will a mother not do for her children! and those children starving!" I am afraid I glanced indiscreetly at the elegance of her mourning attire, but she appeared to take no notice, and asked me if I thought that Count A—— would lend her a small sum to pay the rent of her lodgings for one week. I told her I would take her message to the count, but she stopped me, and laying her white ungloved hand upon my arm, and pouring a whole fire of artillery from her radiant eyes—"Stay," said she, "I would rather receive a favor from *you*. Something tells me that you are generous. I have more faith in youth, with such a countenance as yours, than in the cold, worldly prudence of an older diplomate."

I stammered out something, and put my hand in my pocket—drew out a porte-monnaie, and was quite ashamed on opening it, to find that it contained only two gold napoleons. I told her I hardly ventured to offer so small a sum, but would call at her lodgings in the evening. She took them, however, with a pensive smile, and gave me her direction—"Doña Ana de Gonsalez, Calle de Silva, No. 15, fourth story, to the left hand." Then with another killing glance, she prepared to depart. I handed her into her berlina, and received a sweet "Beso las manos de V. Caballero," as it drove off.

The count was with the Austrian minister when I returned, so I reserved the account of my mission to another opportunity, and in the evening set off, armed with a full purse, to the Calle de Silva. I found the number—mounted to the apartment—poor enough it seemed to be. I knocked—a shrill-voiced maid-servant reconnoitred me through the loop-hole. I asked if the Señora was at home. She threw open the door, and marched on before me through a dark passage, at the end of which she walked into a long low-roofed room, and announced me as *a gentleman—un Caballero.* I found myself, as soon as the light of one flaring tallow candle enabled me to distinguish any thing, in the presence of five old ladies; four with mantillas, and one very deaf, half-blind old lady, the mistress of the house.

They were ranged upon stiff wooden chairs, with their backs close to the wall, and each had a cup of chocolate in one hand, and a small sweet biscuit in the other. Every biscuit remained suspended in its descent into each cup, and all eyes were turned to survey the intruder into their tertulia. I made my respects to the old lady, whose gray hair without a cap turned up with a horn comb, proclaimed her to be the mistress of the domain, and begged to know if the Señora de Gonsalez was at home. "*Mis males?*" said the old woman. "No better. I have suffered a great deal from my rheumatism since last Monday. I went to mass in the rain, and caught more cold. Sit down, Caballero. Take a cup of chocolate." I declined, and repeated "La Señora de Gonsalez," in a louder key. "Señor de Sales," said the lady, "please to be seated. Take a glass of water, and an *azucarillo.*" "You wish to see the Señora de Gonsalez?"

at last said an old lady. "No such person has ever lived here. You have mistaken the number, Señor. Doña Margarita has occupied this apartment for thirty years."

I felt inclined to *execute* the perfidious widow, and besides I saw that the old ladies were dying of curiosity for an explanation, for you must know that I was rather a smart-looking Caballero to appear in this fourth story, being dressed for a soirée at the Austrian minister's. In a few words I explained my errand. "Ave Maria! Caramba! Que picara! La viudita! (the little widow!) with her mourning dress. But you must be tired, Caballero. Sit down—take an azucarillo." A little subdued burst of laughter made me look round, and there on a low stool in a corner, before the table on which the solitary candle was burning, sat the prettiest girl! I am sorry to say, knitting or darning a stocking. Figure to yourself a fine-looking graceful *Andaluza* of about eighteen, with a profusion of dark hair rolled round her head in about fifty plaits, great, full, dark eyes, and a row of pearls in her fresh mouth, which she pursed up very primly when I turned round, seeming very much ashamed of having given audible vent to her mirth. The result of this agreeable sight was, that I sat down, took a glass of clear water and an *azucarillo*, and tried to make myself as agreeable as possible. The hostess received an explanation, given in a shrill, distinct key by one of the ancient Señoras, and much sympathy and indignation was expressed by the venerable Doña Margarita. I could not help thinking how truly polite these good people were, and how perfectly at their ease in the presence of a stranger.

I was just bethinking myself of taking leave, when the first old lady who had spoken, rose up, called her daughter, the fair knitter, and prepared for her departure, saying that her cook had a *pulmonia*, and she must go home to see her.

Such a leave-taking, and kissing, and putting on of shawls, and messages, and promises of return! And as I had risen at the same time, the hostess told me the house was at my disposal, so was the *aunque inutil* (although useless), &c., and yet no one knew my name, or seemed to care to know. I asked permission of the old lady to accompany her and her daughter home. They lived in the Calle de los Espejos. On the way, I received many cautions as to how I listened to imposing widows in future. Doña Dolores walked on demurely in front. I accompanied my new acquaintances up to the fourth story of their house, was requested to walk in, which I declined, and cannot flatter myself that I have made the slightest impression upon the fair Doña Dolores, who, by the way, managed her fan and mantilla in the most bewitching manner. My story was received with much applause next day at the count's table. M—— was in ecstasies at my being so *verdant*. It seems that this class of interesting impostors is not uncommon here.

CHAPTER XXVIII.

The Queen's Drawing-room—The Throne-room—Ceremony of a Royal Reception—News of the Assassination of the Prince of Parma—Sivori—The Principe—"The Black Warrior" Affair—Angry Political Discussion—A Horse-race—La Romería—The Manolas—Hospitality—Aranjuez—Gardens of the Principe—The Palace—Its Environs.

April 27th.

ON the 25th, her majesty held a *besamanos* (drawing-room), to celebrate the birthday of the queen-mother. I copy the Marquesa de M——'s invitation, which I took off her table. She is, as you may remember, the wife of the Minister of the Navy.

EXMA. SEÑORA:

Her Majesty, the Queen our Lady, whom God preserve, has been pleased to appoint the hour of six in the evening of the 25th instant, for the Ladies' *Besamanos*, which is to be held for the plausible motive (*motivo plausible*) of its being the birthday of her Majesty the Queen-Mother. Which I communicate to your Excellency by Royal order for your information (*inteligencia y gobierno*), also making known to your Excellency that the attendance is to be in court-dress and train.

God preserve your Excellency many years.

The Viscountess of Valloria,
Widowed Duchess of Gor.

To the Lady of the Minister of ——.

Palace, 25*th April*, 1854.

The diplomatic corps are invited to attend at an earlier hour. I accompanied Count A—— about two o'clock, first to the queen-mother, before whose doors were crowds of carriages. Those ladies who were not going to court afterwards were in demi-toilette, but the generality were in full court-dress. Queen Christina was very simply dressed in blue silk, with a white shawl; seated, the duke and one lady of honor standing beside her.

The handsomest dresses I remarked, were those of the Countesses of Toreno and Montijo. The latter wore a dress of bright green and gold, which was superb; but the diamonds of the Countess of Toreno seemed to me the finest in the room. All *our* corps were there, always excepting the doyen and his lady; and all the ladies of the cabinet whose husbands go to court early on these occasions, and leave them to follow at six o'clock. Thus, while the cabinet ministers remain beside the throne during nearly all the presentations, their ladies are received the very last, so that, they tell me, the queen takes leave of them after their audience, and retires herself.

The throne-room, or hall of ambassadors, as it is called, is magnificent, the walls and roof covered with fine paintings, chiefly of an allegorical description, the work of Don Juan Bautista Tiepolo. In the cornice are represented the different states and provinces of the Spanish monarchy, with the various costumes of the inhabitants, and the different productions of the soil. In the corners are golden medals contained in vast shells adorned with festoons and cariatidi, and supported by statues representing rivers. The whole salon has a truly regal aspect, with rich furniture of crimson and gold, enormous mirrors, statues, candelabras, curious inlaid-tables, and enormous chandeliers. The throne itself has a magnificent canopy of crimson velvet with gold fringe;

at the foot are four bronze lions, and at either side a statue of Prudence and Justice.

When we arrived the queen had only received her *servidumbre*, the ladies and gentlemen of her household. She sat on her throne, under the splendid dais, the king at her left, the Ynfante Don Francisco on a low seat at the foot of the throne. The scene was certainly very brilliant. The queen herself was in a blaze of jewels, and her ladies seemed to compete with her in splendor. They stood in a long row to the left, and it must be admitted that they are incomparably handsomer than the ladies of any other court which I have yet seen. The uniforms were superb—as were also the dresses of the household and of the grandees; those of the cabinet ministers were also very handsome, especially of San-Luis and Molins—consisting of crimson velvet knee-breeches, with white silk stockings, and coats covered with very rich gold embroidery. The Pope's nuncio and the Archbishop of Toledo stood near the throne. The queen seemed to be in her gayest humor, and I heard her dress very much admired by the diplomatic ladies. It seemed to be composed of some rich and ancient-looking brocade, but further "deponent sayeth not."

The perfect ease of the very youngest Spaniard never ceases to surprise me. They kiss hands and back out, as if they had done nothing else all their lives, and many of them had probably never left their provinces a few days before, or seen the inside of a palace until that moment. Each individual has to walk up the steps of the throne; the ladies, with their long heavy trains, kiss the hand of the queen; then drag their trains along, and kiss the king's hand; back down, and kiss the Ynfante's, then back out through the long hall. The foreign ladies are not expected to kiss hands. How they manage to go backwards with their trains on the floor, is a mystery to me. The Spanish ladies make remarkably graceful courtesies, an art which probably forms part of their education. When we left the hall, the queen retired to her cabinet for rest or refreshment. We found the ladies of the ministers and a few others of the grandees, in the next room waiting their turn for an audience. The ministers themselves had gone home. It was growing dusk, and the servants were beginning to light up the great hall. We staid some time in the king's chamber, as it is called, waiting for the carriage, which had not yet made its appearance.

We remained till the queen and her ladies, with the king and Ynfante, had returned, and resumed their places. The hall was now brilliantly lighted up. The doors were thrown open—the ladies rose, thankful that their hour had come at last, threw down their trains, and went in. We looked on from a distance at this last reception. All the crowd had gone. There were none present but the royal family and their suite. After kissing hands, the ladies backed out, and formed themselves into two lines in an adjoining apartment, further on, and waited till the queen passed out, when they made their last courtesies, and she and her brilliant train disappeared into the inner regions of the palace.

April —.

News of the assassination of the Prince of Parma! Poor young man! Sad end to a gay and reckless life. Strange presentiment that haunted him of an untimely end, thus confirmed. Yet not strange, perhaps, as he knew that this recklessness carried too far in several cases, had made him many sworn foes. The assassin has escaped. All ask whether the crime is more likely to have been committed from private revenge, or from political motives. Most probably from the former. Thus the duchess has seen both her husband and father perish by the knife of the assassin. She is named regent for the young prince. A change of ministry is expected, and especially that she will dismiss the celebrated Baron Ward. The court again goes into mourning.

May is approaching, with her breath of roses, and the weather is perfect. Flowers are blossoming wherever they can find a corner to grow in. The market is filled with every variety of flowers, but still especially with baskets full of the beautiful carnations of Valencia, which arrive in cart-loads every morning. Their size is enormous—the perfume exquisite—the colors of every variety; crimson, pink, straw-color, rose-color, variegated, pure white. It is now a general fashion at soirées, for the girls to wear them in their hair.

Went again to the conservatorio—as usual, good, but tiresome, and lasting till near three in the morning. The queen was there in half mourning, with alternate flounces of white and black lace, and a head-dress of the same. I am flattered to learn that my sisters find me improved in my descriptions of dress.

Sivori, the famous violoncello player, is here. He played a few evenings ago in the palace, before the king and queen, who were delighted with his performance. The king especially is a good musician. The queen has sent Sivori a set of diamond buttons and a cross. He has more soul in his playing than almost any other musician. I know he has played several nights in the Circo, but his music is not of a nature to please the crowd.

Went to the *Principe* to see a new piece, the *Ricahembra,* in which La Teodora is excellent. Her struggles between virtuous pride (though the pride is overstrained) and affection were well rendered. "Rather a contrast to the *hembras* of the present day!" said the sarcastic ——.

Accompanied Señor E—— to the church of the Salesas,

to see a great *funcion* in honor of three lately canonized saints: Juan de Britto, Andres Bobola, and Mariano de Parede y Flores, surnamed the Lily of Quito. The sermon upon the last saint was preached by Father Cumplido; the crowd was immense, and the service lasted from ten till half-past one. A revolution is predicted for the *Dos de Mayo*. Being predicted, it will probably not occur; but the very belief in such an event is bad. It accustoms the mind of the people to the idea, and proves, that the foundation of the government is unstable. Meanwhile the affair of the "Black Warrior" forms an episode which has in some measure distracted public attention from matters of a more purely local nature. It is only when a case of this sort occurs, that one discovers that patriotism is not wholly extinguished in Spain, or swallowed up in a mass of petty intrigues for power and place. The solution of the question depends upon the result of the negotiations opened by Mr. Soulé with this government. The cabinet of Washington insist upon obtaining reparations which the Spanish government consider it an indignity on their part to grant; and whatever be the true state of the question, or upon which side justice lies, a point upon which I do not pretend to give any opinion—here, at least, all parties, of whatever denomination, seem to have but one feeling; a circumstance so uncommon as to be worthy of record.

Vehement political discussion last evening at the table of ——. He himself affects to belong to no party, and invariably invites members of every political *sect*, perhaps with the amiable object of setting them by the ears. The conversation arose from an expression in one of the opposition papers which appeared that morning; in which the government was compared to "an unknown comet of sinister influence, whose irregular and capricious course perturbed the harmony of the stars, and overthrew the laws of nature!" This remark was cited by G——, who seemed to think that the company required something to enliven them.

"After all," said our host quietly, "the government has passed triumphantly through a difficult crisis."

"And by what means?" said an angry editor. "By force—by intimidation."

"Even if it were so, which I deny," said another, "forcible aggressions must be repressed by forcible measures. The cabinet of San-Luis has simply extricated itself from all the difficulties with which the opposition endeavor to embarrass its march. It has done all that can be required of a government, when it finds itself surrounded by difficulties and obstacles. It has got rid of these obstacles by the only means in its power. It has acted upon the principle of self-defence, a right conceded to all individuals when attacked.

"The circumstances in which this government found itself were such, that nothing but unwavering energy and an iron will could have produced a favorable result. They were not natural circumstances; they were created by the opposition. Every act of severity on their part has been more than justified. Had they given way at the first cry of passion, at the first appearance of danger, they would have proved themselves weak and despicable, and unworthy of the confidence of their sovereign and of the nation.

"They did not resolve the crisis of the bank by intimidation. Their object was merely to repress those scandalous intrigues which were put in movement to produce the appearance of a monetary crisis; and when this pretended crisis terminated, it did so merely because it was proved to the public by official documents that they had nothing to fear, and that the panic had been solely the result of stratagem; and therefore, while the abettors of the crisis assembled hundreds before the doors of the bank, public funds rose in the *Bourse.* In my opinion, this cabinet is now more firmly established than ever, and if it is to be overthrown, it will only be by a military revolution."

Went yesterday to see the races at the Casa de Campo; rode there with M—— and S——. The queen and her suite were in a covered *tribune* with some of her ministers. The ladies remained in their open carriages, which had a good effect, as they were all in full *toilette de matin.* The whole affair was rather cold and very aristocratic, forming a contrast to the excitement and enthusiasm of the spectators in the *plaza de toros.* Some of the horses were English, *pur sang.* The jockeys rode well, dressed English fashion, and many of them English in fact. The horses were in the names of the Dukes of San Carlos and Riansares, Marquis of Bedmar, &c., but those of the two first belonged to the queen and queen-mother. Horse-racing is evidently an engrafted taste here, and people in general are very indifferent about it. The weather also was cold and disagreeable for Madrid. The queen staid till eight o'clock, having, as usual, arrived late.

Another *besamanos* on account of the king's birthday, which passed off like the other. The little princess is generally sent into the country on these occasions—a wise measure.

Countess —— told me, that when she returned this evening, she desired very gravely to see the Intendente of the palace, and told him that she had observed that morning, that one of the fountains in the *Pardo* (a royal country-seat) was not playing; and that he must attend to it. Rather precocious for two years old!

May 14th.

Day in which the Viaticum is carried to the sick, who have not been able to make their Easter communion. A grand and solemn procession. All the balconies were hung with covered draperies; those of the grandees with rich and ancient brocades, which, if they could speak, might tell many a tale of the various occasions on which they have displayed their gold and crimson glories, now faded, to the sun. The *Santísimo* was carried in one of the royal state carriages. The streets were strewed with flowers, and bouquets were carried along, of such enormous size, that one could scarcely be lifted by four men.

The queen-mother is dangerously ill with measles; and all communication cut off between her house and the palace.

A great many evening receptions, and various diplomatic dinners; amongst others, one at the Marquis Turgot's, who is now able to walk slowly with the aid of crutches.

May 16th.

Went yesterday to the country fête of San Ysidro, called *la Romería*, where the whole population of Madrid were dancing, on the banks of the river, jotas, fandangos, or boleros; guitars and castanets sounding in every direction; *Manolos* and *Manolas* in a state of intense enjoyment. The dress of the *Manolo*, as well as his character and manners, are no doubt greatly modified since the days when Don Ramon de la Cruz introduced the type into his amusing *sainetes*, the Spanish farce. The dress is now a tight short jacket, with a multitude of silver buttons; an open waistcoat also, with innumerable buttons; an embroidered shirt, the collar lined with red and tied round with a bright-colored handkerchief, the ends passing through a ring; a yellow or scarlet belt, wide pantaloons, white stockings, and well-fitting shoes. A *calañes* hat, flat at the top, and turned up all round the brim, has been substituted for the former pointed high-crowned hat, which is now seldom seen, but was more graceful. A stick in his hand and a knife by his side, and you have the actual costume of the Manolo; the shoemaker, the butcher, the *calesero*, or whatever may be his trade.

The *Manola*, proverbial for her grace, wit, and independence—her indomitable pride, ignorance, abhorrence of foreigners, and vicious and dissipated habits—is still a type apart, but has undergone many modifications since those days when, to walk through certain streets of Madrid, where these dames chiefly congregated, was an affair of some danger, especially for a stranger. In vain, women of a higher class have endeavored to parody the true Manola. Her wit, her repartees, her grace, her dress, are all her own; so are the bell-shaped, embroidered petticoat, the pearl-colored stockings, the high-cut shoe, the striped mantilla, thrown back with an inimitable air; the plaited hair, the peculiar walk, and especially that sweet, rather drawling intonation with which she makes the most witty and insolent remarks.

Venders of flowers and fruit, or officiating in the cigar-shops, certain of these Manolas were celebrated for their grace and beauty. *Geroma*, the chestnut-seller (*la Castañera*); Pepa, the orange girl; Marica, the embroiderer; had their day of fame, and attracted as customers all the distinguished *pollos* of the capital. Within late years, however, their fierceness in certain revolutions, in which they proved themselves worthy rivals of the French poissardes, attracted the attention of the authorities. The progress of civilization has extended itself to this redoubtable class. Their children have been received into various schools of gratuitous instruction, and the type, as it originally existed, is gradually wearing out. A well-dressed stranger may now walk in the district called the *Lavapies*, without being insulted. The Manolas still sell flowers, chestnuts, and cigars, but no longer keep up a war of wit and insolence with their customers. They have not entirely lost their local physiognomy; but, according to my friend M—— and other authorities, they have greatly improved in morals, manners, and habits; both sexes always retaining their taste for dancing and bull-fights, their love of dress, and a certain contempt for every thing that is not Spanish. The original type, in all its perfection, is now confined to the stage, and may be seen in certain pieces occasionally given in the *Circo*, the witty productions of Don Ramon de la Cruz, such as *La casa de Tócame-Roque*, or the Enraged Chestnut-sellers.

I took up my position to-day under a spreading tree by the banks of the river, near the chapel of San Ysidro, and lay there smoking for hours, watching the various groups who were celebrating the *Romería*—the unwearied dancers, the untiring guitar-players, all good-humored, gay and careless, singing, laughing, and enjoying themselves, yet always with perfect decorum. Tired with a long walk in the heat of the sun, I fell fast asleep to the music of the seguidilla. When I awoke, the sun had gone down, a breeze was blowing from the river, and a group of people seated on the grass within a short distance of my retreat, were drinking chocolate, a heap of roasted chestnuts beside them, which a number of children were busily devouring, burning their mouths and fingers with great glee. A very handsome woman, with short petticoats and little feet, a small blue China crape shawl and a mantilla, large pearl ear-rings and a fan, seeing me look towards the party, rose, and coming up to me with an air as graceful and dignified as that of any high-born lady of sixteen quarterings, said to me, " Caballero, you look fatigued. Will you honor us by taking a cup of chocolate?" I rose up and took off my hat, upon which all the men took off theirs, and requested me to put on mine, hospitably enforcing the invitation of Doña Carmen.

An excellent cup of foaming chocolate was handed me, and, sitting down on the grass between two pretty girls—the daughters, I conclude, of Doña Carmen—I accepted their hospitality as frankly as it was offered. As for them, they continued to talk, laugh, and sing, as if there were no interloper in their party, yet always treating me with the most respectful attention. When I rose to leave them I knew the Spanish character too well by this time to venture upon any offer of money; so I merely thanked them, praised their chocolate, and received in return a thousand expressions of good-will, assurances of their being always ready to serve me, and a hearty "*Vaya V. con Dios Caballero*" from the whole group. Suddenly I recollected that I had an acceptable offering in my pocket, and producing my cigar-case, emptied its contents, which were received by the men with many thanks, and we parted the best friends in the world.

To-day the ministers were to have gone to the inauguration of the new railroad from Aranjuez to Tembleque; but, in consequence of the critical condition of the queen-mother, the ceremony is deferred. Another brilliant party at the Peruvian minister's.

May 20th.

On Wednesday last a diplomatic party was formed to visit Aranjuez, a place almost fabulously beautiful. As the Escorial is the grandest and most gloomy of royal residences, Aranjuez is the most enchanting—a very temple of pleasure. The one is well fitted to be the tomb of the Spanish monarchs; the other to be the theatre of their amusements. The railway, certainly, does not seem a poetical enough mode of approach to these gardens of Armida; but inasmuch as the carriages are comfortable, spacious, and well-arranged, and carry the traveller with the speed of thought over a dusty uninteresting road, they are not to be quarrelled with.

The day was warm, but not sultry; and from the moment of entering Aranjuez, we breathed an atmosphere of flowers. Situated on the left shores of the Tagus, the city itself contains upwards of five thousand inhabitants, though more than twenty thousand are said to be accommodated there in the season, that is, during the queen's visit, which is not expected to take place this year.

Formerly this royal retreat belonged to the knights of Santiago, and was the residence of the grand-masters of the order. Philip II. was its first royal owner, and the construction of the palace was begun by his orders, under the direction of Juan de Herrera, a celebrated architect. It was continued during the reigns of Philip V. and Ferdinand VI. and concluded in that of Charles III. All these sovereigns contributed to the formation and beautifying of the gardens and fountains which embellish Aranjuez; but Charles IV. it was who more especially adorned and extended the pleasure-grounds of this his favorite domain. The first sight of the beautiful valley in which Aranjuez lies, fertilized by the waters of the Tagus and Iarama, shows to the traveller like an oasis in the desert, especially as contrasted with the arid and stony country surrounding Madrid.

We took carriages in the village, for it is little more, in spite of its churches, military governor, hospital, theatre, *plaza de toros*, inns, cafés, and post-houses; and driving through the *Calle Larga*, or Long Street, shaded on either side with fine trees, entered the beautiful plaza de San Antonio, leaving on our right the palace with its parterres and waterfalls, and to the left the *Calle de la Reina* and the new garden of Ysabel Segunda; and following the advice of

Count G——, who acted as our guide, directed our way to the gardens of the Principe.

In these beautiful gardens stands the pretty palace called the "*Casa del Labrador*," the house of the workman, ironically, it is said, on account of the many rare and valuable objects which it contains. It was built by Charles IV., and looks like a pretty country-house, standing in the midst of groves and flower-gardens. It is full of curiosities and objects of art, all of Spanish workmanship. The rooms are long and low-roofed, some very small, but covered with paintings, chiefly by Luca Giordani. The staircases are narrow, with gilt balustrades. In the first salon, is a long plateau of alabaster, covered with vases and statuettes of alabaster and porphyry; an ingenious clock, with a diamond star to mark the hours—beautiful candelabras, of which the mould was broken, that the form might not be repeated—marble pillars of different colors, &c. All is jasper and porphyry, and curious marbles and precious stones; a rare and costly bijou.

We made, however, rather a hurried inspection of the numerous apartments, and went out to walk in the gardens of the Principe, several miles in circumference, a labyrinth of the most brilliant and exquisite flowers of every color, shaded by the loftiest and noblest trees, brought from every quarter of the world, and flourishing in these favored regions as in their native soils. We particularly admired the gigantic poplars, and cedars which five men can scarcely span.

The fragrance of the flowers is wonderful, an essence of roses and jasmine. Nowithstanding their immense extent, these gardens are kept in perfect order. A strong dyke of mason-work defends them from the incursions of the Tagus; every species of fruit is cultivated within their precincts;

clear tanks, shady islands, fountains of great architectural beauty, every where refresh the eye, and form a scene of constant and pleasing variety.

Towards mid-day the sun became oppressive, in spite of trees and fountains; and Mesdames —— proposed that we should return to our carriages, and drive to the palace in the *Jardin de la Ysla.* The Tagus, on whose banks this beautiful palace stands, was now a dark muddy color, but the waterfalls into which it forms in front of the palace, were clear as crystal. It is a charming residence; the rooms lofty and spacious—the views from the windows, one maze of groves and fountains, and flowers of the brightest colors. This extreme brightness of tint is remarkable, and was observed upon by all our party. There is something tropical in the color. The roses are redder, the carnations a deeper crimson, the trees a more flashing green, than can be seen elsewhere.

The queen's sleeping-apartments called forth general admiration, especially her dressing-room, fitted up with white Valencian silk, embroidered all over with bunches of pink roses. The carving of the bed, the elegance of the toilette-tables, were all commented on. Her Majesty's *Despacho*, where she receives her ministers, is a charming room, looking out upon the river; and the throne-room is a noble apartment. The walls are covered with yellow damask, and large mirrors. The furniture is entirely composed of dark ruby velvet and gold; chairs, sofas, curtains, &c. Fine paintings, as in the Casa del Labrador, adorn the roofs; chiefly by the indefatigable Luca Giordani. The chapel is handsome—the altar-piece a fine Annunciation by Bayen, a Spanish artist. "In the palaces of the Spanish monarchs," as Count A—— observed, "it is not so much the grandeur of the furniture or the size of the apartments that we admire; it is the intrinsic value and rarity of the objects which they contain; the fine paintings, the Flemish tapestries, the inlaid tables, the precious stones, so much that is rich and ancient and rare, lavished in every direction with an unsparing hand."

Here, however, one must always leave art for nature, though it would seem that both have striven together in amicable contest. But the "Garden of the Island" is the crowning charm of Aranjuez. The island is formed by the junction of the river with a canal. The fabled gardens of Armida, which inevitably present themselves to the imagination in wandering through this scene of beauty, cannot have had a fairer model than this, even in the mind of the poet.

The delicious shade of the lofty and spreading trees, impervious to the fiercest rays of the sun—the temples, fountains, and marble statues—the distant sound of the waterfall, the songs of myriads of birds, undisturbed inhabitants of these groves, the exquisite fragrance of the atmosphere,—every thing that can charm the senses is united here, to a degree that is almost overpowering. I wandered away from our party, who, tired of walking, had seated themselves in the temple beside the great fountain, agreeing to meet them at the house of S——a, where we were to adjourn before our departure.

Nothing could be more oppressive than the stillness. Not a sound but the murmuring water, and the songs of the birds. Turning the corner of a shady alley, I came upon so pretty a picture, that I would gladly have made a sketch of it. A beautiful boy of about four years old, brown, and with the eyes and hair of Murillo's children, was lying fast asleep with his head upon the knees of a grave little girl about three years older, seated upon the grass, by the margin of a dry stone fountain, and busily engaged in making up little bouquets of wild roses and corn-flowers. A man was mowing the grass at a little distance. Both children, though dark as gypsies, bare-legged and bare-footed, were eminently handsome, and had so noble an air, that one might have fancied them a couple of little Moorish captives, of the race of Boabdil.

The sun had set, and a soft breeze was rippling the waters of the Tagus, when I left these enchanted gardens, and made my way to the house of S——a, in time to partake of the refreshments which he had prepared for our party, whom I found seated before a feast of strawberries, purple grapes, and champagne—ices, and iced beverages of every description. It was dusk when we bid adieu to this paradise, and returned to the railroad and scenes of common life. I recommend all *nouveaux mariés* to take a house at Aranjuez in the month of May. The families from Madrid, however, who have country-seats there, complain of it as being extremely dull. Besides it is now decided that the queen will not visit Aranjuez this summer—a great disappointment to the residents. She intends going to La Granja, the Spanish Versailles—and Count A—— has sent there to secure lodgings. Already the heat begins to be felt at Aranjuez; in a short time it will be sultry.

Although it is probable that a long residence there might cloy upon the senses, proving only that we are no longer fitted to pastoralize in Arcadia, I mark down this day in rose-color upon the tablets of my memory, as I do that spent in the Escorial in inky black; yet for a continuance, I should prefer to live in the gloomy precincts of the Escorial, but surrounded by mountains and with bracing air, rather than in this monotony of beauty and sweetness.

CHAPTER XXIX.

The Verbena—The "Bat"—Its attacks on the Government—The Queen visits the Escorial—Agitation—Revolt of the Cavalry—O'Donnell at their Head—History of the Conspiracy—O'Donnell and the Military—Public Anxiety—The Queen's Return—Madrid declared in a state of Siege—Proclamations—Rumors—Defeat of the Rebels.

June —.

WENT to see the *Verbena*, the fête on St. John's Eve. How the good people of Madrid do amuse themselves! Holidays enough they have to make the despair of all utilitarians. Theatres, fairs, bull-fights, moonlight dances,—with them life is nearly a perpetual fête. I cannot imagine them engaged in a revolution. It seems to me that they would dance it off to the music of the Jota. But what a fine brave-looking set of men they are! how frank and independent! and even in their amusements, as I have so often had occasion to observe, how much earnestness in their character! a gayety of spirit, yet no *légèreté*, and especially no indecorum in their conduct.

Here was the Prado on this bright moonlight night, crowded to excess, and a strange scene is presented. Some were playing guitars, some singing the national songs—some dancing,—*manchegas* or *jotas*,—some cooking *buñuelos*, a species of hot cake, upon a small furnace, with quantities of hot oil—some eating them as fast as they were manufactured. Some were drinking at the booths—fresh water with *azucarillos*, or tumblers of water, colored with red wine. The women were all in their working-dresses—the dancers, as usual, rather serious than otherwise, caring apparently very little for their partners, but trying to outshine each other in the variety and complication of their steps. One young man seemed to bear away the palm in a manchega, and was gravely applauded several times. We met rows of young girls, taking each other's arms, and all playing the castanets—no man accompanying them. All were indefatigable; dancers, players, sellers, buyers. We staid till three in the morning—not the slightest disorder up to that hour; probably they became more noisy towards the end.

On the 26th of April, a letter, which appeared like an invitation to a funeral, was left at the Legation, which upon being opened, was found to contain a small printed newspaper, called the *Murciélago* (the Bat), containing a series of attacks against the government. Since then, it drops mysteriously into people's houses, is left at their doors in various forms, and is said to have appeared on the king's table, and even in the queen's toilet-chamber. It has very little wit or talent, but its constant abuse of the ministry and their party, makes it a weapon of some importance. The ministry and their adherents are designated under the name of *polacos*, but what the precise origin of the term is, I cannot discover, unless it be, as some say, that the family name of *Sartorius*, Count of San-Luis, is supposed to be of Polish origin.

In the first number there appeared under the head of advertisements, several of this nature:

"Any persons desiring an office, can call at the Department of *Fomento*, where Don Juan Perez Galvo will attend to them. *Notice.*—The money must be paid beforehand."

"*War Department.*—Employments, grades, crosses, honors. Apply to Don Saturnino Parra, commissioner of the sub-secretary of war to treat of their price." And so on.

At the end we read:

"Responsible Editor, Don José Salamanca. Printing-office of the Count de Vilches."

The government in vain endeavors to discover the author, and offers rewards to that effect. I have it from good authority, that he is an Englishman. Salamanca, Domenech, Collantes, Quinto, and Vista-Hermosa, come in for a large share of abuse; also the Duke of Riansares and the queen-mother. All the measures of the government are unsparingly criticised in its columns. In the number of this morning it is said:

"It seems that a forced loan of 180 millions is demanded. All that astonishes us, is, that the Señores Molins, Blaser, and Calderon de la Barca, should have associated themselves in this responsibility."

In another we read: "A painting has disappeared from the *Museo*. The Duchess of Riansares had it carried to her palace to copy, and has either kept or sold it."

This very painting, copied by the queen-mother with a degree of skill and fidelity which would do honor to a professional artist, and which copy I have seen in the ball-room of her palace, is now in the *Atelier* of the artist Madrazo, who is engaged in restoring it. If all the accusations printed in the columns of the *Murciélago* are equally well-founded, they are not worthy of much credit. But these columns, no doubt, produce a great effect upon the minds of the people.

Another number has come out, in which the throne itself is attacked; the queen is reminded of the attempt of *Merino*, and a change of dynasty is more than hinted at. The abuse of the president of the council, however, chiefly fills the columns of the *Bat.*

June —.

I had almost forgotten to mention the great procession on the day of *Corpus Christi*, when all the balconies were hung with draperies of extraordinary magnificence, and the sun shining on these vivid tints of scarlet, blue and gold, produced the most brilliant effect. The streets were crowded at an early hour, and the Calle Mayor especially presented an appearance really imposing and splendid. The state-coaches with the gorgeous liveries and gayly-caparisoned horses—the troops in their brilliant uniforms—the clergy in their vestments—the people in their bright-colored dresses—the ladies on the balconies, formed an ensemble of rich and varied coloring which would have charmed the eye of a painter. The *Santísimo* was carried under a magnificent canopy of crimson velvet and gold, all falling on their knees as it passed.

June 26th.

Their majesties went off this morning at four o'clock to the Escorial, which they are to visit on their way to La Granja; with the little princess, and a small suite. Two of the ministers, the Count of San-Luis and the Marquis of Molins, accompanied the royal party. The others follow in a few days to La Granja. The queen heard mass in her oratory before setting off. They reached the Escorial in four hours. The queen was received with great enthusiasm, and accompanied to the palace by a procession of young girls dressed in white, and strewing flowers before her. The monks whom she has lately restored to the Escorial, came out to meet her; and before entering the palace, she assisted at a solemn Te Deum in the church. Count A—— thinks of setting off for La Granja next week.

June 28th.

Tremendous agitation in Madrid! Early this morning news was brought to the Legation that the whole cavalry had revolted, with their general, Dulce! At their head is General O'Donnell. The minister of war, General Blaser, immediately sent for his colleagues to his department, where they are now holding a council. As I before mentioned to you, General Dulce, director of the cavalry, had already been strongly suspected of holding a traitorous correspondence with the discontented oppositionists who have been sent from Madrid. General Blaser, a frank soldier, informed him of these suspicions, and showed him several anonymous warnings which he had received on the subject. Dulce, with an affectation of wounded honor, assured Blaser, his hand upon his heart, that he would be loyal till death—and as a proof of his sincerity, confessed that he had received proposals from certain of the absent generals, which he had treated with all the scorn which they deserved.

General Blaser's suspicions were instantly lulled, and from that time forward he reposed the most entire confidence in the traitor. Meanwhile, General O'Donnell had been concealed ever since the 17th of January, sometimes in one house, sometimes in another, but always escaping the vigilance or rather the want of vigilance of the police; in close correspondence with the Generals Dulce, Messina, Serrano, and Manzerno, as well as with the Señores Rios Rosas, Cánovas, and Orlando. It appears that four months ago, the nomination of Dulce as director-general of the cavalry, filled the conspirators with hope, knowing, as they did, his character and opinions. Nor were they deceived. He accepted the post, and betrayed his trust.

Now that the conspiracy has broken forth, it is utterly astonishing to find how many were in the secret. Señor —— has given us this morning the whole history of the plot, as coolly as if he were relating some events which had occurred in the days of Rodolph of Hapsburg.

The first plan of the conspirators was to corrupt the troops. Cánovas, a friend of O'Donnell's, discovered that in the regiment of Estremadura were two discontented lieutenants. A conference was held with these men, who engaged themselves to gain over a certain number of the soldiers of that regiment, beginning with those under their immediate command. O'Donnell was at this time concealed in the house of the Marquis of Vega Armijo, but hearing that this place of retreat was suspected, he removed to that of Don Angel de los Rios in the Calle de Carbon; and finally to one in the Passage de la Ballesta, where he remained up to this memorable 28th of June.

Meanwhile Vega de Armijo was busily engaged in endeavoring to gain over the Brigadier Echagüe, colonel of the regiment of the Principe, and to persuade him to revolt with all the troops under his command, as soon as the conspiracy should be ripe. According to my informant, he did not succeed for some time, the brigadier expressing his horror at the idea of dishonoring himself by so disloyal an action. However a private interview with General O'Donnell removed his scruples.

While this underhand work was going on, O'Donnell fell ill with a nervous attack, and some alarming symptoms having appeared, it was necessary to call in a physician, of course one of the opposition party; and Dr. Seoane, a medical man of some eminence, was privately sent for. The illness of O'Donnell was at that time constantly spoken of in Madrid; he was regularly attended by this physician for a whole fortnight. Dr. Seoane was frequently followed by the police; yet O'Donnell remained undiscovered. Of course there are but two inferences to be drawn. Either they were wholly incompetent, or they were bribed to keep their eyes shut.

There is, however, a remarkable facility for concealment in the old houses in Madrid. The house where O'Donnell was hidden, in the Passage of La Ballesta, communicated with another, the rez-de-chaussée of which was occupied by one Allear, a tin-smith. This man was in O'Donnell's interests, and had the police entered the house where he was hidden, it was easy for the general to escape by this private passage into the neighboring house.

O'Donnell having recovered his health, and the conspirators considering their projects ripe for execution, it was resolved to profit by the first circumstance which should afford an excuse for conducting the troops outside the walls, as a *pronunciamento* within the city was too dangerous and doubtful an enterprise. The 13th of June was the day at first fixed upon by the conspirators for the revolt.

On that day, at half-past four in the morning, the cavalry, with Dulce at their head, were assembled for military exercises in the *Campo de Guardias*, and Echagüe, with the regiment of the Principe, occupied a post near the gate of Alcalá. At five o'clock O'Donnell left his retreat, and entered the carriage of Vega de Armijo, who had engaged to convey him in safety to the *Venta del Espíritu Santo*, about half a league from Madrid, where another carriage was in waiting to carry him to the village of Canillejas, where he was to wait for the troops. This time, however, the conspiracy was a failure. Three hours of fear and anxiety were passed by O'Donnell at Canillejas, in company with one officer, waiting for the troops, who never arrived; anxiously watching each cloud of dust, and in momentary expectation of being discovered and arrested. Dulce, whose instructions were not to undertake his march until he was joined by more troops, remained in the Campo de Guardias, commanding the evolutions of the cavalry, till the expected hour having passed and no auxiliaries arriving, he found himself obliged to return to the barracks and dismiss the troops. Echagüe, on his side, having also waited in vain till half-past eight, had no other resource but to follow the example of Dulce. The regiment of the Principe returned to their barracks, and the business of the day went on in Madrid as usual, the government little imagining the immediate danger from which they had escaped.

O'Donnell, disappointed and alarmed, got into the carriage which was waiting for him at Canillejas, returned to Madrid, and regained his hiding-place without being discovered. That night the conspirators held a meeting in a certain house in the Calle de Tudescos, and it was agreed that they had now gone too far to retreat, that too many persons were in the secret to prevent the possibility of its remaining undiscovered, and that as a second failure would be their death-blow, every thing must be risked to insure the success of the next attempt. They counted upon the cavalry, the regiment of the Principe, one battalion of the regiment of the *Reina Gobernadora*, and several of the officers of the regiment of Estremadura. It was proposed that the signal for revolt should be given within the walls of Madrid on the 23d of June; but as their chief reliance lay on the cavalry, a force very ineffective in the streets of a city, this proposal was *vetoed* by the majority. We must hope also, that even those reckless and ambitious men were not wholly destitute of the common feelings of humanity, and that they felt some reluctance at the idea of rendering Madrid a theatre of carnage and bloodshed.

Days passed on, and various measures were taken by the government, disadvantageous to the plans of the conspirators. Orders were given that the remaining battalion of the regiment of the Principe was to march on the 28th to Torrelaguna; the other had already been sent to garrison Toledo and Ciudad Real. One regiment of cavalry also had received orders to set off for Alcalá. In order to profit by the departure of the battalion of the Principe, the conspirators were of opinion that the revolt should be fixed for the morning of the 28th. Meanwhile one battalion of the regiment of the *Reina Gobernadora* had preceded the queen to La Granja, to await her arrival there; the other, with their commander Señor Cuadros, was in the barracks of San Mateo, in the city, and upon them the conspirators counted, although, as it afterwards appeared, this regiment remained faithful to the government.

About one in the morning of the 28th, Quesada, the military governor, began to conceive some suspicions of what was going on, and the conspirators had a moment of alarm, which almost induced them to abandon their enterprise. But it was too late. Too many were now compromised. It was evident that the suspicions of the government would speedily be aroused; and the enterprise must be carried forward at any risk.

A new kind of saddle had been made for the cavalry, and Dulce, under pretence of trying it, asked and obtained the permission of the minister of war to review the troops outside the walls. That very morning, at daybreak, Dulce passed the house of General Blaser, and seeing him on the balcony, called out: "Good morning, General: will you not accompany us?" "I would gladly," said Blaser, "but it is impossible; I have too much business on hand." "Well, Adios," said Dulce, "*Hasta luego!*"

At three in the morning this *loyal* officer led the cavalry towards the Campo de Guardias. At the same time the battalion of the Principe went out with Echagüe at their head. About an hour after, O'Donnell left Madrid by the gate of Bilbao, in the carriage of Vega de Armijo, who himself acted as coachman, and drove to the Church of Chambery, where he deposited his precious freight in another coach which awaited him there.

Already the cavalry were assembled in the *Campo de Guardias*, together with the battalion of the Principe, awaiting the arrival of the regiment of the Reina Gobernadora, until, finding that it did not appear, the officers ordered the troops to march towards Canillejas, where they arrived about half-past five, followed by the carriage containing O'Donnell. Here they received orders to halt; and their loyal chief, accompanied by the Generals Ros de Olano and Messina, informed the troops that they had revolted, and presented to them General O'Donnell, in a citizen's dress, as their commander-in-chief.

What the conduct of officers should be in a situation of this nature, there can be no doubt of; but the soldiers find themselves in a terrible predicament. Accustomed to obey their superiors blindly, unacquainted with politics, and not knowing on which side their duty lies, their position is worthy of pity. These constant military revolutions must necessarily destroy the principle of honor at its very root; and the men, aware that they will be punished or rewarded according to the party which has the upper hand, decide for that which appears the strongest.

One officer alone, the Count de la Cimera, colonel of the regiment of Santiago, refused to follow the rebels, and was permitted to retire with his son, an officer in the same regiment. Another disappointment, besides that occasioned by the loyalty of the regiment of la Reina Gobernadora, awaited the rebel chiefs. The regiment of Estremadura, on whose assistance they had counted, also remained faithful to the government. At four that same morning, an attempt had been made by some of the officers to leave the city secretly with their respective companies. This was prevented by the bravery and firmness of Captain Fernandez, who commanded the *Guardia de Prevencion* (Police Guard), and positively refused to allow the troops to pass the gates, until he had received an order to that effect. Perez, a lieutenant in the regiment, discharged a pistol at Fernandez, and wounded him in the head; but finding that he still kept his post, savagely struck him with the butt-end of the pistol, until he fell, bathed in blood.

Then a tumult arose, Perez and one Segui, and others, endeavoring to open the gates; the soldiers of the guard making desperate efforts to keep them closed. In the midst of the confusion, the soldiers refusing to obey the orders of their superiors, returned to Madrid in haste and confusion, and presented themselves at their quarters. The Lieutenants Perez and Segui made their escape, and contrived to join the rebel forces. Various officers were put under arrest; amongst others, Captain Montero, who, with one of the companies, had eluded the vigilance of the guard, and passed the gates, having returned to discover the cause of the delay of his companions, was disarmed and arrested by orders of his colonel.

" Treachery, thy name is *Dulce!* " said M——, throwing himself into an arm-chair in the chancellerie. " O'Donnell was opposed to the government. He had disobeyed orders—had set the example of a breach of military discipline. He and the Conchas are desperate. Nothing but a revolution can bring them into power, or restore their forfeited honors.

It is true that, by this revolt, they more than justify the severity of the government, but at least they were not, like Dulce, in its confidence, intrusted with its secret measures, holding a high and responsible situation under them. Neither friends nor foes can excuse his conduct, for even his own party, while making use of him, must despise him."

Of course all sorts of rumors, true and false, are in circulation. The absence of the queen and two of her ministers at this juncture, makes the position very critical. A telegraphic message has been sent to the Escorial, requesting their immediate return, but their return in safety is doubted. It is reported that the cavalry, headed by Dulce and O'Donnell, have gone towards Alcalá de Henares, in hopes of raising two more regiments of cavalry, destined to march upon the Escorial, where the rebel chiefs hope to force the queen to sign whatever they please to impose. But it is more generally believed that their forces are not sufficient to permit them to take so desperate a step. It is said that the rebels have cut the wires of the telegraphs, so that the queen may not be aware of her danger.

The city has remained wonderfully quiet until now, but the people look sad and uneasy, and the Puerta del Sol and the Calle de Alcalá begin to be crowded in expectation of the return of the queen. It is said that the agents of O'Donnell are trying to raise the people. Towards evening the Calle de Alcalá presented a strange aspect. Expectation and anxiety were painted on every countenance. Many fully believe the report that O'Donnell would attack Madrid that night. Soldiers are posted at the gates, round the palace, and at the corners of the streets. One rumor is, that the president of the council and the minister of the navy have been attacked and shot on their way from the Escorial. We have been at Count G——'s, who lives in the Calle de Alcalá, and whose windows consequently command a good view of all that occurs. He had just returned from the Calle del Barquillo, where he had gone to offer his house to the family of the minister of state in case of any danger, and had passed up there with great difficulty. The captain-general, Lara, has declared Madrid in a state of siege.

29th.

Last night, about eleven o'clock, when anxiety was at its highest, all the bells of the city pealed forth in concert. At the same time, the sound of wheels and the tramp of horses, and loud shouts of "Viva la Reyna!" mingled with the music of the Royal March, broke in upon the lugubrious silence in which Madrid had been sunk for a few hours. The queen had passed the gates in safety. The entrance was very fine—twelve or thirteen coaches, and a splendid troop, the balconies crowded with ladies. The ministers had gone to the gates to meet her majesty, and a council was held in the palace that night. The Marquis —— told Count A—— this morning, that the queen had returned, "covered with dust, and full of courage." The journey had necessarily been slow, on account of the escort which accompanied the royal party the whole way without changing horses. The ministers, he says, tendered their resignation, which the queen positively refused to accept, saying that, at the present juncture, it would be regarded as a proof of weakness.

The following royal decree has issued from the war department, where the council of ministers is held at present.

"The unheard-of disloyalty of General Dulce, who, ungratefully abusing not only his authority, but the confidence which we had deigned to place in him, has caused the revolt of a part of the troops whose direction had been confided to him, must be treated with all the rigor of the law. We have therefore resolved to deprive General Dulce from this time of all his offices, honors and crosses, and to blot out his name from the list of officers, reserving his future judgment for a Council of War.

Given in the palace this 28th of June, 1854.

Signed by the royal hand.

A second decree declares the Peninsula in a state of siege, establishes military commissions in all the provinces, and takes measures for punishing all persons found guilty of conspiring against public order.

An address to the people of Madrid is published by General Lara, the military governor, expressing the horror which should be felt by all loyal subjects at the conspiracy of General Dulce;—and the perfect confidence reposed by her majesty in the loyalty of her people and in the fidelity of her troops, &c.

There is also a proclamation from the same source declaring that a permanent Council of War is established in the Casa de Correos (general post-office) now occupied by the *Ministerio de la Gobernacion*, for the trial of all who directly or indirectly shall conspire against public order; forbidding the reunion of more than three persons at a time in the public streets, prohibiting the use of arms, without exception of persons, and the circulation of all printed papers tending to propagate alarming reports.

Another decree deprives the revolted generals of their rank, crosses and honors. General Blaser is himself to head the troops that are going out against the rebels who are supposed to be encamped in the neighborhood of Madrid, near the village of Vicálvaro.

Last evening, the queen reviewed the troops in the Prado.

In the morning a proclamation had been issued, addressed to the army, to the effect that her majesty, offended in her person and dignity by the revolt of certain disloyal individuals, would place herself and her throne under the protection of her faithful and valiant soldiers.

The queen arrived in an open carriage, accompanied by the king and princess, and escorted by her guards; General Blaser riding by the door of her carriage. The Prado was crowded—a fine sight, but a melancholy one under the circumstances. The queen looked sad, and her eyes were swollen as if from tears. She gave crosses to some of the men—raised one to the rank of an officer, and after the review, went to the barracks, and tasted their supper—wished to send them a magnificent supper from the palace, but was advised to send them money instead—to which advice she yielded.

It is said on good authority, that Colonel Nulans del Bosch was sent in the name of the government to treat with the rebel generals; offering them, on the part of the queen, pardon and the restoration of their rank on condition of their returning to Madrid, and delivering up General Dulce, to be tried by a Council of War. As may be supposed, these offers were not accepted. O'Donnell and his party have gone too far to recede; and would consider any thing preferable to the humiliation of throwing themselves on the clemency of those whom they have injured. It is also affirmed that Nulans finding his embassy unsuccessful, dined with the officers, and offered them his services!

A document was then drawn up by the revolted generals, addressed to the queen, setting forth the causes which had induced them to take up arms, and their resolution not to lay them down, until the present ministry was dismissed, and the government had "satisfied the exigencies of public opinion, and conformed to the principles of liberty, morality and justice;" high-sounding words by which the authors of all revolutions endeavor to justify their rebellion against lawful authority. This document was intrusted to Nulans del Bosch.

Meanwhile rumors are industriously spread abroad, that the troops of the government, especially a large part of the artillery, will only keep up the appearances of a combat, when led against the rebels, and that the cavalry will immediately join their companions. These rumors are said to be firmly believed by the revolted generals, and are circulated by them amongst their soldiers.

30th.

Reports follow reports, but little reliance can be placed on any thing that is rumored at present. This morning the rebel troops were said to be advancing on the city. It was a melancholy sight to see the regiments go off with their generals, Blaser, Lara, and Vista-Hermosa; the infantry (followed to the gates by their wives and children); the fine cavalry regiment of Villaviciosa, the civil guard, and various pieces of artillery. Nothing is more disheartening than the aspect of a civil war. Meanwhile a report is spread that Valladolid Saragossa, Victoria and Burgos have revolted, but this is no doubt an invention of the opposition party. O'Donnell has issued a proclamation "in the name of the queen," dispensing all who shall join him, from two years' service.

The streets are crowded, though quite orderly. All business is suspended; people go about asking questions which no one can answer. About eight o'clock this evening we heard the beat of drums, the tramp of cavalry, and the sound of military music. There was a universal buzz of voices, "The queen's troops have been driven back by the rebels!" If that be so, then at least the report of their having deserted to the enemy is false. Then—"There has been immense bloodshed, but the result on both sides remains doubtful." Finally—"The queen's troops have gained a complete victory."

From the camp at Vicálvaro, the following was received from General Blaser. "The garrison of Madrid is a model of bravery and enthusiasm. It has destroyed the revolted cavalry; both infantry and artillery receiving a close fire from them, and from the regiment of Villaviciosa. The camp is full of dead bodies, wounded men and horses; many prisoners are taken—amongst others Colonel Garrigo, who commanded the *Farnesio* regiment of cavalry. The troops have not ceased to cry 'Viva la Reyna!' The rebels are dispersing. I have no time for more."

Not only was the news of their desertion false, but they fought like lions, as indeed did the poor soldiers on the other side, casting themselves into the very mouth of the cannon, in their endeavors to take at least one of these formidable engines. They fell like sheep in every direction.

The queen and her ministers had passed an anxious day in the palace; when the news of the victory arrived, she ordered her carriage, and insisted upon going out to meet and thank the troops. Just as she was stepping into it, an aide-de-camp rode into the court full gallop, with the news that her troops had been intercepted by the rebels; and the poor queen sadly retraced her steps up the great staircase. But soon after arrived General Blaser, and explained the mistake which had occurred in the darkness, by which her troops had turned upon one of their own regiments, mistaking them for the insurgents, and had wounded several of the poor fellows. The news of the revolt in the provinces is also false, so far at least; assurances of fidelity having been received from every quarter, and especially from the cities supposed to have revolted.

CHAPTER XXX.

The Rebels disheartened—False Reports—The Diplomatic Corps congratulate the Queen—"Justice, Liberty, and Morality" in the Rebel Camp—Retreat of the Insurgents—Visit to the Battle-Field—Assurances of Loyalty—The Insurgents desperate—Colonel Garrigo pardoned—Letters from his Family—Energy of Salamanca—Dinner Party—Political Discussion—Becomes Uproarious—Blaser and the Insurgents—Public Works—Parties—The Duke of Bailen.

July 1.

THE rebels have abandoned Alcalá de Henares, and all the points which they occupied yesterday in the neighborhood of the city. To-day they are said to have cut the telegraph and destroyed large portions of the railroad leading to Aranjuez. They have halted at Valdemoro, about three leagues from Madrid, and are said to be living in a state of constant alarm; several officers have deserted the ranks, and have returned to Madrid, and amongst others the cashier of the regiment of Santiago, with all the funds under his charge. Dulce and O'Donnell are said to be greatly dispirited, having calculated upon the desertion of the garrison from Madrid.

Meanwhile, the city remains perfectly quiet, but the *Café Suizo* has presented the appearance of a nest of hornets ever since the 28th. About two in the morning, the regiment of María Cristina, tramping hurriedly through the streets, excited a fresh alarm. A report had been spread that the insurgents were to attack Madrid that night. The queen and her ministers passed the night in a state of anxiety caused by these rumors. The queen is said to be out of spirits, and tormented by false reports, purposely spread to frighten and excite the people. No enemy has appeared, and the troops, fatigued from having been under arms all night, have returned to their quarters.

July 3d.

The intrigues in the palace are in full force. Some surround the queen, entreating her to dismiss her ministers; others endeavor to frighten her by false reports. The diplomatic corps went to congratulate her on the successful result of the affair at Vicálvaro. She received them in her dressing-gown, which I heard criticised, but no Spanish woman ever thinks of her toilette when she is agitated. The heat has been excessive. This evening a tremendous thunderstorm cleared the atmosphere. The troops are encamped at Aranjuez, their chiefs said to be greatly dispirited. If all fail, they will probably retreat to Portugal. M—— does not believe in the fidelity of the provinces, and thinks the conspiracy very widely extended. O'Donnell has taken up his quarters in the house of Salamanca at Aranjuez, and is making free with his champagne. His troops are said to be very much discouraged. He gives them extra pay and plenty of wine to keep up their spirits. Salamanca takes this ravaging of his cellars very coolly. Several regiments entered the city yesterday—an agreeable sight, as we have now some force in Madrid.

A letter received by the minister of the treasury from the Director General *de Rentas estancadas* (of monopolized goods) in Aranjuez, gives some curious details of the ideas of "justice, liberty, and morality," which prevail in O'Donnell's camp. The insurgents surrounded the office, and forced the director to deliver up all the funds in his possession. Shortly after, he was ordered to appear before O'Donnell, and by him sent to one Don Leon Medma who holds the office of intendant to the forces, who informed him that more money was necessary. Upon his assurances that he had no more in his power, the *estanqueros* (those who retail the government tobacco) were sent for, and forced by threats and violence to deliver up the sum of two thousand reals, the imposts of the tobacco, which he was obliged to give them. O'Donnell then proceeded to order that all the tobacco should be given up for the use of his soldiers, who having already brought a large supply from Alcalá, obtained money by selling it at their own prices to the peasants of Aranjuez.

On the 4th, according to the letter of the unfortunate functionary, the cavalry with their four generals, evacuated the premises by the break of day, leaving the infantry to block up the roads, and to prevent any one from leaving Aranjuez. The letter is accompanied by a note of the money and effects of which the office has been pillaged.

A committee of young men are meanwhile left in Madrid, whose object is to excite the people, and keep up a constant agitation in the public mind. Their names are Cánovas, Tasara, Vega de Armijo and Rios, while one Ortiz de Pivedo is charged with performing the duties of a courier between the rebel camp and these agents.

5th.

The insurgents are retreating towards Andalusia. Blaser goes out to-morrow at the head of a large force to pursue them. The regiment of the *Reyna Gobernadora* went out this morning—the men in good spirits. Several rewards have been given to those who distinguished themselves at Vicálvaro; the grand cross of Charles III. to General Campuzano; that of Ysabel the Catholic to Field-marshal Quesada; to General Lara, the grand cross of the military order of San Fernando. The Count of Vista-Hermosa is raised to the rank of lieutenant-general. Many question the prudence of rewarding men for simply doing their duty.

M—— proposed that we should ride out this morning, and visit the field of battle, which is but a few leagues from Madrid. Though most of the spoils have been cleared away, and the dead bodies removed, we still found many traces of a bloody affray. There were dead horses not yet carried away, saddles broken and blackened, pieces of clothing and soldiers' caps matted with blood. Fifty-eight wounded men have been carried to the military hospital, the greater part belonging to the rebels, none of whom are very dangerously wounded. As M—— is an old acquaintance of Colonel Garrigo's, he requested admission into the hospital to pay him a visit. We found him in a hall destined for the officers, guarded by a sentinel, and surrounded by every comfort. His wound is very slight, but his one eye gives him rather a sinister appearance. Beside him was Don Fernando Prerraro, another officer of the same regiment of *Farnesio.* He and Garrigo were freely allowed to receive the visits of their friends and companions in arms.

Several of the newspapers in giving an account of the action at Vicálvaro, are liberal enough to do full justice to the bravery of the revolted troops. "All agree," says the *España*, "that it was difficult to know which to admire most—the headlong courage of the enemy's cavalry, or the serenity and steadiness of our own cavalry and infantry."

The fate of Garrigo, who will inevitably and, according to military law, deservedly, be condemned to suffer death as a traitor, excites great sympathy amongst the queen's troops. Much interest will be made to save him, and the queen is always ready to pardon. It will be natural that

General Blaser, who must feel deeply irritated at finding himself deceived on all hands, should be opposed to any act of lenity towards this officer; but few capital punishments will take place in the reign of Doña Ysabel Segunda, so long as she really governs.

Letters have arrived for the government from all the captain-generals of the various military districts throughout Spain, protesting the indignation which the disloyalty of the revolted generals and troops has produced in all the forces under their command, and their enthusiastic desire to assist in the defence of the throne and of public order, wherever and by whomsoever they may be threatened. The civil governors daily send assurances of the "unalterable tranquillity" which reigns in every city throughout the provinces, and express their indignant surprise at the treachery and ingratitude of the conspirators, and the deep sentiment of irritation which universally exists against the disturbers of the public peace. These letters are published, and signed by the different governors. Yet the knowing ones amongst the opposition party sneer at what they term the blind confidence of the government. But if all this is a mass of treachery, in whom can they confide? If all the governors, civil and military, are so many *Dulces*, then honor in Spain has become a name—loyalty a mere pretence.

One does not require to be possessed of the wisdom of Solomon, to observe that the result of the action at Vicálvaro has disappointed several of the grandees. In their blind hatred of San-Luis, they rejoiced at the prospect of a revolution, which they fancied must at least produce a change of ministry, forgetting that, like Samson when hurling on his enemies the gates of Gaza, they are liable to be crushed themselves along with their foes.

Blaser went out on the 7th. In the opinion of many,

he should have gone sooner, and followed up the defeat at Vicálvaro. This delay has given the insurgents time to recover from the shock, and their chiefs time to combine some new plans. Many desertions continue to take place from their ranks.

The family of Colonel Garrigo has had an audience of the queen. She and they wept together. She is resolved to pardon him, at least the capital punishment. Wise or otherwise on her part, this exercise of compassion comes with good grace from an offended sovereign and a woman.

The Casino is now the focus of political discussions. Both there, and at the Café Suisse, the most important questions are argued freely and publicly. I have seen groups of men openly sneering at what they call the infatuation and blindness of the government, first in having trusted the professions of Dulce, and next in believing the assertions of the governors of the provinces. It is now generally known that the discontented officers have been working zealously and underhandedly for the last six months at least, to bring about a revolution—and that the military insurrection in Saragossa was promptly put down, merely from the want of chiefs to head it. Now these are not wanting.

Meanwhile, however, the situation of the insurgents is desperate, unless they strike some unexpected *coup de main.* General Serrano has joined them with *six* servants instead of the magnificent force upon which he counted. Some wise heads are of opinion that in this position, they will coalesce with the *progresistas*, and call in Espartero to their aid. But this will be a step replete with mortification to the O'Donnell party.

This state of things is sad to contemplate. The love of change has grown into a mania. Even if tranquillity ensues, it will probably be of short duration. O'Donnell has published a manifesto, which shows that he is reduced to adopt extreme measures. He decrees *en Souverain* that the national guard shall be restored. This measure, entirely at variance with his political principles, is calculated to render him extremely popular with the masses. The diligences now travel through Spain without passengers. Parties of robbers make all travelling unsafe.

The queen has signed the pardon of Colonel Garrigo. A letter from his wife and family is published in the Herald, expressing their gratitude to her majesty and to those who have sympathized with him in his troubles. The first is to the editor of the Herald:

"We but fulfil a sacred and agreeable duty in sending you a copy of the letter in which we return thanks to her majesty for the act of clemency by which she has dried the tears of a disconsolate family; and we should disobey the warmest impulse of our grateful hearts were we not to profit by this occasion to manifest our deep gratitude towards the government, which has comprehended and carried into effect the magnanimous sentiments of her majesty;—towards the corps and individuals of the army who have made so many efforts in favor of an unfortunate officer;—and towards those of all classes who have shown him such lively sympathy, and such instinctive hope that his blood would not be shed;—and in the impossibility of manifesting these feelings to each individual separately, as we should wish to do, we hasten to employ this means of doing so to all.

Your obedient servants *L. S. M. B.*

Francisca Montero de Garrigo,
Dolores Garrigo de Capablanco,
Encarnacion Garrigo,
Antonio Garrigo,
Joaquin Maria Garrigo,
Raphael Capablanco.

The letter to the queen is as follows:

"Madam:

"The undersigned would be wanting in the sacred duty imposed upon her by the magnanimity with which your Majesty received her petitions in favor of her husband, Don Antonio María Garrigo, were she not to hasten to manifest to your Majesty her deep and eternal gratitude for your Majesty's goodness.

"Your Majesty, by an act of innate and unequalled clemency, has calmed the grief of a desolate family, has dried up their tears, and has averted from them an incalculable tissue of misfortunes. One word pronounced by your Majesty has raised them to joy, in the very midst of their grief and despair.

"Nor is this all, madam, that they owe to your Majesty. Even before this was done, they saw tears flow from your Majesty's eyes, caused by participation in their grief. Your Majesty then lavished upon an unfortunate family the most tender and touching consolations, and made them conceive the grateful hope that their misfortune might not be consummated; and the value of such kindness, madam, the deep impression which it leaves in the hearts of those capable of appreciating it, can only be conceived by one who, like she who addresses your Majesty, has obtained such signal favors.

"She and her children will never forget them. Her life is your Majesty's; and as long as they exist, they will rejoice to publish to the world all that they owe to your Majesty, and their own unbounded gratitude. God grant, madam, that their prayers may obtain from the Almighty, that He may pour forth upon your Majesty all the blessings which such magnanimity and clemency deserve.

"At the royal feet of your Majesty,

"Francesca Montero de Garrigo."

Whatever misfortunes may befall the queen in these turbulent days—whatever calumnies may be propagated against her—whatever faults even she may be led to commit—the remembrance of these acts of clemency will always throw a gentle radiance round her name, and will be like a healing balm to her own mind,—like a ray of light on which to turn her eyes, in the darkest hour that may yet overtake her.

June 10th.

And now once more Madrid is as quiet as if nothing had occurred—as if Dulce and O'Donnell had gone on a hunting-party, followed by Blaser with the intention of joining in the chase. No sooner had O'Donnell and his disorderly troops abandoned Aranjuez, than Salamanca, with that wonderful promptitude and energy which make him so remarkable, instantly began to have the railroad repaired, which the rebel forces had destroyed, and the telegraph renewed; and such was the celerity with which he proceeded, that although whole *kilomètres* of the railroad had been dragged off, and the telegraph cut in twenty places, by the 6th every thing was in order—the queen's troops went by railway to Velasqüilla, and the telegraph is in use as before.

Two solemn *funciones* have been held at the church of Atocha, by orders and at the expense of the queen—the one for the repose of the souls of those who fell at Vicálvaro; the other for the peace and tranquillity of the kingdom, and for the cure of the wounded.

Dined yesterday at S——'s. This time the conversation was purely political. *Bisque* and *vol-aux-vents* went down ungrateful throats—hock and burgundy only sharpened the tongues of the drinkers. As usual, the guests were of every political *color*, consequently there were many discordant notes in the general harmony. Of course, the late revolt, its causes, its probable result, formed the theme—mingled with criticisms or eulogiums of the actual administration, according to the speaker. During dinner, and while the servants were present, there was only a slight skirmishing between the opponents; but no sooner was the coast clear than R——, a personal friend of Señor Collantes, struck the war-signal by qualifying the late insurrection as the abortive effort of half a dozen discontented and ambitious men. Murmurs of disapprobation from some—of cordial assent from others. Our host smiled innocently, and lighted a cigar. "I repeat it," said R——, "the criminal ambition of half a dozen generals, aided by the suggestions of a few political men, more criminal if possible than they, has alone caused that revolt, which is another stain upon our history. We all foresaw it—the government were perfectly aware of the names of those who were conspiring against order and against the throne." "And took no measures to prevent the revolt?" said one. "The conspiracy was too widely extended. They could not make their ministry a reign of terror." "But why employ Dulce? Why give him so golden an opportunity? It was putting a sack of money in the way of a robber." "To their honor be it spoken, they would not believe that a Spanish officer could be so black a traitor." "But why do they not resign?" "Because this is not the moment—and also because their names are a mere pretext. It is absurd to suppose that this conspiracy is directed against the ministry. These men fly at higher game. Is it with this ministry that the system of opposition began? As San-Luis said with truth when he addressed the Senate: You have only to go back to the ministry of Narvaez, and you will see the same game played, and the same opposition on the part of those who are now in rebellion. It is true, their ambition was then only in its bud; but the same tendencies may be seen under the last ministry of the Duke of Valencia as those which have led to this military revolt. During that cabinet, we all heard the same declamation as now upon "illegality, violence, and immorality." Then came the cabinet of Bravo Murillo, and for a little while the opposition seemed quieted, and their members accepted high military posts. But when their services were dispensed with, the opposition arose with greater force than ever. The laws, the throne, the constitution, *morality*, their favorite watchword, all were in danger, and as usual, they alone were the champions of these sacred objects, and this solely because their self-love was wounded. Next comes the Alcoy cabinet, endeavoring to conciliate all the discordant elements of the Moderado party, and to give them all a share in the public administration. The constitution was reformed in a liberal sense, and perfect liberty of the press decreed. Did the opposition of these very generals cease? On the contrary, they declared war to the knife against the ministers, who in self-defence then treated them as enemies. Then came fresh declamations, fresh accusations, and the most innocent acts of the cabinet were loaded with opprobrium. The Alcoy cabinet ceases to exist, and we have the Lersundi ministry. They desire the union of the Moderado party; they endeavor by moderation, clemency, and concessions, to extinguish the fires of discord. What is the result? These concessions are supposed to proceed from weakness, and the oppositionists endeavor to embitter the lives of the ministry, in return for their good intentions. Their favorite plan is to trammel the march of the cabinets, as may be seen in the absurd accusations raised against them, after the decision on the subject of railroads.

"At last comes the San-Luis cabinet, and here the system of conciliation is carried to its fullest extent. The members of the opposition are favored with the confidence of the government—the Cortes is convoked—useful reforms are proposed—there is tolerance for all opinions, respect for legitimate ambition,—all services are made useful. A period strictly constitutional is inaugurated, and the spirit of reform is visible in every act of the cabinet. The governments flattered themselves that they had disarmed their opponents; that in future they would be met by a rational, prudent opposition in the name of principle. And what has been the result? The opposition became more furious than ever. Their benefits were received with ingratitude. To the idea of conciliation their opponents answered with a cry of war. Nothing was heard but passion, and an unmasked resolution to dispute the authority of the government, and to obtain the power for themselves. Their ambition, grown desperate, burst all bounds, and could no longer contain its bitterness; until gradually it has broken forth into open rebellion, a cause of scandal to the whole civilized world, by the total subversion of every principle of order, discipline, and morality; leaving a blot on the reputation of our army, disturbing the peace of the country, paralyzing its interests, and committing exactions worthy of robbers upon the people, forming an absurd contrast to the great words of morality and public welfare for ever in their mouths. No; depend upon it, the ministry are a mere pretext. What these men aim at, is to humble the throne; it is against the throne that these conspiracies are directed.

"These germs of demoralization which have now been sown—this breach of discipline, without which an army cannot exist—this vandalism, which plunders villages, and procures contributions at the point of the bayonet; which destroys the public works, which pillages inoffensive individuals, because they will not make common cause with their treason; all these scandals, in short, which we have seen within these last few days,—what is their true cause? Here there is no respectable principle, because principles of that nature are incompatible with crime and disorder; there is no self-sacrifice, or there would be no rebellion. The cause is evident—the miserable and criminal ambition of half a dozen generals."

R—— had talked himself out of breath, and continued to speak, in spite of numerous interruptions. Then he leaned back on his chair, and was presently lost in a cloud of smoke, from which he never again emerged, so far as I observed.

Then arose a true Babel of tongues; wholesale abuse of the ministry, diatribes against the Governor Quinto—sneers at his proclamations on one hand—on the other, eulogiums of the San-Luis cabinet, a warm defence of all their measures, and denunciations against military traitors.

"For my part," said the grave Conde de C——, who had been talking apart with S——a during all the uproar, "I take no part in politics. I care very little for the ministers personally, having but a slight acquaintance with any of them, though I am of opinion that in point of talent they form a remarkable combination. But be this as it may, I abhor and deprecate these military revolutions, which make our race a by-word throughout Europe, and which almost make me ashamed of the name of Spaniard."

"*Caramba!*" said a little bilious-faced man, with a hairy countenance; "so we are to sit with our arms folded, and smile benignantly at all these corruptions, and submit to have the press trammelled, María Cristina enriched at the expense of the country." Here a number of voices chimed in. "Arbitrary government, political gangrene, corrupt administration, fundamental reform, liberty of the press, the *knout* of the *polacos*," &c., were the most distinguishable words. There was, in fact, such an uproar, that it was surprising to see them, half an hour afterwards, shake hands and depart in peace.

The weather is now extremely warm, but not oppressive. The royal circle, no doubt, regret that they are forced to relinquish their projected visit to La Granja, at least for the present. The Marquis Turgot returned to Madrid on account of these disturbances. He had gone to try the effect of mineral waters for his lameness. The Fuente Castellana and the Prado are now crowded to an advanced hour of the night. Every thing in appearance is the same as before the 28th of June. For the first few days succeeding the revolt, there were no carriages there and no ladies. Men with anxious faces and a hurried look walked along in close conference, with an air quite unlike the usual easy and contented style observable in the frequenters of the Prado. But now the chairs placed along the salon are all occupied, and groups sit there *al fresco*, till eleven or twelve o'clock at night.

Nevertheless, it may be imagination; but it seems to me that there is an uneasy and distrustful look in people generally. Blaser has not yet come up with the insurgents, who retreat before him. It seems that on the 4th, O'Donnell and his troop left Tembleque, and directed their course to Manzanares, about twenty-two leagues from Aranjuez, from whence he directed his bulletin, announcing his intention of re-establishing the national militia. News has arrived from Cuenca, the capital of the province of that name, distant twenty-nine leagues from Madrid, that one Buceta, at the head of a party of insurgents, had entered the city, and taken possession of it in the name of O'Donnell, had driven out the guard, and filled the inhabitants with fear and anxiety. It appears that the authorities were taken by surprise; totally unaware of the approach of this band of rebels, who consist, it is said, of armed peasants from Madrid and the environs. It is supposed that O'Donnell, unable to reduce them to any kind of military discipline, has permitted them to do a little business on their own account. The principal body of the insurgents are retiring towards Andalusia, followed by General Blaser.

The democratic party here are evidently alternating between hope and fear. The news from the provinces is eagerly read. Printed papers are circulated with the news constantly received from the governors, containing assurances of the perfect tranquillity which reigns every where, but they are read with distrust. Yesterday, at the Puerta del Sol, I saw a young lady, who was walking down the Calle Mayor, desire her attendant to buy a proclamation which one of the blind men was hawking about. As she stopped for a moment to read it, a man said to her, "Señorita, *me da lástima*, it makes me sorry to see you spoil your pretty eyes reading such lies!"

The great works going on at the Puerta del Sol, which it is to be supposed will embellish the city when concluded, and which in the mean time give occupation to numerous workmen, are probably among the most unpopular measures of the government. The loungers have no other place so convenient for them to congregate in. Mason work, lime and dust, make it unpleasant to remain there any length of time in this warm season. Then the clock is taken down, a great resource for the idle. Two young men were smoking there as I stopped yesterday to look at the works. "*Que barbaridad*," said one, "to have no clock! One never knows the hour. I lost the *Coro de los Alguaziles* at the Circo yesterday." "Have you no watch?" said the other. "*Toma!*" said his friend. "Do you expect a man to be at the trouble of taking out his watch every moment?"

July 15th.

News of some slight troubles in Valencia. The governor writes: "Yesterday was dispersed a party of one hundred insurgents, twenty-one of whom were taken prisoners, amongst them one of the ringleaders. I am not aware of the existence of one other rebel in the district under my command." There are one or two other little affairs of the same sort, proving that the "perfect tranquillity," of which the government sent so many assurances, has been slightly disturbed. It is already a remarkable fact that the example given in the capital should have produced so little effect in the provinces. I was present yesterday at a conversation between Count A—— and a gentleman from Bayonne, who assured the count that, some time before the San-Luis ministry came into power, General Concha, being then at Bayonne, expressed his firm determination to use all his efforts to bring about a revolution; and that on his return from Madrid, when he passed through the same city full of wrath and indignation, he assured the same gentleman that a revolution would break forth in a very short time,—a proof, if any were wanting, that a change of ministry is a mere pretext.

Unhappy Spain! thus torn to pieces by her own children. Here we have a Republican party—a Carlist party—a party for the accession of Don Pedro Quinto of Portugal—a Montpensier party, and a loyal party, who will defend the dynasty of Doña Ysabel Segunda. The Republican party is small; and as for the Montpensier party, the duke, with that practical good sense which he inherits from his father, has publicly declared that his wife renounces for herself and her children all pretensions to the throne of Spain, under any circumstances. The Conchas are supposed to favor the Portuguese plan. Meanwhile the insurgents continue to retreat before General Blaser, levying contributions as they pass, and quartering themselves and their horses wherever they find it convenient. As many have deserted and few have joined them, and as in spite of the money forwarded to them by Sevillano the rich banker, and others, their funds are said to be very low—it seems probable that they will, however unwillingly, throw themselves into the arms of the Progresistas, and obtain the coalition of Espartero.

July 16th.

The governor of the province of Cuenca is dismissed from his office. Buceter and his party have evacuated the city. The minister of war has arrived at Bailen, a city celebrated as being the scene of the victory gained over the French by the Spaniards under their celebrated general, Don Francisco Castaños, afterwards created Duke of Bailen, in which the French lost three thousand men, and had twenty thousand soldiers and seven generals taken prisoners. It is pleasant to repose for one moment amidst all the scenes of treachery now passing before our eyes, and to reflect upon the loyalty and disinterestedness of this brave old general, who died loaded with years and honors but a few months ago, at the advanced age of ninety-seven, scarcely leaving sufficient funds for his interment. But magnificent funeral honors were rendered him at the expense of the queen, who herself accompanied the cortege, and his memory lives enshrined in the hearts of the people, as well as in that of the sovereign.

The old duke was as pious as he was brave and honorable, and never failed to assist daily at early mass, frequently taking upon himself the part of assistant to the priest. I am told that, on one occasion, when the usual curate was not in attendance, and his place was taken by a young priest to whom the duke was unknown, he assisted as usual, being then upwards of ninety. When they entered the sacristy, after mass, this priest, turning impatiently to the sacristan, said, "I will thank you not to employ this old man again to serve at mass. He is so slow, that I am perfectly out of patience with him." "Father," said the sacristan, "this is his excellency the Duke of Bailen!" The priest was confused, and stammered out some excuses. "No matter," said the old duke, laughing; "it is near seventy-five years since I have been scolded, and I rather like it from its rarity." The old Duke of Castro-Terreños, now ninety-seven, is the last remaining veteran who is contemporary with General Castaños.

CHAPTER XXXI

Bursting of the Storm—Resignation of the Ministry—Insurrection in Madrid—Fury and Violence of the Mob—Plundering—The new Ministry—Destruction of Life and Property—Terror and Dismay—Juntas—Periodicals—Inflammatory Addresses—Patriotic Orgies—Flight of the Administration—The Fugitives.

July 18th.

THE storm has come! The clouds that have been gathering on the political horizon have rolled together, and are now pouring down their phials of wrath on this misguided land. On the 16th news arrived from the provinces, was hawked about the streets, and greedily devoured by the multitude. Catalonia had *pronounced;* and at Barcelona the captain-general himself had headed the movement! In the Basque provinces, and in Arragon, the Revolution had declared itself. The cavalry regiment of Montesa, which had received orders to join General Blaser, had refused to obey their chiefs, and had gone to join the camp of the insurgents.

It seems that the ministry immediately took their determination, and having assembled in the State department, resolved that no pretext should be afforded, on their part at least, for a civil war. At half-past twelve they were received by her majesty, and gave in their resignation, which the queen, willingly or otherwise, had no choice but to accept. No sooner had this news circulated, which was with the quickness of an electric shock, than a kind of *sourde* agitation was visible throughout Madrid. Groups collected in the

Puerta del Sol and in the mercantile parts of the city. There seemed a general expectation of some unusual occurrence. Printed papers began to be circulated, and crowds collected round the venders of these inflammable productions. Still no one seemed to fear any outbreak amongst the people. It was rather supposed that the resignation of the ministry would give sufficient satisfaction, and that every thing would pass off quietly. Still those "hojas volantes" (flying leaves) were dispersed abroad; each café had its orator, each group its tribune, and it appeared to me very evident that a storm was brewing in the atmosphere.

In a few hours it was known that the queen had named General Córdova president of the council, and had charged him to form a new cabinet. This nomination gave satisfaction to no party. It was one of those temporizing measures which rarely succeed, when taken in any great emergency. Neither his talents nor his political opinions were sufficiently marked to enable him to guide the helm of state in the storm that was approaching. A bull-fight had been announced for this day—no doubt with premeditation. The *plaza* was crowded, and before the *spectacle* had proceeded very far, some of the *manolos* called for the hymn of Riego. The band did not venture to disobey, and the revolutionary music was played amidst shouts of applause.

About five o'clock, M—— and I went on foot towards the Plaza de Toros, and it was evident that an unusual agitation prevailed amongst the multitudes who were pouring out of the enclosure, and gradually forming themselves into groups in the Calle de Alcalà and in all the principal streets leading from the Puerta del Sol. The Prado, however, was crowded as usual, even by ladies, who remained there till eight or nine o'clock. About eight o'clock, we were joined by M. de —— of the French embassy, who was of opinion that there would undoubtedly be a popular insurrection that night. Occasional cries were now heard of "Viva la Libertad!" "Viva O'Donnell!" and gradually the groups of people assumed a more formidable and threatening aspect. Papers were now circulated in every direction, calling upon the people to attack the houses of the ministers and of the queen-mother, and then arose cries of "Death to San-Luis!" "Death to Cristina!" "Death to the *ladrona!*" "Death to Quinto!" &c. Cordova, it was said, was unable to form a cabinet; as it turned out, was unable to do any thing—unable or unwilling. There were comparatively few soldiers in Madrid. Between the rebels and their pursuers, the city was well-nigh abandoned by the military forces. Enough, however, there were to put down any popular tumult, had the general chosen to exert himself. But whatever may have been his motive, it seems that he thought it expedient under the circumstances to let the fury of the mob have an outlet (*desahogarse*), as he expressed it. Much gratitude is due to him from those upon whom this fury was discharged.

As time passed on, it was evident that the mob had the game in their own hands. The cries of "Muera Cristina! Muera San-Luis! Muera Quinto! Mueran los ladrones!" grew louder and louder. An immense fire was kindled in front of the general post-office, before the department of the president of the council. Here an infuriated crowd, composed of people of all ages and sexes, were endeavoring to penetrate into the building, by burning down the door. Within was a company of the civil guard, and another of the grenadiers of the crown. These brave men stood at their post, impassible as statues, while the bonfire steadily increased. Suddenly the door gave way with a crash, and the yelling populace rushed in like a torrent, overpowered the guard, took possession of the arms, and illuminated the balconies with the candelabras which they found in the office of the minister.

Other groups directed themselves meanwhile to the Calle Mayor, and breaking into the offices of the civil governor, got possession of the arms deposited there. Bonfires were now seen all over the city, which was besides almost entirely illuminated, and lighted up such a sea of sinister faces, as I could not have believed were in existence in Madrid.

In the Calle del Prado are situated the apartments of San-Luis and Collantes. They occupied the first and second floors of the house which forms the corner with the Calle de Leon. The light of the bonfires at a distance, showed us what was going on there. The mob had disarmed some half-dozen soldiers of the municipal guard, who stoutly opposed their entrance, and rushing in, dashed down the furniture into the fire. Tables, beds, chairs, paintings, mirrors, came pouring down to feed the flames. The wardrobes of Madame Collantes were emptied from the windows, and furious-looking women, decking themselves in satin petticoats and fine shawls, danced round the fire like so many harpies.

Similar scenes took place at the house of Salamanca in the *Calle de Cedaceros.* He was from home—his wife and children took refuge in the oratory. A brave Englishman, whose name I do not know, together with G—— and several others, resolutely defended the door of Madame Salamanca's bedroom, until she and her children had escaped by a back-door in safety. Gold and silver plate made a royal bonfire here. Rich and elegant furniture was dashed into the flames; mingled with masterpieces of painting and sculpture, and all that the taste and wealth of the Spanish Monte-Cristo had accumulated for years.

The same fate awaited the house of Domenech, minister of the treasury. His wife and daughters escaped amidst the insulting cries of the mob, half-dressed into the streets, and the house was pillaged—linen, plate, furniture, &c., reduced to ashes. The house of Count Vista-Hermosa, now absent in pursuit of the insurgents, was also sacked and plundered—that of Count Quinto pillaged from garret to cellar. The finest paintings and tapestries fed the flames. The diamonds of Salamanca vanished that night. The box which contained them was found empty. A million of reals belonging to Count Vista-Hermosa, also disappeared. Even the house of his brother was attacked, and his mother, aged and infirm, with her little grand-child, escaped, through the fidelity of a dependent, by a back-door which led into a neighboring garden. The Countess of Quinto made her escape in disguise through the gallantry of one of the chiefs of the riot, who assisted her to pass through the crowd.

But the most formidable mob had rushed towards the palace of the queen-mother, who, warned in time, had taken refuge in her daughter's palace, round which the troops of the garrison had concentrated themselves, rendering it for the moment an impregnable fortress. All this time the mob had been suffered to yell, burn and destroy without opposition, as if the new government was paralyzed. We had allowed ourselves to be carried down by the current, without waiting to see the result of the invasions of the ministerial habitations. When we arrived in front of Queen Cristina's palace, it presented a terrible spectacle of desolation. The vestibule of colored glass had been broken in pieces by showers of stones. The royal guard opposed a firm resistance to the mob, and for some time prevented their entrance. This was at length forced by bands of infuriated women, who, relying upon the courtesy due to their sex, all unsexed as they were, poured into the palace, driving back the guard, so that when we arrived, the balconies were filled with a multitude of men and women of the lowest class—rich furniture was dashed into the square—mirrors were flying in shivers on the pavement—the curtains had been set on fire—the flames were spreading rapidly—and the work of destruction was going on amidst a chorus of yells and curses truly appalling.

Suddenly a discharge of musketry was heard. There was one moment of silence, succeeded by cries of rage and terror. Don Joaquin de la Gándara was, I believe, the officer who headed the troop which had at length marched to oppose the madness of the people. The mob now began to disperse in every direction. After a time the fire was got under, and with some difficulty we made our way from the smoking ruins, and about three in the morning reached the Legation. The minister and two of his colleagues were in the *Chancellerie*, and I found that a personage of some importance, who had escaped with difficulty and in disguise, was lodged in a small room adjoining mine. It is probable that no one slept very soundly last night in Madrid. M—— and I passed the remainder of the night watching from the windows, and occasionally dozing in our arm-chairs. My guest, who was naturally in very low spirits, moodily smoked a cigar. For a few hours all was tolerably tranquil, and we began to hope, vainly, as it appeared, that the worst was over.

July 21st.

For some days it has been impossible to write. Events have succeeded each other so rapidly—the whole change in the aspect of Madrid is so sudden and extraordinary, that it is difficult to believe that so few days have elapsed since the 17th. On the 18th the *Gaceta*, the government paper, announced the resignation of the ministry, and the nomination of General Córdova as president of the council. The same *Gaceta* announced the resignation of General

Córdova, and the nomination of the Duke of Rivas as president of the council and minister of the navy—his colleagues being Don Luis Mayans, a deputy, minister of state—Don Manuel Cantero, a senator, minister of the treasury—Don Antonio de los Rios y Rosas, minister of *la Gobernacion*—Don Miguel Roda, minister of *Fomento.* At the same time, Colonel Garrigo was put at the head of all the cavalry in Madrid! Thus in three weeks he has seen himself in arms against the queen's troops, a prisoner, condemned to death as a traitor, pardoned, and rewarded. *Ainsi va le monde* in the land of the Cid!

On the morning of the 18th confusion reigned triumphant throughout the city, and it was evident that the disorders of the night were but a prelude to disasters of greater importance. The people forming into groups at the corners of the streets, armed with muskets, sabres, stones, whatever they could lay their hands upon, could no doubt have been reduced to order, had energetic measures been taken in time. Mounting upon the roofs of the houses, they discharged showers of tiles and stones upon the heads of the soldiers, and whenever one fell, a round of applause ensued, as if from the spectators at a theatre.

In the Plaza Mayor the civil guard for some time succeeded in driving back the people, and helped by the guard of the *Correos* and others, got possession of that point, which was an important advantage on their side. At that moment Colonel Garrigo, waving a white handkerchief as a flag of truce, rode through the principal streets, and for a few moments the firing ceased. The soldiers, profiting by this truce, took possession of several houses in the Calle de Preciados, and the civil guard fortified themselves in their quarters. Colonel Garrigo, however, ordered the troop to abandon their positions, which they did amidst the shouts and jeers of the multitude. But the truce there was of short duration. The firing broke out again, and M——, S—— and I had some difficulty in escaping from the balls and stones which were flying in every direction. Garrigo then rode down to the Plaza Mayor, and gave orders that the civil guard should be disarmed. Their muskets passed into the hands of the people.

A division, commanded by Gándara, and composed chiefly of artillery, after passing along the Prado, turned into the Carrera de San Gerónimo, where a company of the civil guard were intrenched on the balconies of the Casino. The troop passed on to the Calle de Atocha, where a captain of artillery was killed, and a shower of stones, balls, tiles, and even furniture, fell upon the heads of the unfortunate soldiers, who fell wounded in every direction. At nightfall, by orders of their colonel, they took refuge in the houses in that street, and the firing ceased. In other parts of the city, the mob gradually overpowered the soldiers. The government made this easy, by recalling nearly all the troops disseminated throughout Madrid to defend the neighborhood of the palace. In the evening the whole city was illuminated. The people were busily employed in constructing barricades. Every one asked what the new ministry were about, a question which no one could answer.

On the 19th the agitation had greatly increased. The people and the soldiers were exasperated against each other. Numerous barricades had risen as if by enchantment. The people had got possession of arms—muskets, sabres, and pistols, and the balconies were covered with multitudes armed with another formidable missile, sharp and heavy paving stones.

But the most desperate state of affairs was in the Calle de Toledo, where one Pucheta, a bull-fighter, had put himself at the head of several hundred of the lowest of the populace, who had named him their captain, disarmed the carabineers who guarded the gate of Toledo, and made their way into the powder-magazine, where they seized the gunpowder, and were now filling the neighborhood with dismay.

Barricades had been formed in all the avenues leading to the Puerta del Sol, so that the troops in the *Correos* were actually hemmed in, and it was evident that hunger would at last oblige them to submit. The troops, shut up in their quarters at San Mateo and el Soldado, were in the same predicament. They had not tasted food since the preceding day. The streets were now intransitable except on foot. The barricades began to assume a formidable appearance. A number of French *republicains rouges* were busily imparting their experiences to their fellow-demagogues. The firing continued in every quarter of the city; but especially in the streets of San Gerónimo, el Prado, the Príncipe, la Cruz, and others in that direction. Each street was converted into a separate field of battle. Balls were whistling in every direction, and it was an affair of some danger to pass along the streets. A ball passing into the Casino had struck and dangerously wounded the Count de la Cuba.

At length some attempt was made to restore order. A Junta was held in the house of Sevillano, the banker, General San Miguel chosen as its president, calling itself "A Junta for the safety, armament, and defence of Madrid, whose object is to give a successful direction to the popular movement, to economize blood, and to save the institutions trampled on by the most barbarous and unheard-of tyranny." This popular Junta published a document, calling upon all the armed citizens to cease firing, unless in case of provocation, and upon all the officers to give the same orders to their troops.

At the same time a Gazette Extraordinary was issued informing the public that the queen had accepted the resignation of the Rivas ministry, which had lasted eight-and-forty hours, and had named president of the council of ministers, Don Baldomero Espartero, Duke of Victoria! General San Miguel being charged to fill the office of captain-general of Castile, and minister of war *ad interim*.

The members of the Junta with San Miguel at their head, directed their steps the following day to the Puerta del Sol, the heroes of the barricades permitting them to pass solely on condition that they would carry no food to the guard in the *Casa de Correos*, as they were resolved to force these brave fellows to capitulate by hunger and thirst. They had cut the pipes, and for two days these soldiers had not even been refreshed by a drop of water. On entering the house, the Junta found the battalion of the grenadiers of the crown and other two companies of infantry worn down by fatigue and hunger. San Miguel going out upon the balcony, addressed the people, and appealed to their generosity in favor of these poor men, but was answered with furious shouts, that the soldiers should remain there till they died of hunger, or gave up their arms. On hearing these words, each soldier without uttering a complaint, resumed his position, and prepared to continue the combat; but the officers, after some parley with the members of the Junta, resolved to accede to the demands of the people. The soldiers were disarmed, and passed out, one after the other, with sad and dejected countenances. The people rushed in and took possession of the arms, and the Junta prepared to celebrate its sessions in the same building.

A counter-Junta was formed in the *Plazuela de la Cebada* (the barley-market), of a purely democratic character, under the auspices of the doughty Captain Pucheta, now the most powerful and important personage in the state.

As barricades are a mode of defence hitherto unknown in Madrid, a new periodical called "*El Miliciano*," undertakes to instruct the people of the "Heroica Villa," as to what they are good for.

"The barricade," it says, "is a bulwark raised by patriotism, to defend itself against the aggressions of tyranny.

"The barricade is a wall against which the sanguinary fury of the executioners of the people is broken.

"The barricade is a majestic castle, a superb fortress, on whose towers waves the flag of liberty, of honor, and of the laws, trampled on and scorned by those who should be its most loyal and firm defenders.

"The barricade is in short an impregnable rock, raised by the powerful hand of the people, against which are broken in pieces the waves of ambition, which boil in the breasts of the barbarous conquerors, thirsting for liberal and virtuous blood, because they do not respect candor, old age, or misfortune. Their object is to exterminate the freemen, whose peaceful dwellings fall under the bullets launched forth by their fatal cannons."

In the *Diario Español* we read: "The General Cortes, which will soon be convoked, has to decide the four following questions:

"Is it expedient that the House of Bourbon should continue?"

"Is it expedient that Don Pedro V. of Braganza should be called to govern the constitutional Spanish throne?"

"Is it expedient that the Peninsula should be constituted into a Republic, or are we to give ourselves up to Montemolin?"

"This is what the electors must determine by their votes in the election which is going to take place, and which is as, or more important than the re-establishment of the national militia."

Meanwhile it is decided that till the national guard is established, the people shall neither abandon their barricades nor give up their arms. Madrid remains therefore for the present in the hands of an armed mob.

On the 21st an order was issued by the Junta, ordering the immediate organization of the national militia, including in it all the citizens now under arms. The most inflammatory addresses to the people circulate through the city. As a specimen of their style, I give you a few words of the following:

"People! After eleven years of slavery, thou hast broken, with noble and daring pride, thy chains. This triumph thou owest to no party, not to the army, nor to the gold, nor to the arms of those who so often have arrogated to themselves the titles of thy defenders and chiefs. This triumph is due to thy own strength, to thy patriotism, to thy daring, to the valor with which from thy fragile barricades thou hast overwhelmed, in a whirlwind of fire, the bayonets, the horses, and the cannons of thy enemies, &c., &c."

This address terminates with, "Long live the individual liberties, people of brave men! Long live the national militia! Long live the constitutional Cortes! Long live universal suffrage! Long live the radical reform of the taxing system!"

The people continue to strengthen the barricades. All the streets are torn up, and the heat, the dust, the odor of the heaps of refuse from the houses, the crowds of *patriots* with their muskets, which they flourish about in a manner equally endangering their own and their neighbors' lives, form a union of sight, smells, and sounds, far from agreeable. The chiefs of the barricades look dark and sinister. Their wives bring them their *puchero*, and they lay aside their muskets, or deliver them over to their faithful spouses, and brighten up a little, while they hastily swallow the smoking soup. All these heroes have names well known amongst the people. There in front of the Correos, stands Don Fernando Obregon, where the barricade was formed, says "the Miliciano," "amidst a deluge of red-hot balls." In the street of the *Humilladero* "our valiant countryman, Don Narciso Roco," proudly displays a range of handsome muskets, taken from the palace of the Duke of Osuna.

But the district of the *Lavapiés* presents the most patriotic spectacle. There, barricades have arisen like small fortresses, and the *manolas* are in their glory, carrying stones, mattresses, chairs, tables, whatever first comes to hand to strengthen "the bulwarks of patriotism." Through the streets of Toledo, Captain Pucheto, the bull-fighter, directs his half-savage band, amidst the shouts and *vivas* of the populace. As night comes on, the confusion and noise increase. The soldiers are now disarmed—the bands play the hymn of Riego—the city is illuminated, even the empty habitations of the ex-ministers. True to their habits, the people begin to dance, and sing wonderful improvisations. "La Donna è mobile" is screamed in chorus, with new words adapted for the occasion, by some patriotic minstrel.

"Muera Cristina
Muera la Ladrona,
Viva Espartero," &c.

Pictures of Espartero crown the barricades, and men and women are dancing and singing round them. Blind men have been shrieking all day through the streets, "Life and Miracles of the Count of San-Luis!" Sleep is impossible amidst the light, the noise, the heat, the ringing of bells, the buzz of voices, the cries, the songs of liberty! But towards four in the morning there is a lull, for even patriots must sleep for a few hours.

General San Miguel, and Captain Pucheta, the bull-fighter, are the popular heroes—the one a fine old man, trying to restore order and to curb the popular fury, ever received with shouts and acclamations, yet not able, though head of the Junta, to enforce order—at least unable to induce the people to lay down their arms, or to abandon their barricades; the other omnipotent in his section. It is evident that he must be gained over, and flattered into compliance with the dictates of the Junta now sitting in the *Correos*.

Meanwhile where are the ex-ministers of the crown? Concerning them and their whereabouts the reports are various. It is known that Calderon de la Barca, Molins, San-Luis, Domenech, and Collantes, were in the palace when the *émeute* began. The day following that night of disorder, we made our way through the confusion, and went to make inquiries at their various houses. That of San-Luis and Collantes presented nothing but a scene of desolation; also that of Domenech, and no one could tell us where their families had taken refuge. In the *Casa de Astrarenas*, the residence of Molins, we heard only that the Marquesa and her children had escaped, and that the house, though threatened by the mob, had been spared. In the Calle del Barquillo, where the minister of state lived, we found every thing *in statu quo*—the furniture untouched, the porter at his post, a tall and grave individual, with a face of unmistakable honesty. We inquired for the family. "They are gone," said the functionary. "Where have they gone to?" "They gave me no orders," said the man. "But we are their friends; you have seen us in their houses. We wish to see them, to be of service to them." "I am sorry, your excellency," said the man; "but I only know there is no one in the house." No arguments could elicit any thing more from him. We have since heard that they are in the "house of the seven chimneys," the Austrian legation; and that Calderon de la Barca himself has escaped from the palace, where he was hidden for three days, to the French embassy.

I went with Mr. de —— this evening to the French embassy, where it is said that about sixty persons are concealed; among others, the Ynfantas have taken refuge there. It presents a curious scene. Doors are locked and double-locked. We met, as we passed through the corridors, several ladies closely enveloped in mantillas, gliding along in the darkness, no doubt going to visit their captive husbands or friends. It is rumored that San-Luis himself is concealed in a room opening upon the garden. His life is, no doubt, in danger. If he or the queen-mother were to fall into the hands of the mob, no pity would be shown them. Against Molins and Blaser there seems little feeling of hostility—against Calderon de la Barca, none.

CHAPTER XXXII.

Decrees of the Junta—A Horrid Scene—Espartero—The Queen insulted—Resolves to abdicate—Expected Arrival of Espartero—The Queen's Manifesto—The Mob—Cristina—Proclamations and Vivas—Barricades—Condition of Madrid—Chapel of our Lady of Solitude—The Manolas quarrelling—Espartero arrives—O'Donnell and Espartero—The new Cabinet—The Fugitives—Gymnastics of the Spanish.

24th.

THE Junta, which has taken the title of "Superior Junta of the Province," does all in its power to keep the people in a good humor, for, at the present juncture, they are the masters; and we may thank Heaven that it is a Spanish and not a French mob which now governs in Madrid. The Junta decrees an order, "immortalizing the great deeds which have saved liberty and public morality." It concedes a grade to all the officers who, alone or with troops, have adhered spontaneously to the popular movement (that is, to all who have revolted); the deduction of two years' service to the soldiers who have done the same, and offers to recommend to the government all those who, in the civil and military branches of the administration, have aided the popular cause, on the three days—the 17th, 18th, and 19th. They suppress the provincial council and the municipal guard, and all the ministerial offices. They decree that the general direction of the treasure and the deposits and payments belonging to the State, shall pass their funds to the Spanish bank of San Fernando, and put them at the disposal of the Junta. They also suppress the royal council. They revoke the sentence of banishment imposed on Don Enrique de Borbon, the Ynfante; and after many other decrees, they conclude by issuing one, to the effect that "the persons of the ex-ministers forming the San-Luis cabinet, as well as that of the Count of Quinto, the ex-governor of Madrid, shall be detained and put at the disposal of the Junta, to be submitted to the tribunal by whom they are to be judged."

On the 23d I was witness to a horrid scene. I and several of the Legation had gone down early to the street of Toledo and the *Barley-market*, the denizens of which, under the direction of the savage Pucheta, form at present a kind of independent population, ruled by their own laws, and blindly obedient to their own chief. You may be sure that, when curiosity leads us to these quarters of the city, our dress is not very foppish. It was evident that, amidst the ragged groups who were swarming in the Plaza, something was going on of more than usual interest. It soon appeared that, by orders of Pucheta, a band of these patriots had gone to the *Plazuela de los Mostenses*, to arrest the person of Don Francisco Chico, an old man well known as having been the head of the secret police during the ministry of Narvaez and others. His zeal in performing the duties of his office had made him an object of intense hatred to the lowest part of the population, by whom he was equally feared and dreaded. For many years he had abandoned his office, and having accumulated some fortune during the long period in which he occupied his difficult post, he lived with his wife and family in a well-furnished house, and had laid out considerable sums in the purchase of paintings, of which he was a true amateur. For some time past he had been bed-ridden, from old age and infirmities, and was now on his death-bed.

The mob rushed fiercely down to the house of the dying man, gathering impurities as it went—fierce, brawling women, with their imps of children, precocious in wickedness. From every dark nook and passage men rushed out to join the band, and the cries of "Death to Chico!" overpowered all the other sounds, whether of bells or drums or music, or shrieking blind men, which made the air *vocal* with discord that day.

Arrived before his house, they summoned the porter to admit them. The man imperturbably declared that he had no knowledge of where his master was. A pistol-shot, which laid the faithful dependant weltering in his blood, announced to the old police-officer that his time was come. A priest was passing by. "He is dying," said he to the mob; "he has but a few hours to live!" "Has he confessed?" "He has." "Then he is all ready!" cried the mob, and rushing up the stairs, they burst in the door, dragged the unfortunate man out of bed, and, as he was unable to stand, they threw him on a mattress, and, amidst shrieks and curses, jeers and applauses, he was carried down and hoisted on the shoulders of his ferocious persecutors. "*Picaro! bribon!* Rascal! scoundrel! You'll put my brother in the *Saladero* again!" "You'll have my husband *garotted!*" And a shower of stones and filth is launched by a female fury at the head of the prisoner. Not a word escaped from his mouth. He gazed at the crowd with a stupefied air, but uttered no complaint—no cry for mercy. Thus the horrid procession passed on till it reached the Plaza de la Cebada, and there, amidst taunts and jeers and cries of "To hell with the miscreant!" the bull-fighter gave the signal, a shot was fired, and the sufferings of poor old Chico were ended. I felt sick and stupefied. Was this Madrid?—that gay, busy, prosperous city, so few days since? Were those squalid, filthy men and women, with matted hair and fierce eyes, part of that well-dressed, joyous population with whom life seemed but a prosperous, long summer-day?

Nor was this all. Numbers of the secret police had already suffered death without more form of trial than had been vouchsafed to Don Francisco Chico; and the mob, not satisfied with his death, returned and murdered other members of his family. His wife and daughters were said to have escaped.

But now old General San Miguel found that it was time to interfere, and put a check to this popular despotism. As his health would not permit him to go on foot, he was carried on a chair to the Plaza de la Cebada, and a mission of some danger it was. But the gallant Captain Pucheta imposed silence on his followers, and the allocution of San Miguel was listened to with respect. He denounced the crimes of which they had been guilty as stains upon the glory which they had acquired in the late memorable days, and demanded their promise that similar assassinations should henceforward be unknown amongst them. He was responded to by cries of "Viva San Miguel!" and the old hero, having obtained the promise of the captain that he should no longer take "justice" into his own hands, was carried along amidst enthusiastic cheering.

At length a messenger has arrived from Espartero, in answer to the telegraphic message received by him from the queen, calling him to her aid. He was certainly not happy in the choice of the emissary charged to inform her majesty upon what conditions he would accept the charge which she proposed to confer upon him. About eleven o'clock that morning Count A—— received a message from the palace, to the effect that the queen requested the diplomatic body to meet there as soon as possible. Upon arriving there, the count was informed that her majesty could not receive the diplomatic body. He and the other ministers who had accompanied him retired, greatly surprised at this unusual and unceremonious treatment. However, the explanation which has been given, has fully satisfied them. It seems that General Allende Salazar, having demanded an interview with her majesty, delivered to her a paper containing the conditions of Espartero, which were of a nature greatly mortifying and irritating to the queen; one of them being, that she should dismiss all the individuals of her household, without exception. Upon her expressing to the general her disinclination to comply with this condition, it appears that he broke out into a series of abusive charges against the queen's private conduct. Utterly astonished and confounded, she could only falter out a few words. "I do not know what you mean; I have never been spoken to in this way." "I have no doubt of it, madam," said the envoy; "it is not often that truths are told in this palace." As he continued his accusations of levity of conduct, the king, who was in the next apartment, hearing his voice raised in an insolent manner, walked in, and demanded how he dared to insult the queen. Salazar muttered some words purporting that he was a plain soldier, &c.; and the queen, bursting into tears, said, "I am too much agitated now to give an answer. I shall retire and consider of it." No sooner was she alone than she impetuously resolved to abdicate rather than submit to the conditions of Espartero or to the insolence of his emissary, and sent for the diplomatic corps with the intention of declaring to them her resolution. It happened, however, that the first who arrived was the French ambassador; and his representations, but especially his reminding her majesty, that although she could abdicate for herself, she could not do so for her child, and that she would be under the necessity of leaving the little Princess in the hands of the new chiefs, produced a reaction in the mind of the queen. "Rather would I be dragged through the streets!" she exclaimed, "than separate from my child." Consequently, when the ministers arrived, they received the message which had at first surprised them.

Therefore, also, was General Allende Salazar again admitted to the royal presence, and charged with a communication to his chief, purporting that her majesty acceded to his conditions, "returning to Saragossa," says the *Gazette*, "fully satisfied (*altamente satisfecho*) with the interview which he had with her majesty."

And now, every one awaits with impatience the next scene in the drama—the arrival of Espartero, Duke of Victoria. Even those most opposed to him in political feeling, are anxious for his arrival—for the arrival of any one who will assume the reins of government, and put an end to this extraordinary phase in Spanish annals—a country without any government at all. Every one is aware, that but for the energy and prudence of San Miguel, no one would dare to lay his head upon his pillow in peace. But even the prestige of his name may fail—and no day passes without some tale of outrage, no night closes in without scenes of disorder; and were it not for that pure atmosphere which is the boast of Madrid, the present dirt and stench arising from the state of the streets, would long since have engendered an epidemic under this fierce July sun.

A manifesto is published by the queen, which has been but coldly received. It is so evidently the result of her situation, that it excites no sympathy amongst the people. She throws herself on their protection—she declares her complete adhesion to the ideas of Espartero—she praises the sacrifices which the people have made to recover their liberties, &c.

Meanwhile, what are the feelings of O'Donnell, Dulce, and the other chiefs of the revolt? Have they made a revolution in favor of Espartero? Little, indeed, can they have foreseen that this should be the end of such a beginning! Those amongst the grandees who desired the fall of San-Luis, did they believe that they were working in favor of Espartero and the Progresista party? But who in a revolution shall say—"Thus far shalt thou go, and no further!" Who that "sows the wind" shall not "reap the whirlwind?"

25th.

The young Ynfante, Don Fernando de Borbon, who accompanied his sisters to the French embassy, is dead, and it is said of typhus fever. The ambassador and his lady are full of attention and courtesy to their uninvited guests, but it is a heavy responsibility, this mingling of discordant elements under their roof. And every now and then, rumors arise, that the mob will attack the Benavente Palace, and will not understand or respect diplomatic rights, in searching for certain of the late ministers. It is also reported that the diamonds of the queen-mother are there for safe-keeping—saved from the flames by the bravery and fidelity of a Swiss attendant of her majesty, who mingled with the crowd, entered the apartments of Queen Cristina, and filling her apron unobserved with the precious tiaras and necklaces of her mistress, contrived to escape with them at the peril of her life. And it is rumored that therefore the mob will attack the embassy, and will not respect the rights of nations, of which they know nothing, but will force the ambassador to deliver up to them the person of the count, and the brilliants of the queen-mother.

Yesterday was *Santa Cristina*, and many of the barricades were hung with black, and orders were given that the city should not be illuminated as usual. Meanwhile the object of this popular hatred remains in the palace, tranquil and serene, as the few who have been admitted to see her, testify, uneasy for her children, but for herself dauntless, as one accustomed to the variations of popular favor.

"Ten years ago," said Count A—— to us this morning, "I witnessed the arrival of Queen Cristina in Madrid, after the downfall of Espartero. It is well known that when forced to abdicate the regency, and to leave the country, she said to him those memorable words at parting: 'Adieu, Espartero. I have loaded you with honors—I have raised you to the highest rank—I have made you every thing but *a gentleman. Eso nace, no se hace.* That one must be born—not made.' But again the wheel of fortune had revolved, and the royal exile was recalled.

"The balconies were hung with rich stuffs to celebrate the return of the popular idol. Flowers were strewed beneath her feet. Cries of frenzied enthusiasm greeted her approach. Her children, so long deprived of the guidance of their mother, clung to her with tears and sobs, especially the little queen, whose majority had been declared by the Cortes, at the early age of thirteen. Tears of joy streamed from her own eyes as the triumphal carriage in which she was seated, slowly made its way amidst the devoted crowd, whose cries of 'Viva Cristina!' rent the air. Peasants from the different provinces performed the national dances in front of the palace. The grandees of Spain crowded to welcome her, and when she appeared on the balcony of the palace between her two children, accompanied by Narvaez and a brilliant crowd of uniforms, one would have thought, like Burke of another unfortunate queen, that 'a thousand swords would have leaped from their scabbards to avenge even a word that threatened her with insult.'

"I remembered all this, when, admitted into her presence a few days ago, I found her nearly alone in an inner apartment of the palace, while the execrations of the multitude were borne towards her in yells that drowned all other sounds. She stood at the window, calmly surveying the destruction of her palace. No tears were in her eyes then—not a cloud upon her brow. She stood serene and calm, though thinner and paler than before the dangerous illness from which she has hardly recovered. Whatever her feelings were, she had crushed them back into the inmost recesses of her heart. She talked calmly of the events that had occurred, without anger, without bitterness. One of her ladies spoke of the possibility of her effecting her escape in disguise. 'I will leave Madrid as a queen,' said she, calmly, 'or I will remain there.'"

The manifesto of the queen has in so far satisfied the people, that her picture now appears on the barricades, between that of Espartero and O'Donnell.

The situation of General Blaser, when the news from the capital reached him, must have been far from agreeable! By despatches received yesterday it is known that he has delivered up the command of his troops to General Rendon.

The newspapers are filled with proclamations, whose object seems to be to encourage the people, and especially to keep them quiet, and in a good humor, till the arrival of the hero of Luchana. There are manifestoes from San Miguel—from the Junta—addresses to the national guards—to the heroes of the barricades—accounts of the sympathy of the provinces—abuse of all the late cabinets—praises of the loyal Dulce, of the valiant O'Donnell, of the glorious Duke of Victoria, and generally concluding with a long string of *Vivas:*

"*Viva* the national sovereignty!

"*Viva* the armed people!

"*Viva la Reina!*
"*Viva* Don Baldomero Espartero
"*Viva* the patriarch of our liberties!
"*Viva* the Junta of safety, armament and defence!"

To give you an idea of the state of Madrid in its external aspect, you must know that there exist within its walls no less than two hundred and eighty-four barricades according to statistical enumeration, 264 of which are considered first-class barricades, each one of which forms the centre of eight, twelve, or fourteen redoubts; all these *improvised* fortifications composing a formidable system of defence. Boards, bricks, mattresses, paving-stones, bags of sand, flint, mortar, carts, coaches, diligences and private carriages are the materials employed in erecting, says the *Diario español*, "the robust pedestal of our liberties."

Banners and standards float from their summits, and crowds gather round them at night, and sing the hymn of Riego by the light of the illumination. "It is eleven years," exclaims the *Diario*, "since we have seen so animating and inspiring a spectacle in Madrid."

28th.

Still expectation increases, and Espartero comes not—neither does O'Donnell, and still we are at the tender mercies of the people. O'Donnell is said to be at Andergai, and travelling post towards Madrid. "Why tarry the wheels of his chariot?" It is a case in which each of the champions is willing to *céder le pas* to the other. But here are ten days in which those who have made the revolution know the danger to which all peaceable citizens are exposed—in which the queen remains a prisoner in her own palace, defended by troops who can no longer know in what loyalty consists, surrounded by multitudes thirsting for the blood of her mother

—depending for her safety upon the influence of one old general, infirm of health—and still no one hastens to relieve her—and if she is saved, and if the streets of Madrid are not deluged with blood, the situation is not the less critical, and their apathy is not the less blamable.

Yesterday the Junta made the following announcement: "Her majesty the queen will go out this evening at six o'clock, to visit her loyal people of Madrid; the Junta of safety, armament, and defence, will accompany the royal person during her promenade, which will be guarded by the national guard and the army. The queen will thus go through the *Plaza de la Armería*, the Calle Mayor, the Puerta del Sol, the street of Alcalá and the Prado, returning to the palace by the Carrera de San Gerónimo, and the Calle Mayor. This promenade of her majesty, after the grave conflict through which the people of Madrid have passed, will be a manifestation of the alliance which fortunately reigns between the people and the constitutional throne."

Whether the queen really intended to take this step, or whether it was merely announced with the intention of occupying the minds of the people, I cannot say; but it is certain that her majesty very wisely remained within the palace walls. Besides her personal danger, it is said that she fears to leave the palace whilst the queen-mother is there, lest the mob should take advantage of her absence, and force their entry. It is now given out that she will defer her *paseo*, till the arrival of the heroic Duke of Victoria. Two companies of the national militia are now guarding the palace, with as many more of the regular troops, their party-colored dresses forming a grotesque contrast with the handsome uniforms of the soldiers. Men, women and children may now be seen dancing round the barricades, which are ornamented with flowers and green branches. Guitars and muskets lie together, side by side. Manolas, with their arms a-kimbo, strut about the streets, occasionally taking the arms of the gallant chiefs of the barricades. In the Calle del Cármen, where, in peaceful times, the fair Madrileñas pass their mornings in cheapening silks and laces, no business goes on now. At the door of a large magazine, fronting a frowning barricade, a shopkeeper, fraternizing with the militia, stood this morning, rubbing his hands and exclaiming, "*Gracias á Dios!* We are free at last!" "And sell nothing!" said his neighbor in a lower tone, and with a doleful face.

And still, when night approaches, the illumination, suspended only on one occasion for Saint Cristina's day, begins; perhaps a wise precaution. The fine-music of the regiments of the garrison, escorted by an immense mob, play the patriotic airs, the hymn of Riego or the hymn of Luchana. As a popular revolution invariably throws up the scum to the surface, it is not to be supposed that all the respectable portion even of the people sympathize with these demonstrations. Many a sad face may be seen behind the balconies of many a poor house, even in the fine old street of Toledo, picturesque in its destruction. Many a respectable matron, her honest eyes looking out from her mantilla, casts a glance of disgust at the champions of the barricades, and her wit overstepping her prudence, makes a sarcastic remark to them, upon the profitable way in which they are spending their time.

The little chapel of Our Lady of Solitude, in the street of La Paloma, near the Gate of Toledo, celebrated for the miraculous image, called the Virgin of La Paloma, is crowded from morning till night. It is a beautiful little chapel, with one aisle adorned with Corinthian pillars, and the image of Our Lady of Solitude painted on canvas above the altar.

At the lower end of the chapel hang a multitude of votive offerings. Though it is situated in one of the worst parts of the city, I found, on trying to make my way in there, a few days ago, that it was crowded, not only by women of a lower class, but by ladies enveloped in their mantillas, who had braved the difficulties of the unpaved streets and the chances of attracting the attention of Pucheta and his band, in order to pray for the intercession of Our Lady of La Paloma.

As I passed down the Calle del Cármen this morning, the shops looked desolate, and their owners somewhat lugubrious. "Caramba! if this goes on," said one, "we may shut up our shops. Every thing is covered with dust, and we have not had a customer for the last ten days." "I am glad of it," said a young damsel, with a pale face and great black eyes. "You wished for it, and you have got it."

"*Tú te metiste fraile, Padre Mosten; tú lo quisiste, tú te lo ten.*" (You put yourself in it, Friar Mosten; you wished for it, and now you have got it.)

"Come along, Mariquita!" said her prudent mother. "Adios, Señores!" cried the girl, heedless of her mother's signs and warnings. "This is only the beginning. Let us see how you will like the end!"

In the *Plaza de la Cebada*, a quarrel between two Manolas attracted my attention. It was a war of tongues, but threatened, as it waxed louder and louder, to end more seriously. A crowd had gathered round the disputants. It appeared that the lover of the one was in the regiment of Montesa, which had joined the insurgents; the son of the other was one of the municipal guard. The lover had got a grade, and a deduction of two years' service; the other had got a ball in his knee, and was dismissed. Therefore the quarrel was personal and political. The first cried the Revolution to the clouds; the other anathematized it. "There lies my

Pepe," said the elder woman, "lame for life, and dismissed for doing his duty!" "For firing on the patriots," said the other. "And that good-for-nothing Juan of yours has got a grade for deserting!" "For fighting for liberty!" "*Caramba* with your liberty! Will it give us bread? All my customers gone;—Count A—— and his family off to Bayonne—the Condesa de —— away this morning. They took her for Queen Cristina, and made her get out of the diligence and take up her veil, and sent for half-a-dozen of the Nationals to look at her! Good eyes they've got." "*Cristina*," said a fierce-looking dame with a basket on her arm, "was sent off this morning to the hospital, to be kept under lock and key, and guarded by the Nationals till Don Baldomero has her tried." "Who told you that, Mariquita?" said a number of voices. "I saw her myself," said the dame, "in a carriage, with all the windows shut and the blinds down, and an escort of soldiers guarding it." "*Ca!*" said the washerwoman. "It was no more Queen Cristina than it was me. Catch her falling into the hands of these *pícaros!*" "*Cállate, bruja!*" (Hold your tongue, witch!) "Come, Cármen," said the same prudent old woman who had tried to silence her daughter, a few minutes before, coming up with that black-eyed damsel; "come and let us see Pepe;" and at the remembrance of her son, the anger of poor Cármen was quenched in tears, and she suffered herself to be drawn from amidst the storm of tongues, and led unresistingly away. But I must do her adversary the justice to say, that no sooner had she seen this gush of tears, than all her fury at the municipal soldier and his mother vanished and melted away; and seizing a bottle of orgeat which was keeping cool beneath the shadow of her booth, to wet the throats of thirsty patriots, she ran after her, and with many soothing words, thrust upon her the bottle of cooling drink for "poor

Pepito" (el pobrecito de Pepito), which act the Nationals, many of whom had no-doubt good hearts beating under their party-colored jackets, gravely applauded.

"On the 20th of July, and before receiving the appeal of the queen, the Duke of Victoria, responding to the invitation of the revolutionary Junta formed at Saragossa, had entered that city, where he had been received with immense applause, popular acclamations, and military serenades. Upon the return of General Salazar from his mission to the queen, it was published in all the journals of the capital, that the hero of Luchana would immediately direct his march towards the capital. It is now asserted that to-morrow he will positively make his entry into Madrid, accompanied by Don Leopold O'Donnell, the hero of Lucena. Patriots are waxing impatient The Junta, like an orchestra, striving to allay the popular excitement, while the actors are tardily arraying themselves behind the scenes,—by playing their favorite airs, blowing themselves out of breath, tearing away at their violins, and trying to drown the clamor and stamping of the feet, are well-nigh at the end of their resources; and if the curtain does not draw up speedily, we shall have one universal uproar, which even the fine old director himself, Don Evaristo, with uplifted arm, guiding the movement of French horn and violin, will not be able to avert.

30th.

The curtain has drawn up! and, amidst hand clapping, loud huzzaing, and vociferous *vivas!* Don Baldomero has made his bow to the audience. Yesterday morning the street of Alcalá was crowded, almost since day-break. The Junta, headed by its president, had gone out as far as the *Venta del Espíritu Santo* to meet Espartero *le Desiré.* The president directed a discourse to the hero, in the name of the people, and received the following reply:—

"*Madrileños:* You have called me to strengthen for ever the liberties of the country. Here you have me (*aquí me tenéis*), and if any one of the enemies of our most holy liberty tries to tear it from us, with the sword of Luchana I will put myself at your head, at the head of all the Spaniards, and I will teach you the way to glory."

Hereupon the chief alcalde congratulated the duke in the name of the Ayuntamiento and of the national militia, to which he replied nearly in the same words.

After many hours of fruitless expectation, the shouts of the people, assembled in the Calle de Alcalá, announced that the procession was in sight, and soon after might be descried an open carriage, in which stood a figure with its hand on the region of its heart, bowing in acknowledgment of the prolonged *vivas.* And now we could more plainly distinguish the figure, though not the features of the hero of Luchana, but the hero of Lucena was not with him. Several officers rode beside the carriage, and a company of unwashed patriots, the defenders of the barricades, followed with tumultuous cries; thronging round the carriage, impeding the progress of the horses, and shouting "Viva la Libertad! Viva Espartero!" Espartero opened his paternal arms, as if he would gladly have taken the whole population to his heart in one embrace; as if he wished, like Nero, that they had but one head, not that he might, like that ancient tyrant, lop it off at one blow, but that he might lay his outstretched hand upon it, and bless it for the thoughts it had conceived and the deeds that it had done. Mingled in amicable confusion, were the companies of the national militia and of the army, marching in time and out of time to the music of the hymn of Riego. Scarcely a house that did not display a rich hanging on its balcony—scarcely a throat that was not hoarse with shouting.

Slowly the triumphal chariot passed on, enveloped in clouds of dust, through the streets of Alcalá (re-baptized Street of the Duke of Victoria), down the Calle Mayor, slowly from the press of the multitude and from the state of the streets, and at length entered the court-yard of the palace, and Espartero mounted the grand staircase which eleven years ago he had so hastily descended, and was received by the sovereign who, sore beset, had called him to re-establish order. What both felt at that moment, we may never know. What the queen-mother and ex-regent felt, shut up in her distant apartments, who can say? The visit was short. In a few minutes Espartero again descended the staircase and entered his carriage, and the queen appeared on the balcony, with the king and little princess, and saluted the people; and a few faint cries of "Viva la Reina Constitucional!" were mingled with the vivas to liberty and Espartero.

The carriage continued its route to the house prepared for the reception of the popular hero, the *Casa de Mathieu*, in the street of Espoz y Mina, which he entered under a canopy of waving flags and flying colors, and there, after a few words to the populace, he saluted them, and retired to repose from his fatigues.

But now it was rumored that the valiant General O'Donnell would arrive in the evening train, and the members of the Junta and Ayuntamiento, headed by General San Miguel, repaired to the landing-place to receive and welcome the prime mover of the Revolution. He, in his turn, was conducted in triumph to the house of Espartero, and in a little while the two heroes of Luchana and Lucena appeared together on the balcony, locked in a fast embrace, typifying the fusion of the Moderado and Progresista party, *Lucena*, in a physical point of view, towering above *Luchana*. How cordial was the embrace, let those judge who know their antecedents. But the people comprehend only what they see, and patriots and Nationals rent the air with one simultaneous shout in honor of O'Donnell, Espartero, and Liberty.

This morning the men of the barricades defiled in presence of the Duke of Victoria, and felicitated him upon his return. The variety of their costumes, banners, and arms, presented a grotesque but sufficiently formidable appearance. As for the new cabinet, it was formed with tolerable promptitude, under the auspices of the new president of the council. General O'Donnell, in spite of the ardent desire which he manifested to retire into the shades of private life, "unwillingly accepted the post of minister of war and the rank of captain-general." Collado, a rich capitalist, was made minister of the treasury; Lujan, minister of *Fomento;* General Allende Salazar, minister of the navy. It is to be presumed that the inclinations of the queen were not particularly consulted in this last appointment. Don Joaquin Pacheco was named minister of state; Señor Santa Cruz, like Collado and Lujan, hitherto unknown to fame, minister of *La Gobernacion;* and Don José Alonso, minister of grace and justice.

What, meanwhile, has become of the members of the San-Luis cabinet? a question constantly asked, but as yet not satisfactorily answered. San-Luis is reported to be still in close confinement in the French embassy. Domenech is said to be concealed in the innermost recesses of the palace, receiving refreshments from the royal table, through the attention of his royal mistress. No one seems to have ascertained the whereabouts of Collantes. Sometimes it is reported that he is taken, at others, that he is concealed in the house of an ancient friend; for here, at least, fallen ministers have firm friends, who would risk their lives to save them, and faithful servants, who would die sooner than betray them. Quinto and his countess are supposed to have sought shelter at the Portuguese Legation. Salamanca has escaped in the disguise of an *Aguador*. Molins is concealed in a friend's house, and his family have returned to occupy their apartments in the *Casa de Astrarenas*. Calderon de la Barca is still, according to some, concealed in the French embassy; according to others, is with his family in the "house of the seven chimneys." The editor of the "Herald" is reported to have taken refuge in the English Legation. The two eldest daughters of Queen Cristina have passed the gates in safety, disguised as peasant-girls, and have taken the route to Portugal, under the care of a trusty friend. The youngest is to be conveyed, under the care of another friend of the queen-mother, to Bayonne.

"It is a positive fact," said Mrs. ——, an English lady, at a tea-party this evening at the Countess G——'s, "that all public men in Spain should learn gymnastics." The tea-party, with the exception of this lady, and a certain celebrated marquesa, who told us she had come through the Prado, taking the arm of one of the chiefs of the barricades, was entirely composed of men. "Not a man of any note," continued the lady, "who at one time or another has not had to escape at the risk of his life, climbing over roofs, coming down chimneys, and performing feats worthy of Grimaldi. Concha was at one time concealed for weeks in the French embassy behind a heap of wood, and, as I have been credibly informed, his escape was miraculous. Salamanca, with troops watching for him on the street below, clambered over the roofs like a cat, and owed his preservation to his wonderful facility in climbing." "General ——," added the marquesa, "was hidden for weeks at the Duke of ——'s, and it was a regular game of hide-and-seek with him and his pursuers. Sometimes crouching in the cellar, at others in the coalhouse, or half suffocated in a sofa-bed. At least twenty times all the apartments were searched, and when at last the house was filled with soldiers, and it was evident that his hiding-place must be discovered, he leaped from the balcony into the garden, hid himself all night in a loft over the stable, changed clothes with the coachman, drove the duchess next evening to the opera, and when it was over, and her carriage was called for, the coachman was missing, and it was at least three months before the manner in which General —— had escaped, was discovered." "Therefore," said Mrs. ——, "it's a positive disadvantage for public men here not to be accustomed to climbing. Imagine," said she, lowering her voice, "what I saw this evening! I went to the Austrian Legation, to make inquiries after the Calderons, who are staying there, and, *entre nous*, I rather think the minister is there also. Well, I observed in the garden a ladder placed against the wall which separates the Danish minister's garden from the Austrian, and I am convinced that this ladder is intended to be used by him, in case the mob take it into their heads to search the Legations, which has been threatened half-a-dozen times. Now, *he* probably never climbed in his life, or tried to make his escape before. The consequence is, that he may break his neck. As I said before, the young men here ought to have a peculiar physical education, to prepare them for these emergencies."

CHAPTER XXXIII.

The Cabinet in Trouble—Official Changes—Beggars—Situation of Cristina—Union Club—Catalonia—Office-seeking—San Miguel—Funcion at the Circo—Espartero and O'Donnell—Results of the Revolution—The Clubs—Departure of Cristina—Popular Discontent—Escape of the San-Luis Ministry—Cristina's Palace—Espartero, O'Donnell, San Miguel, and Ros de Olano—A Letter from my Guest—Character of the Spanish—Adieu to Madrid.

August 1st.

THE new cabinet is by no means upon a bed of roses. The sovereign people have been masters too long, to submit easily to any legitimate authority. Each province has its *Junta*, which the people consider entirely superior in authority to the central government. In Madrid the people have been persuaded, though with some difficulty, to destroy the barricades, and the intransitable condition of the streets at this moment of transition, may be imagined.

With regard to the Provincial Juntas, the government have taken a kind of *mezzo-termine*. An exposition is drawn up, addressed to the queen, and signed by the new ministers, in which after stating that the Juntas cannot continue to govern, they add that "they may yet do great service to the executive power, as well as to the nation." "We wish them," adds this rather embarrassed document, "not to trammel the executive, but to subsist by its side, enlightening it by its counsels, until the Cortes is convoked, which will be in a very short space of time." Then follow the articles decreed by the cabinet—purporting that all the Juntas throughout Spain are to continue with the name and character of Juntas consultive and auxiliary to the central government, and to the provincial authorities, to be consulted by them whenever they find it expedient, especially in regard to the formation of the electoral lists."

August 2d.

To-day appears an interminable list of changes in the various departments, especially in that of war. Colonel Echagüe, Generals Messina, Ros de Olano, Serrano, Infante, Zavala, and others who have assisted in the revolution, are, of course, amongst the first who receive new military honors. A list is ordered to be made out of all those who have distinguished themselves in the barricades, that they may receive "the just reward of their services!" General Pezuela is recalled from his post of Governor of Cuba. General Concha is named in his stead.

The extraordinary influx of beggars in Madrid, is a new feature in the present situation of affairs. Ragged, hungry, and threatening in their aspect, they have poured in from all the surrounding cities and villages, and demand alms in a tone which would almost indicate that they have some strong argument at hand with which to back their request. They swarm especially in the street of Toledo, and there as well as in many other parts of the city, it is now by no means safe to go unarmed after a certain hour.

The great and most pressing difficulty, the question which the government is now more especially called upon to resolve—more pressing even than the formation of a new constitution, than the convocation of the *Cortes Constituyentes*, is that which refers to the queen-mother. Demands, couched in threatening language, are made to the cabinet, on the part of the people, instigated by their revolutionary leaders, that until the tribunal destined to judge her majesty shall have met, she shall be confined in the Alcazar of Segovia, in Saragossa, or in some stronghold in Madrid, where she shall be guarded by the patriots. No doubt the government would feel relieved could this question be solved for them, by the voluntary escape of the queen-mother, but if even this were possible, nothing, it is said, will induce her to attempt it. Her children are in safety, and she awaits her fate with calmness.

To the popular clamors, Espartero has responded with the assurance that "Doña María Cristina de Borbon, shall not leave the city, *neither by day, nor by night, nor furtively.*" But the people are suspicious, and all the avenues to the palace are strictly watched, and every coach, and diligence, and cart—nay, every horseman, and foot-passenger, male or female, who goes through the gates, is subjected to a close examination, in case either the queen or one of the ex-ministers should attempt to escape in disguise. And if any one were discovered, there is little doubt that those most obnoxious would meet with such justice as was shown to the members of the secret police; and at the very least, as daily examples prove, the offender mounted upon an ass, exposed under a burning sun to the insults of the rabble, would be conducted before the "consultive and auxiliary Junta," and by them delivered over to the executive power; and if the government did not deal *justice* upon those whom the people have been taught to regard as their enemies, their days would be numbered; for the people are still masters; and though now there is a strong military force in Madrid, the soldiers have seen too recently the result of doing their duty by opposing that many-headed sovereign, to venture upon it unadvisedly.

Therefore while the situation of Queen Cristina and of the ex-ministers is critical, that of the new government is no less so. An outrage upon the person of the queen's mother would be a stain upon them for life, while her departure in safety may cost them their offices, at the very least.

And therefore, the heroes of Luchana and Lucena sit moodily in council, and know not what course to pursue. Espartero, it is said, takes occasionally to his bed, perhaps taking counsel of his pillow. But their word is given—*neither by night, nor by day, nor by stealth*, is the royal lady to be permitted to escape; and worse than all, neither by night, nor by day, nor furtively, will she attempt it. And in truth, were she even to consider such an attempt as compatible with her dignity, it would be one fraught with danger. To the lowest of the people her features are familiar; those eyes which many tears shed in secret have not yet dimmed, those dimples, that smile which in happier days poets have sung, and painters have never succeeded in representing,—every lineament of her once-loved face is as well known to each patriot now thirsting for her destruction, as the features of his own mother.

But some measure must be taken, and that promptly. Some choice of evils must be made. The queen will not leave her palace while her mother is there, and while her absence might expose her to danger; and the queen's health is said to suffer from this long confinement, this monotony of anxiety and agitation. The health of the princess also is supposed to suffer from want of air and exercise, but her majesty will not permit her to leave her presence; not an unnatural decision in the actual circumstances.

The *Union Club*, a political society self-formed, and calling itself the auxiliary of the Junta, agitates the most important questions, and especially occupies itself with that relating to the queen-mother. From its stormy centre issues an exposition directed to the Duke of Victoria, demanding that justice shall be done upon the person of Doña María Cristina de Borbon, and declaring that the government which shall facilitate the departure or flight of that lady, will be "the first traitor, the first who will throw a handful of mire upon the splendid standard hoisted in Manzanares and Saragossa." This document of considerable length has a multitude of patriotic signatures, and is widely circulated throughout the city.

August 4th.

Some days ago, important affairs called my friend M—— to Barcelona. By a letter received from him this morning, though very guarded in its expressions, it would seem that all the plagues of Egypt had fallen upon Catalonia. The captain-general, La Rocha, after his constant assurances of the "unalterable tranquillity" of the province, had himself headed the popular movement, but as might naturally be expected, inspired little confidence in the people.

To solve the social problem, the workmen of Barcelona discovered that the shortest method was to loose the Gordian knot, by setting fire to the manufactories. All machines which by facilitating labor diminished the necessity of employing more than a certain number of hands, were burnt. Some of the ringleaders were shot, but not before several of their employers had fallen victims to the popular fury. An alarm of cholera was spread; and in the midst of all these occurrences, General Manuel Concha, Marquis of Duero, having arrived from the Canary Islands, where he had been sent by orders of the San-Luis cabinet, was elected captain-general in the place of La Rocha, who no doubt fell unpitied by any party.

But Don Manuel de la Concha soon discovered that he

was unequal to the situation. He found himself an object of suspicion to the people; the troops under his command were undisciplined and insubordinate, and having ordered all the forces dispersed throughout Catalonia to concentrate themselves in the capital, it was rumored that he intended to give a *coup d'état*, and to propose himself as dictator, in opposition to Espartero and O'Donnell. In the midst of all these disorders—a rebellious army, fierce workmen, the cessation of all trade, and a population compared to which those of Madrid are as lambs led to the slaughter, the new Governor of Catalonia probably regrets his tranquil life in the Canary Islands.

To-day the following paragraph appears in the *Clamor Público.*

"MOORS ON THE COAST.

"Yesterday it seems that Doña María Cristina was to have taken her departure for a foreign country; but suspended her journey in consequence of having observed that the avenues of the palace leading to the *Campo del Moro* were watched by a considerable number of armed peasants, who, without doubt, would be happy to take leave of the *Mother of the Spaniards.* Last night a group of from 60 to 80 men stopped and searched, near the *Hospicio*, all the coaches which had taken the direction of the road to France; others traversed the neighborhood of the *Pradera de Guardias;* whilst other groups kept watch in different directions."

It is characteristic of the state of the times, that we find in the same journal, that Señor Güel, a *Habanero*, married to the Ynfanta Josefa, is named President of the popular Junta in Valladolid!

August 9th.

But nothing now occupies the attention of at least the feminine portion of the inhabitants of Madrid more, than the necessity under which the queen finds herself of dismissing her whole household, and supplying their places with persons chosen by her *guardians.* From the mistress of the robes down to the smallest scullion, there is to be what M—— would call a "clean sweep" of the whole *servidumbre.* Neither long services, nor personal attachment, nor any qualities whatsoever will find grace in the eyes of these new masters. Even the head cook, first officer of the mouth to her majesty, undisputed sovereign of the culinary department since the days of her royal father, must resign his sceptre into the hands of a stranger, a new "Minister of the Interior." The dismissal of old and faithful servants, who cannot influence the queen in political matters, certainly seems a wanton exercise of power; but patriots must be rewarded, and there are not pensions and places enough in all Spain to satisfy a third part of the applicants.

Nothing is spoken of this morning but the scenes which took place in the palace, when the queen took leave of her ladies and *gentilhombres;* of the tears that were shed on all sides; and it is even rumored that her majesty had the courage to say in a loud voice, "I hope to see you all again in happier days." The places of the dismissed ladies and grandees are to be filled by those who belonged to the opposition party in the Senate.

Nearly the whole Spanish diplomates are also changed. The Gazette of to-day gives the following nominations:

Señor Gonsalez is named minister to London—Olózaga, to Paris—Mon, to Vienna—Rios Rosas, to Lisbon—General Infante, to Rome—Gonsalez Bravo, to Constantinople—Pastor Diaz, to Turin.

"When," exclaimed the *Clamor Público*—"when is the question of giving offices to be ended, and when is that of reform to begin?"

The queen having sent for General San Miguel to express her gratitude to him for the services he had rendered to her during the days of the barricades, asked him what reward she could bestow upon him. "Madame," said the old general, "the greatest reward your majesty could give me, would be *un abrazo.*" "Willingly," said the queen, and suiting the deed to the word, she gave a hearty embrace to the old man, who retired from the audience probably more "fully satisfied" than General Allende Salazar when he returned to give an account of his mission to his commander. It is said that the gallant Captain Pucheta is now entirely on the side of the queen, and is losing his popularity with his own party in consequence.

August 10th.

The minister of war has named his loyal friend General Domingo Dulce, Captain-general of Catalonia, in the room of General Manuel Concha.

Señor Mon has declined the nomination of minister to Vienna.

It is announced that on Sunday next, a patriotic *funcion* will take place in the *Circo*, under the auspices of the Countess of Lucena (wife of O'Donnell), of the Countess of Campo Alange, of the Señora Dulce, of the mother of General Serrano, and other patriotic ladies, at which will be sung various patriotic hymns, and at which will be represented amongst other pieces, "A Hero of the Barricades."

The Jesuits have been expelled from Valladolid and Burgos.

Señor Moltinedo, director of the gas company in Madrid,

declares in the name of that body, that the influence attributed to Doña María Cristina de Borbon in that enterprise is false, and that neither she nor any one representing her, has ever had a single share in the gas company. Pity that it is not for the interest of other public associations to refute in the same way all the other accusations against her majesty!

August 18th.

Disorders continue in the provinces; disorders in Madrid. The Prado presents itself under a totally new aspect; equally crowded, but apparently by a different population. The open carriages are filled by over-dressed women, but the elegant equipages of the aristocracy are absent. Every now and then, in a hired *berlina*, passing through the least frequented streets, may be seen some well-known face, enveloped in a mantilla, evidently anxious to preserve its incognito. Every diligence is crowded with families of distinction hurrying from the capital. Nothing is talked of but politics—the changes in the various departments—the elections—the reunion of the *Cortes Constituyentes*—the position of the queen-mother—the news from the provinces.

The *funcion* at the Circo took place as announced. The patriotic hymns were interrupted by vivas from the most tumultuous audience perhaps ever seen in a Spanish theatre. The "Hero of the Barricades" was received with enthusiasm, although listened to with as little attention as it deserved. Long before it was ended, the audience broke out in shouts and groans—"Death to the Tyrants!" "Death to the *Concordato!*" Death to Religion!" This last seemed rather to shock the occupants of the boxes, and the ladies began hurriedly to put on their cloaks and shawls, and to hasten from the theatre, fearing some more energetic demonstrations of independence on the part of the patriots.

Amidst the crowd that now figure in public affairs, whether of new names, or of names which the wheel of fortune has again brought into notice, and who have returned white-washed and "as good as new," there are in fact but two which fix the general attention—Espartero and O'Donnell. The few who, taking no part in political affairs, may be supposed to judge with a certain degree of impartiality, augur no good to Spain from their forced union. Espartero now sixty-two, a brave soldier before the enemy, but totally destitute of political talent, feeble in health, and indolent by his nature, retained few friends in any party, after remaining for two years in the regency. O'Donnell, daring and ambitious, is considerably younger than his coadjutor, being now in his forty-sixth year. But Espartero stands at present in an incomparably higher position than his colleague. He has responded to the call of his sovereign, to put an end to the disorders occasioned by the revolution brought about by O'Donnell. It is true that he had already also responded to the invitation of the insurgents in Saragossa, but he was not openly at least, like O'Donnell, the prime mover of the insurrection. There can be no doubt that nothing was further from the intentions of O'Donnell than to coalesce with Espartero and the Progresista party; and still less did he expect to find himself acting in a secondary position, in the cabinet of which his ancient enemy was the chief.

So far the two generals have agreed in one point—in distributing rewards to all who have aided or abetted in the last revolution. But it is evident that the Spanish cabinet is at the mercy of its own indecision, as well as of the general state of uncertainty in which the political affairs of the country are plunged, and that they are blindly pursuing a system of reaction against all that has been done for the last ten years.

After having accused the last ministers of violating the institutions and the laws of the country, they are following in their footsteps, or rather greatly overstepping them. Already they have suppressed the council of state—abolished the provincial councils; and, unable to decide for what constitution the revolution has been made, whether for that of 1845 or that of 1837, they have discovered that it was for neither, and have convoked the *Cortes constituyentes* to decide the question; a cortes to be composed of only one Assembly.

As for the situation of the queen, her person is probably in safety; but as queen, her authority is null. Obliged to make excuses to the people, to reward an insurgent general "for his brilliant conduct at Vicálvaro," to dismiss the friends of her childhood, her position is truly worthy of pity.

It remains to be seen whether Espartero will now give evidences of the talent and decision which in his younger days he was devoid of, or whether O'Donnell, new to government, will be able to direct the circumstances into which he has brought himself. One thing is certain. For the present, their only safety consists in their union. Neither is strong enough to govern alone, and the conviction of this fact may keep these heterogeneous elements united for a longer period than might at first be expected. Their complete fusion is evidently impossible.

25th.

In the mean time the fruits of the revolution, so far, have been, in Madrid, disorders and confusion, furious clamors and excesses on the part of the press, violence and pretension on that of the clubs. In the provinces the result has been anarchy in every form; properties and persons daily menaced—popular seditions in Cadiz—the authorities murdered at Tolosa—the goods of the commonwealth distributed amongst the people by socialist communities in various other places—at Algesiras, the custom-house duties abolished.

The Duke of Victoria has accepted the presidency of the Union Club. This club demands that the constitution shall proclaim the sovereignty of the people; it reclaims the suppression of indirect contributions, the establishment of one only tax, the abolition of conscription and capital punishments, the reduction of the standing army, the universal arming of the people, and the trial of Queen Cristina before the Cortes.

A banquet was given by the press to the two heroes. Various toasts were proposed by Espartero, but none to the health of the queen! The omission was afterwards repaired by O'Donnell.

This revolution of "morality and liberty" has produced such a universal *scuffle* for places, and the changes are so numerous, that the whole world goes about congratulating and condoling with one another; and it requires a good memory, or rather it is necessary to keep a sharp eye upon the news of the day, to know which are the losers and which the winners in the game. Diplomacy, magistracy, administration,—all has been totally renewed; even the judges have been replaced by others. As all pretensions cannot be satisfied, the most inveterate amongst the democrats are loud in their denunciations against many of the new nominations. Those made by Pacheco in the State department are declared by some of the Republican journals to be "worthy of Sartorius and Bravo Murillo." The government are desired to show more "tact" in distributing offices, and the insolence of the press has increased to such an extent, that the two generals are beginning to consult upon the measures necessary for curbing its excesses, as well as for abolishing some of the most violent of the revolutionary clubs. But as long as Queen Cristina remains in the palace, her name will be made a pretext for riot and disorder, and it is rumored that some desperate step is about to be taken by the government for having her majesty conveyed beyond the frontier in safety.

28th.

This morning, at seven o'clock, an early riser might have observed, as I did from my window in the Plaza del Oriente, a travelling-carriage with four horses enter the palace by the eastern gate, and drive into the court-yard. A curious person, as I was on this occasion, passing into the court-yard of the palace, might have observed this carriage drawn up at the foot of the grand staircase, and might have wondered to see, at this early hour, two squadrons of the regiment of Farnesio in rapid march towards the royal dwelling; moreover, he would have noted, that these two squadrons were commanded by Colonel, now General Garrigo, by the same Garrigo—the rebel, the condemned, the pardoned, the loyal, the rewarded; and it would have been evident to the same curious individual, that these troops were destined to escort that travelling-carriage, and that consequently that carriage was destined to convey to a place of safety some precious and even royal freight. And one who was within the palace that memorable morning, which I was not, faithfully related to me the scenes of which he was an eye-witness at that early hour, and of which the *dramatis personæ* were royal and illustrious individuals. First on the scene was Queen Ysabel, who, with swollen eyes and pale countenance, had evidently passed a sleepless night—anxious and trembling—wrapped in a dressing-gown, her hair in disorder. Next enters the royal traveller, plainly dressed. She had received, only the night before, intimation that all was in readiness for her departure, and in all probability had not closed her eyes; but she is grave and calm, and sheds no tear. There was the little princess, sleepy and wondering—the king, in uniform, looking troubled and anxious—the Duke of Riansares, making an effort to appear composed, but evidently full of uneasiness. The generals, and other members of the ministry, stand there in full uniform, hat in hand. Queen Cristina has kept her word. She will leave Madrid "like a queen." The duke whispers that all is ready—Queen Cristina kisses her daughter and the little princess and her son-in-law; but she will not shed one tear before this audience.

The queen clings convulsively to her mother—sobs as though her heart would break—cries out loud, hysterically, and falls, half fainting, on a sofa. The little princess cries for company; still Queen Cristina remains composed—signs to the king to attend her majesty—takes advantage of the half unconscious state of her daughter, and leaves the room with a firm step. The Duke of Victoria walks down the grand staircase by her side; General O'Donnell towers up behind. She bids them adieu in an indifferent tone—inquires, with a slightly sarcastic smile, for their respective ladies—is handed in by the Duke of Victoria, and the Duke of Riansares follows—the postillions crack their whips—Garrigo rides up to the side of the carriage. The escort move in serried ranks—Garrigo rides by the door on the side of the queen, and looks like a man who will be faithful to his trust. They have left the enclosure of the palace, and have taken the route leading to Portugal. Heaven send them safe across the frontier of Spain!

But now comes "the tug of war." How will the people take it? It is probable that none of the ministers, but especially neither of the two heroes, breakfasted with much appetite that morning; nor, indeed, had they much time, for by nine o'clock the news had circulated throughout Madrid. Then, indeed, did the popular lion give a savage roar. Their prey had escaped them—and their own leaders had deceived them—*Et tu Brute?* Then arose a cry for vengeance upon the government; crowds gathered, frantic patriots rushed along the streets, calling upon the citizens to take up arms, and the beat of drum announced to the national guard that the country was in danger. Cries of "Down with the government!" were in some places mingled with "Viva Espartero!" from those who were willing to believe that the popular chief had in this instance been overpowered by his stronger and more energetic colleague. Some rushed to the workshops of the gunsmiths and demanded firearms; others began to construct fresh barricades, and one of the foreign ministers was forced to alight from his carriage, which was dragged away to help in the formation of these ramparts. The Union Club, headed by Orense, Marquis of Albayda, demanded the return of Queen Cristina; various shops were broken into, and their owners, willingly or otherwise, furnished wine and victuals without payment, as an impromptu banquet, for the refreshment of the patriots. The moment was critical; and had any name of sufficient *prestige* appeared behind that of Espartero, his reign and that of the new ministers would have terminated that day.

Orense, heading a commission from the Union Club, presented himself before the Duke of Victoria, and in answer to his indignant reproaches against the ministry, was invited to repair to the department of *la Gobernacion*, together with commissions from all the popular corporations of Madrid, and to present themselves to the council of ministers, which was about to be held in that department, there to manifest the popular wishes to the government.

Accordingly, amidst cries of "Down with the government!" "Death to O'Donnell!" and even "Death to Espartero!" commissions proceeded to the *Gobernacion*, from the auxiliary junta, the provincial deputation, the chiefs of the national guard, the Ayuntamiento, and so on; and together with Orense, who was generally supposed to be the prime mover of the tumult, and who headed the commission from the Union Club, entered the building, while the impatient crowd awaited the result of the stormy conference, and the whole city resounded with shouts of "Death to Cristina!" "Down with the ministry!" and other exhilarating cries.

High words are said to have passed between Orense and O'Donnell. Espartero endeavored to explain the necessity of the step that had been taken. O'Donnell followed up by a speech of more length, terminating by these memorable words: "Two months ago, accompanied by a handful of brave men (a *handful* being rather a poetical license, when speaking of the whole cavalry of Madrid), I despised my life (despreció mi vida) to redeem my country from slavery, to reconquer liberty, far then from thinking that two months would suffice for cries to arise against a government in which the Duke of Victoria and I are as strictly united as we have been in the field of battle. The enterprise is accomplished; come what may, it matters nothing to me. The passions of the moment may cause the services I have rendered to my country to be forgotten, but history will do me justice! No matter what fate awaits me, if liberty is preserved. For it I have exposed my head during two months; for it I will expose my head again, whenever it is threatened."

Again the two heroes appeared on the balcony, locked in each other's arms. The people were addressed in terms of praise and persuasion. For some time the crowd remained moody and discontented, but at length they gradually dispersed. The national guard took possession of several points leading to those streets where the principal focus of the insurrection had formed itself. The parapets were taken down, though cries continued of "Bring back Cristina!" "Down with all the ministers except Espartero!" A commission, composed of Buceta and others, traversed those streets, and gave assurances to the defenders of these barricades that Espartero had no will but that of the people, and that they might put perfect reliance in him. Gradually the barricades disappeared, and towards evening a certain degree of order had been restored throughout the city.

The address of the ministers to the people, the composition of Señor Lujan, contained the following paragraph:

"National Guard! People of Madrid! The government, the lover of liberty, loyal above all, has faithfully fulfilled its promise to the people of Madrid, that *Doña María Cristina should not go away furtively, neither by day nor by night.*"

To this the malecontents reply—"The government did *not* say that Doña María Cristina should not go away secretly neither by day nor by night," but that "Doña María Cristina should not go away *neither by day nor by night, nor secretly.*" They complain bitterly of this transposition, of this play of words, of this witch-like Macbeth's oracle, thus paltering with them in words of double meaning. If they had read Shakspeare, they might exclaim—

"And be these juggling fiends no more believed,
That palter with us in a double sense,
That keep the word of promise to our ear,
And break it to our hope."

It is, however, a clever idea on the part of Señor Lujan, the minister of Fomento, and proves him to be a man of expedients. Meanwhile the royal traveller is on her way to Portugal, and every hour that passes brings her nearer a port of safety.

The cabinet have conducted themselves with prudence and energy on this occasion, and have saved themselves and the country from a great and lasting disgrace. And so concludes the first act of this political drama.

Another source of embarrassment to the new ministry has been removed, in the escape of all the members composing the late cabinet, and of the ex-Governors Quinto and Lara, each of whom has gradually made his exit from the scene, as if by a trap-door, and reappeared in safety on the frontiers of France. Those whose lives were in positive danger, San-Luis, Domenech, Collantes and Quinto, must have passed through adventures fraught with a deep and thrilling interest; while all, worn out as they must be with long concealment, constant anxiety, and the dread of at least imprisonment for an indefinite period, must look back upon the last six weeks as on a strange and troubled dream, a political nightmare. So sudden and unexpected a revulsion of fortune may well try the spirits of the bravest.

All fled in disguise, more or less complete. Fair hair was dyed black, bushy whiskers and fierce moustaches fell under the edge of the razor. If the "diable boiteux" could within the last month have unroofed certain houses where members of the late government lay, *perdus*, the scholar might have imagined that fallen statesmen were preparing themselves to attend a masked ball, had it only been in the height of the carnival season; or that they were rejuvenating themselves for conquest. They would have seen San-Luis divesting himself of moustache and whiskers, and appearing with a closely-shaved countenance and hair like the raven's wing; Calderon de la Barca changing his gray hair to jet black; Molins laying low his bushy *favorites*, and dark moustaches; Collantes performing the same operation; and all arraying themselves in habiliments forming as great a contrast as possible to the brilliant uniforms in which they were wont to meet the public eye. Strange scenes have been enacted, half ludicrous and half lugubrious.

On two different occasions the mob threatened to attack the French embassy, in order to take possession of the person of San-Luis and the diamonds of the queen-mother. The ambassador protested, and despatched a missive to Pacheco, threatening to demand his passports should such an infraction of diplomatic rights be carried into effect. A quarrel with France would not have improved the situation of affairs; and a certain number of the national guard were sent to lodge in the embassy, to defend it in case the people should put their threat in execution. We may imagine the feelings of the ex-president of the council while this discussion was pending. But now the embassy is cleared of its unwonted guests.

San-Luis, acting the part of a valet, let us hope "for this time only," was jolted across the Pyrenees in the rotunda of a diligence. The minister of state, saved through the generosity of a French gentleman, performed the part of a Bordeaux wine-merchant, till he had crossed the Bidassoa. Domenech escaped with difficulty from the palace, but I have not heard under what disguise he, Collantes, and Quinto evaded the eyes of the authorities. At all events, like stout swimmers they have reached the port. The vessel is wrecked, the cargo lost, but the crew are saved.

All the environs of the French frontier are now crowded with distinguished Spanish emigrants. Some are in Bayonne, others at Brarritz or at St. Jean de Luz. M. de ——, who has just returned from Paris, where he was sent with despatches, tells me that he saw more well-known Spanish faces on the principal street of Bayonne, than are to be met with nowadays on the Prado; amongst others, many of the ladies of the palace, the Duchess of Gor, the families of M——a, S——r, &c.

The families of the ministers followed, soon after their departure. The lady of the minister of the navy found herself accidentally in the same diligence with the minister of the treasury; I, amongst others, went to take leave of the family of the minister of state, and saw them off in the diligence at twelve o'clock at night.

Madrid has completely changed its aspect, and without having the miraculous seven years slumber of Rip Van Winkle, it would suffice that one should have fallen asleep seven weeks ago, and awakened this 1st of September, to find an entire alteration in men and things. My friend M—— has returned from Barcelona, escaping from riots, cholera, and misery of every description, and we walk the streets together in moralizing mood, or ride far away into the country, leaving Madrid dust behind us, or rather exchanging the dust of the city for that of the country.

We went yesterday to look at Queen Cristina's palace, which presents a sorry spectacle. We stood there while the moon threw a mellow veil over its ruined walls; and it seemed to me that years must have elapsed since they echoed to the sound of dancers' feet, and to the gay music of the cotillion. How many changes in a short period! How all that gay and joyous society is scattered! Where is the queen-mother, who sat there smiling and gracious?—Driven into exile. Where her charming daughters, the life of that assemblage?—Also in exile. That little Ynfante Fernando, childish and nervous?—Dead. *His* troubles are well over. The Prince of Parma?—Stabbed. The ministers and their families?—Fled. The ladies of the palace?—Dismissed and dispersed? What has become of the queen herself, whose word, however gentle, was a law to her cabinet?—Surrounded by strange faces, deprived of her early friends, and forced to obey and even to thank those who have risen in rebellion against her!

"Where's Brummell?—Dished. Where's Long Pole Wellesley?—Diddled," said M—— irreverently. "The dead will certainly not return, but those who have fled may be back again and in power to-morrow."

Last week I had the honor of assisting at a *grand dinner*, given by the French embassy to the new cabinet. All the diplomates were present, always excepting the representative of the United States. Among the first who arrived was Espartero, in whose outward man there is certainly little to attract the popular fancy. Divested of his uniform and multitudinous crosses, he would appear an ordinary looking individual, rather in feeble health, devoid of strength either moral or physical. His manners are grave, his features in no way remarkable; his hair dyed dark, and rather closely cropped. In conversation he is far from brilliant, and except that he is himself a man of the people, one looks in vain for the qualities which have made him the hero of the popular cause.

O'Donnell, on the contrary, is a showy-looking man, of fine figure, immensely tall, his face remarkably handsome, though heavy and not particularly intelligent in its expression. He is more fluent in conversation, with more ease of manner, and is altogether more brilliant than his colleague. Old General San Miguel has an undeniably honest countenance; his hair, whiskers, and moustaches perfectly gray; strong, rugged features; a fine energetic expression; however one may disapprove of his political principles, it is impossible to doubt his sincerity. General Ros de Olano, wiry and nervous, thin and restless, looks as if some internal fire were wearing him out.

The banquet was long and serious, notwithstanding a sprinkling of agreeable women; but their superb jewels, and the uniforms and crosses of the generals and diplomates, had a brilliant effect. Seated at the lower end of the table, amongst the subaltern members of the diplomatic body, I could only observe that there was a greater flow of wine than of conversation, and a good deal of stiffness and embarrassment on all sides, excepting in the feminine portion of the society. Espartero spake little, and eat less, and looked sleepy and suffering. O'Donnell was grand and condescending. Old San Miguel seemed very well pleased to let the ladies attend to him.

In the evening the addition of several guests gave more animation to the society. Espartero and O'Donnell took leave early. Countess ——, a determined enemy of the new government, remarked, in a loud whisper as they went out, that they reminded her of a peacock and a barn-door fowl.

The guest whom I mentioned as having taken refuge in my dressing-room, suddenly vanished one afternoon whilst I was from home. On my return I found the following note on my table:

MY DEAR FRIEND,

When you read this, I hope to have passed the barrier, and to be some miles on the way to freedom. Accept my warmest thanks for your kindness and hospitality, and put me at the feet of his excellency. I hope never to have it in my power to render you a *similar* service; in all else command me.

You may believe I do not doubt your discretion, but it is better for all parties that no one but Miguel should be in the secret. He has brought me a disguise, in which I hope to baffle all recognition, and now awaits me with a horse, at a certain distance. If I escape, you will hear from me; if I am captured, you will hear of me. I do not take leave of Count A——, who, I regret to hear, is indisposed. It is needless to make him feel anxious, or to mention the matter to him, till the result is decided.

I leave you a box of Havanas, to smoke to my memory, and a portmanteau to be forwarded to the care of our consul at Bayonne, when the times grow peaceful. Comfortable as this little room is, I revel in the idea of fresh air and a hard trot.

Adios amigo mío! till better days. Believe in the affection of your *apasionado*.

A day and night of some anxiety, and then I began to breathe more freely. Yesterday the faithful Miguel appeared, and brought me a few hurried lines from his master, dated from *Urdas*, in Navarre, "on the French side of the bridge." He writes in high spirits, and promises me an account of his adventures, when he has eat, washed, and slept.

October 1st.

The serious illness of my excellent chief, Count A——, has entirely occupied me during the last fortnight. The physicians recommend him the bath of Aix. The new secretary having arrived, the Count proposes that I should accompany him so far, and then make a flying visit to my fatherland! If this plan be carried out, I may be at Castle —— in a few weeks, and the remainder of my news shall be imparted *viva voce!*

At the present juncture I shall leave Spain without regret. Madrid looks sad and desolate—nearly all the best society has emigrated—the people appear gloomy and reckless; yet their noble character has never come out more triumphant than now. Their good qualities are their own—their faults those of their leaders. In what city after all, would fewer disorders have taken place, or less innocent blood have been shed than during that interregnum when the mob had the reins of the government in their own hands? How many instances of faithful devotion, of almost chivalrous disinterestedness I have heard and witnessed within the last two months! of servants who have risked their lives to save their masters—of men and women in the extreme of poverty, who have spurned bribes and even refused reward! To say that no robberies took place during the late disorders would be to advance a fallacy. Gold and silver, jewels and money, were no doubt abstracted during these scenes of riot and tumult; but we must recollect that the lowest scum of the populace not only of Madrid but of the adjacent villages, were then collected together. A large portion of the people, properly so called, never left their houses, or took any part in the insurrection. The soldiers have been brave and enduring—the people, as a whole, moderate and magnanimous.

So far, the government is vainly endeavoring to make its way through all the complications that impede its march. Disorders arise in one place as fast as they are put down in another. Until the reunion of the Cortes, the result of the elections that have taken place must remain problematical. Parties are divided—civil war threatens the country—a manifesto appears from the Count of Montemolin, and the Carlist party naturally conceive hopes of success from the anarchy in which the country is plunged. Even in Burgos, one of the most peaceful of cities, a slight augmentation in the price of bread has occasioned a popular riot. Carts loaded with grain for Santander were set on fire; the houses of the principal merchants were burned and pillaged. The authorities ordered the troops to fire upon the people, and several of the rioters were killed, and many wounded. The spirit of sedition has spread throughout the country. At Malaga, at Jaen, and many other cities, neither person nor property is respected, and to add to all these evils, the cholera, in its worst form, is devastating the provinces.

Would the chiefs of the revolution have paused in their career, could they have foreseen these results? Perhaps not; for it is only a Washington, one guided by no personal motives, who with a cool head, an unbiassed judgment and an honest heart, can weigh and calculate with solemn earnestness the good or evil likely to accrue from a step which scarcely any amount of evil can render justifiable.

What will be the winding up of this drama? We have no prophet or seer to give the answer. The proverb says "Qui vivra, verra;" but amidst all these complications I fear that he who will see the end of this beginning, must live many years; *Qui verra, vivra long-temps.*

October 15th.

The travelling carriage is at the door. Antoine the count's valet, and I, look to our pistols—Madrid is sleeping in the warm haze of the morning sunshine. The Manzanares has dwindled to a silver thread. Many of the fountains have dried up. The sky is blue as a vast hollow turquoise—the tops of the mountains are enveloped in a warm mist. I salute the old palace and the bronze statue, and all inanimate familiar things upon which I have daily looked for more than a year past, and so, for the space of three months, I bid adieu to Madrid and to my Diary.

THE END.

A LIST

OF

NEW WORKS

IN GENERAL LITERATURE,

PUBLISHED BY

D. APPLETON & COMPANY,

846 & 848 Broadway.

*** *Complete Catalogues, containing full descriptions, to be had on application to the Publishers.*

Agriculture and Rural Affairs.

Boussingault's Rural Economy, . . . 1 25
The Poultry Book, illustrated, . . 5 00
Waring's Elements of Agriculture, . 75

Arts, Manufactures, and Architecture.

Appleton's Dictionary of Mechanics vols. . 12 00
" Mechanics' Magazine. vols. each, 3 50
Allen's Philosophy of Mechanics . . . 3 50
Arnot's Gothic Architecture, ... 4 00
Bassnett's Theory of Storms, ... 1 00
Bourne on the Steam Engine, ... 75
Byrne on Logarithms, ... 1 00
Chapman on the American Rifle, . . . 1 25
Coming's Preservation of Health, . . . 75
Cullum on Military Bridges, ... 2 00
Downing's Country Houses, ... 4 00
Field's City Architecture, ... 2 00
Griffith's Marine Architecture, . . . 10 00
Gillespie's Treatise on Surveying, . . .
Haupt's Theory of Bridge Construction, . . 3 00
Henck's Field-Book for R. Road Engineers, . 1 75
Hoblyn's Dictionary of Scientific Terms, . 1 50
Huff's Manual of Electro-Physiology, . . 1 25
Jeffers' Practice of Naval Gunnery, . . 2 50
Knapen's Mechanics' Assistant, . . . 1 00
Lafever's Modern Architecture, . . . 4 0
Lyell's Manual of Geology, ... 1 75
" Principles of Geology, ... 2 25
Reynold's Treatise on Handrailing, . . 2 00
Templeton's Mechanic's Companion, . . 1 00
Ure's Dict'ry of Arts, Manufactures, &c. 2 vols. 5 00
Youmans' Class-Book of Chemistry, . . 75
" Atlas of Chemistry. cloth, . . 2 00
" Alcohol, ... 50

Biography.

Arnold's Life and Correspondence, . . . 2 00
Capt. Canot, or Twenty Years of a Slaver, . 1 25
Cousin's De Longueville, ... 1 00
Croswell's Memoirs, ... 2 00
Evelyn's Life of Godolphin, ... 50
Garland's Life of Randolph, ... 1 50
Gilfillan's Gallery of Portraits. 2d Series, . 1 00
Hernan Cortez's Life, ... 38
Hull's Civil and Military Life, ... 2 00
Life and Adventures of Daniel Boone, . . 38
Life of Henry Hudson, ... 38
Life of Capt. John Smith, ... 38
Moore's Life of George Castriot, . . . 1 00
Napoleon's Memoirs. By Duchess D'Abrantes, 4 00
Napoleon. By Laurent L'Ardèche, . . . 3 00
Pinkney (W.) Life. By his Nephew, . . 2 00
Party Leaders: Lives of Jefferson, &c. . . 1 00
Southey's Life of Oliver Cromwell, . . 38
Wynne's Lives of Eminent Men, . . . 1 00
Webster's Life and Memorials. 2 vols. . . 1 00

Books of General Utility.

Appletons' Southern and Western Guide, . 1 00
" Northern and Eastern Guide, . 1 25
Appletons' Complete U. S. Guide, . . . 2 00
" Map of N. Y. City, . . . 25
American Practical Cook Book, . . .
A Treatise on Artificial Fish-Breeding, . . 75
Chemistry of Common Life. 2 vols. 12mo. .
Cooley's Book of Useful Knowledge, . . 25
Cust's Invalid's Own Book, ... 50
Delisser's Interest Tables, ... 4 00
The English Cyclopaedia, per vol. . . . 2 50
Miles on the Horse's Foot, ... 25
The Nursery Basket. A Book for Young Mothers, 38
Pell's Guide for the Young, ... 38
Reid's New English Dictionary, . . . 1 00
Stewart's Stable Economy, ... 1 00
Spalding's Hist. of English Literature, . . 1 00
Soyer's Modern Cookery, ... 1 00
The Successful Merchant, ... 1 00
Thomson on Food of Animals, ... 50

Commerce and Mercantile Affairs.

Anderson's Mercantile Correspondence, . . 1 00
Delisser's Interest Tables, ... 4 00
Merchants' Reference Book, ... 4 00
Oates' (Geo.) Interest Tables at 6 Per Cent. per Annum. 8vo. 2 00
" " Do. do. Abridged edition, . 1 25
" " 7 Per Cent. Interest Tables, . 2 00
" " Abridged, ... 1 25
Smith's Mercantile Law, ... 4 00

Geography and Atlases.

Appleton's Modern Atlas. 34 Maps, . . 3 50
" Complete Atlas. 61 Maps, . 9 00
Atlas of the Middle Ages. By Kœppen, . 4 50
Black's General Atlas. 71 Maps, . . . 12 00
Cornell's Primary Geography, ... 50
" Intermediate Geography, . . .
High School Geography, . . .

History.

Arnold's History of Rome, ... 3 00
" Later Commonwealth, . . . 2 50
" Lectures on Modern History, . . 1 25
Dew's Ancient and Modern History, . . 2 00
Koeppen's History of the Middle Ages. 2 vols. 2 50
" The same, folio, with Maps, . . 4 50
Kohlrausch's History of Germany, . . . 1 50
Mahon's (Lord) History of England, 2 vols. . 4 00
Michelet's History of France, 2 vols. . . 3 50
" History of the Roman Republic, . 1 00
Rowan's History of the French Revolution, . 63
Sprague's History of the Florida War, . . 2 50
Taylor's Manual of Ancient History, . . 1 25
" Manual of Modern History, . . 1 50
" Manual of History. 1 vol. complete, 2 50
Thiers' French Revolution. 4 vols. Illustrated, 5 00

Illustrated Works for Presents

Bryant's Poems. 16 Illustrations. 8vo. cloth, . 40
" " " cloth, gilt, . 50
" " " mor. antique 90

Gems of British Art. 30 Engravings. 1 vol. 4to. morocco, ... 18 00
Gray's Elegy. Illustrated. 8vo. 1 50
Goldsmith's Deserted Village, ... 1 50
The Homes of American Authors. With Illustrations, cloth, ... 4 00
" " " cloth, gilt, 5 00
" " " mor. antqe. 7 00
The Holy Gospels. With 40 Designs by Overbeck. 1 vol. folio. Antique mor. . . . 20 00
The Land of Bondage. By J. M. Wainwright, D.D. Morocco, ... 6 00
The Queens of England. By Agnes Strickland. With 29 Portraits. Antique mor. . 10 00
The Ornaments of Memory. With 18 Illustrations. 4to. cloth, gilt, . . 6 00
" Morocco, . . 10 00
Royal Gems from the Galleries of Europe. 40 Engravings, ... 25 00
The Republican Court; or, American Society in the Days of Washington. 21 Portraits. Antique mor. 12 00
The Vernon Gallery. 67 Engrav'gs. 4to. Ant. 25 00
The Women of the Bible. With 18 Engravings. Mor. antique, ... 10 00
Wilkie Gallery. Containing 60 Splendid Engravings. 4to. Antique mor. . . . 25 00
A Winter Wreath of Summer Flowers. By S. G. Goodrich. Illustrated. Cloth, gilt, . 3 00

Juvenile Books.

A Poetry Book for Children, ... 75
Aunt Fanny's Christmas Stories, ... 50
American Historical Tales, ... 75

UNCLE AMEREL'S STORY BOOKS.

The Little Gift Book. 18mo. cloth, . . 25
The Child's Story Book. Illust. 18mo. cloth, 25
Summer Holidays. 18mo. cloth, . . . 25
Winter Holidays. Illustrated. 18mo. cloth, . 25
George's Adventures in the Country. Illustrated. 18mo. cloth, ... 25
Christmas Stories. Illustrated. 18mo. cloth, . 25

Book of Trades, ... 50
Boys at Home. By the Author of Edgar Clifton, 75
Child's Cheerful Companion, ... 50
Child's Picture and Verse Book. 100 Engs. . 50

COUSIN ALICE'S WORKS.

All's Not Gold that Glitters, ... 75
Contentment Better than Wealth, ... 63
Nothing Venture, Nothing Have, ... 63
No such Word as Fail, ... 63
Patient Waiting No Loss, ... 63

Dashwood Priory. By the Author of Edgar Clifton, ... 75
Edgar Clifton; or Right and Wrong, . . . 75
Fireside Fairies. By Susan Pindar, . . . 63
Good in Every Thing. By Mrs. Barwell, . . 50
Leisure Moments Improved, ... 75
Life of Punchinello, ... 75

LIBRARY FOR MY YOUNG COUNTRYMEN.

Adventures of Capt. John Smith. By the Author of Uncle Philip, ... 38
Adventures of Daniel Boone. By do. . . 38
Dawnings of Genius. By Anne Pratt, . . 38
Life and Adventures of Henry Hudson. By the Author of Uncle Philip, . . . 38
Life and Adventures of Hernan Cortez. By do. 38
Philip Randolph. A Tale of Virginia. By Mary Gertrude, ... 38
Rowan's History of the French Revolution. 2 vols. 75
Southey's Life of Oliver Cromwell, . . 38

Louis' School-Days. By E. J. May, . . . 75
Louise; or, The Beauty of Integrity, . . . 25
Maryatt's Settlers in Canada, ... 62
" Masterman Ready, . . . 62
" Scenes in Africa, . . . 62
Midsummer Fays. By Susan Pindar, . . . 62

MISS McINTOSH'S WORKS.

Aunt Kitty's Tales, 12mo. 75
Blind Alice; A Tale for Good Children, . . 38
Ellen Leslie; or, The Reward of Self-Control, 38
Florence Arnott; or, Is She Generous? . . 38
Grace and Clara; or, Be Just as well as Generous, ... 38
Jessie Graham; or, Friends Dear, but Truth Dearer, ... 38
Emily Herbert; or, The Happy Home, . . 37
Rose and Lillie Stanhope, ... 37

Mamma's Story Book, ... 75
Pebbles from the Sea-Shore, ... 37
Puss in Boots. Illustrated. By Otto Specter, . 25

PETER PARLEY'S WORKS.

Faggots for the Fireside, ... 1 13
Parley's Present for all Seasons, . . . 1 00
Wanderers by Sea and Land, ... 1 13
Winter Wreath of Summer Flowers, . . 3 00

TALES FOR THE PEOPLE AND THEIR CHILDREN.

Alice Franklin. By Mary Howitt, . . . 38
Crofton Boys (The). By Harriet Martineau, . 38
Dangers of Dining Out. By Mrs. Ellis, . . 38
Domestic Tales. By Hannah More. 2 vols. . 75
Early Friendship. By Mrs. Copley, . . 38
Farmer's Daughter (The). By Mrs. Cameron, 38
First Impressions. By Mrs. Ellis, . . . 38
Hope On, Hope Ever! By Mary Howitt, . 38
Little Coin, Much Care. By do. . . . 38
Looking-Glass for the Mind. Many plates, . 38
Love and Money. By Mary Howitt, . . 38
Minister's Family. By Mrs. Ellis, . . . 38
My Own Story. By Mary Howitt, . . . 38
My Uncle, the Clockmaker. By do. . . 38
No Sense Like Common Sense. By do. . . 38
Peasant and the Prince. By H. Martineau, . 38
Poplar Grove. By Mrs. Copley, . . . 38
Somerville Hall. By Mrs. Ellis, . . . 38
Sowing and Reaping. By Mary Howitt, . . 38
Story of a Genius. 38
Strive and Thrive. By do. 38
The Two Apprentices. By do. 38
Tired of Housekeeping. By T. S. Arthur, . 38
Twin Sisters (The). By Mrs. Sandham, . . 38
Which is the Wiser? By Mary Howitt, . . 38
Who Shall be Greatest? By do. . . . 38
Work and Wages. By do. 38

SECOND SERIES.

Chances and Changes. By Charles Burdett, . 38
Goldmaker's Village. By H. Zschokke, . . 38
Never Too Late. By Charles Burdett, . . 38
Ocean Work, Ancient and Modern. By J. H. Wright, ... 38

Picture Pleasure Book, 1st Series, . . . 1 25
" " " 2d Series, . . . 1 25
Robinson Crusoe. 300 Plates, ... 1 50
Susan Pindar's Story Book, ... 75
Sunshine of Greystone, ... 75
Travels of Bob the Squirrel, ... 37
Wonderful Story Book, ... 50
Willy's First Present, ... 75
Week's Delight; or, Games and Stories for the Parlor, ... 75
William Tell, the Hero of Switzerland, . . 50
Young Student. By Madame Guizot, . . 75

Miscellaneous and General Literature.

Title	Price
An Attic Philosopher in Paris,	25
Appletons' Library Manual,	1 25
Agnell's Book of Chess,	1 25
Arnold's Miscellaneous Works,	2 00
Arthur. The Successful Merchant,	75
A Book for Summer Time in the Country,	50
Baldwin's Flush Times in Alabama,	1 25
Calhoun (J. C.), Works of. 4 vols. publ., each,	2 00
Clark's (W. G.) Knick-Knacks,	1 25
Cornwall's Music as it Was, and as it Is,	63
Essays from the London Times. 1st & 2d Series, each,	50
Ewbanks' World in a Workshop,	75
Ellis' Women of England,	50
" Hearts and Homes,	1 50
" Prevention Better than Cure,	75
Foster's Essays on Christian Morals,	50
Goldsmith's Vicar of Wakefield,	75
Grant's Memoirs of an American Lady,	75
Gaieties and Gravities. By Horace Smith,	50
Guizot's History of Civilization,	1 00
Hearth-Stone. By Rev. S. Osgood,	1 00
Hobson. My Uncle and I,	75
Ingoldsby Legends,	50
Isham's Mud Cabin,	1 00
Johnson's Meaning of Words,	1 00
Kavanagh's Women of Christianity,	75
Leger's Animal Magnetism,	1 00
Life's Discipline. A Tale of Hungary,	63
Letters from Rome. A. D. 138,	1 90
Margaret Maitland,	75
Maiden and Married Life of Mary Powell,	50
Morton Montague; or a Young Christian's Choice,	75
Macaulay's Miscellanies. 5 vols.	5 00
Maxims of Washington. By J. F. Schroeder,	1 00
Mile Stones in our Life Journey,	1 00

MINIATURE CLASSICAL LIBRARY.

Title	Price
Poetic Lacon; or, Aphorisms from the Poets,	38
Bond's Golden Maxims,	31
Clarke's Scripture Promises. Complete,	38
Elizabeth; or, The Exiles of Siberia,	31
Goldsmith's Vicar of Wakefield,	38
" Essays,	38
Gems from American Poets,	38
Hannah More's Private Devotions,	31
" " Practical Piety. 2 vols.	75
Hemans' Domestic Affections,	31
Hoffman's Lays of the Hudson, &c.	38
Johnson's History of Rasselas,	38
Manual of Matrimony,	31
Moore's Lalla Rookh,	38
" Melodies. Complete,	38
Paul and Virginia,	31
Pollok's Course of Time,	38
Pure Gold from the Rivers of Wisdom,	38
Thomson's Seasons,	38
Token of the Heart. Do. of Affection. Do. of Remembrance. Do. of Friendship. Do. of Love. Each,	31
Useful Letter-Writer,	38
Wilson's Sacra Privata,	31
Young's Night Thoughts,	38

Title	Price
Little Pedlington and the Pedlingtonians,	50
Prismatics. Tales and Poems,	1 25
Papers from the Quarterly Review,	50
Republic of the United States. Its Duties, &c	1 00
Preservation of Health and Prevention of Disease,	75
School for Politics. By Chas. Gayerre,	75
Select Italian Comedies. Translated,	75
Shakespeare's Scholar. By R. G. White,	2 50
Spectator (The). New ed. 6 vols. cloth,	9 00
Swett's Treatise on Diseases of the Chest,	3 00
Stories from Blackwood,	50

THACKERAY'S WORKS.

Title	Price
The Book of Snobs,	50
Mr. Browne's Letters,	50
The Confessions of Fitzboodle,	50
The Fat Contributor,	50
Jeames' Diary. A Legend of the Rhine,	50
The Luck of Barry Lyndon,	1 00
Men's Wives,	50
The Paris Sketch Book. 2 vols.	1 00
The Shabby Genteel Story,	50
The Yellowplush Papers. 1 vol. 16mo.	50
Thackeray's Works. 6 vols. bound in cloth,	6 00

Title	Price
Trescott's Diplomacy of the Revolution,	75
Tuckerman's Artist Life,	75
Up Country Letters,	75
Ward's Letters from Three Continents,	1 00
" English Items,	1 00
Warner's Rudimental Lessons in Music,	50
Woman's Worth,	38

Philosophical Works.

Title	Price
Cousin's Course of Modern Philosophy,	3 00
" Philosophy of the Beautiful,	62
" on the True, Beautiful, and Good,	1 50
Comte's Positive Philosophy. 2 vols.	4 00
Hamilton's Philosophy. 1 vol. 8vo.	1 50

Poetry and the Drama.

Title	Price
Amelia's Poems. 1 vol. 12mo.	1 25
Brownell's Poems. 12mo.	75
Bryant's Poems. 1 vol. 8vo. Illustrated,	3 50
" " Antique mor.	6 00
" " 2 vols. 12mo. cloth,	2 00
" " 1 vol. 18mo.	63
Byron's Poetical Works. 1 vol. cloth,	3 00
" " " Antique mor.	6 00
Burns' Poetical Works. Cloth,	1 00
Butler's Hudibras. Cloth,	1 00
Campbell's Poetical Works. Cloth,	1 00
Coleridge's Poetical Works. Cloth,	1 25
Cowper's Poetical Works,	1 00
Chaucer's Canterbury Tales,	1 00
Dante's Poems. Cloth,	1 00
Dryden's Poetical Works. Cloth,	1 00
Fay (J. S.), Ulric; or, The Voices,	75
Goethe's Iphigenia in Tauris. Translated,	75
Gilfillan's Edition of the British Poets. 12 vols. published. Price per vol. cloth,	1 00
Do. do. Calf, per vol.	2 50
Griffith's (Mattie) Poems,	75
Hemans' Poetical Works. 2 vols. 16mo.	2 00
Herbert's Poetical Works. 16mo. cloth,	1 00
Keats' Poetical Works. Cloth, 12mo.	1 25
Kirke White's Poetical Works. Cloth,	1 00
Lord's Poems. 1 vol. 12mo.	75
" Christ in Hades. 12mo.	75
Milton's Paradise Lost. 18mo.	38
" Complete Poetical Works,	1 00
Moore's Poetical Works. 8vo. Illustrated,	3 00
" " " Mor. extra,	6 00
Montgomery's Sacred Poems. 1 vol. 12mo.	75
Pope's Poetical Works. 1 vol. 16mo.	1 00
Southey's Poetical Works. 1 vol.	3 00
Spenser's Faerie Queene. 1 vol. cloth,	1 00
Scott's Poetical Works. 1 vol.	1 00
" Lady of the Lake. 16mo.	38
" Marmion,	37
" Lay of the Last Minstrel,	25
Shakspeare's Dramatic Works,	2 00
Tasso's Jerusalem Delivered. 1 vol. 16mo.	1 00
Wordsworth (W.). The Prelude,	1 00

Religious Works.

Title	Price
Arnold's Rugby School Sermons,	50
Anthon's Catechism on the Homilies,	06
" Early Catechism for Children,	06
Burnet's History of the Reformation. 3 vols.	2 50
" Thirty-Nine Articles,	2 00

Bradley's Family and Parish Sermons, 2 00
Cotter's Mass and Rubrics, 38
Colt's Puritanism, 1 00
Evans' Rectory of Valehead, 50
Grayson's True Theory of Christianity, 1 00
Gresley on Preaching, 1 25
Griffin's Gospel its Own Advocate, 1 00
Hecker's Book of the Soul,
Hooker's Complete Works. 2 vols. 4 00
James' Happiness, 25
James on the Nature of Evil, 1 00
Jarvis' Reply to Milner, 75
Kingsley's Sacred Choir, 75
Keble's Christian Year, 37
Layman's Letters to a Bishop, 25
Logan's Sermons and Expository Lectures, 1 13
Lyra Apostolica, 50
Marshall's Notes on Episcopacy, 1 00
Newman's Sermons and Subjects of the Day, 1 00
" Essay on Christian Doctrine, 75
Ogilby on Lay Baptism, 50
Pearson on the Creed, 2 00
Pulpit Cyclopædia and Ministers' Companion, 2 50
Sewell's Reading Preparatory to Confirmation, 75
Southard's Mystery of Godliness, 75
Sketches and Skeletons of Sermons, 2 50
Spencer's Christian Instructed, 1 00
Sherlock's Practical Christian, 75
Sutton's Disce Vivere—Learn to Live, 75
Swartz's Letters to my Godchild, 38
Trench's Notes on the Parables, 1 75
" Notes on the Miracles. 1 75
Taylor's Holy Living and Dying, 1 00
" Episcopacy Asserted and Maintained, 75
Tyng's Family Commentary, 2 00
Walker's Sermons on Practical Subjects, 2 00
Watson on Confirmation, 06
Wilberforce's Manual for Communicants, 38
Wilson's Lectures on Colossians, 75
Wyatt's Christian Altar, 38

Voyages and Travels.

Africa and the American Flag, 1 25
Appletons' Southern and Western Guide, 1 00
" Northern and Eastern Guide, 1 25
" Complete U. S. Guide Book, 2 00
" N. Y. City Map, 25
Bartlett's New Mexico, &c. 2 vols. Illustrated, 5 00
Burnet's N. Western Territory, 2 00
Bryant's What I Saw in California, 1 25
Coggeshall's Voyages. 2 vols. 2 50
Dix's Winter in Madeira, 1 00
Huc's Travels in Tartary and Thibet. 2 vols. 1 00
Layard's Nineveh. 1 vol. 8vo. 1 25
Notes of a Theological Student. 12mo. 1 00
Oliphant's Journey to Katmundu, 50
Parkyns' Abyssinia. 2 vols. 2 50
Russia as it Is. By Gurowski, 1 00
" By Count de Custine, 1 25
Squier's Nicaragua. 2 vols. 5 00
Tappan's Step from the New World to the Old, 1 75
Wanderings and Fortunes of Germ. Emigrants, 75
Williams' Isthmus of Tehuantepec. 2 vols. 8vo. 3 50

Works of Fiction.

GRACE AGUILAR'S WORKS.

The Days of Bruce. 2 vols. 12mo. 1 50
Home Scenes and Heart Studies. 12mo. 75
The Mother's Recompense. 12mo. 75
Woman's Friendship. 12mo. 75
Women of Israel. 2 vols. 12mo. 1 50

Basil A Story of Modern Life. 12mo. 75
Brace's Fawn of the Pale Faces. 12mo. 75
Busy Moments of an Idle Woman, 75
Chestnut Wood. A Tale. 2 vols. 1 75
Don Quixotte, Translated. Illustrated, 1 25
Drury (A. H.). Light and Shade, 75
Dupuy (A. E.). The Conspirator, 75
Elten Parry; or, Trials of the Heart, 63

MRS. ELLIS' WORKS.

Hearts and Homes; or, Social Distinctions, 1 50
Prevention Better than Cure, 75
Women of England, 50

Emmanuel Phillibert. By Dumas, 1 25
Farmingdale. By Caroline Thomas, 1 00
Fullerton (Lady G.). Ellen Middleton, 75
" " Grantley Manor. 1 vol. 12mo. 75
" " Lady Bird. 1 vol. 12mo. 75
The Foresters. By Alex. Dumas, 75
Gore (Mrs.). The Dean's Daughter. 1 vol. 12mo. 75
Goldsmith's Vicar of Wakefield. 12mo. 75
Gil Blas. With 500 Engravings. Cloth, gt. edg. 2 50
Harry Muir. A Tale of Scottish Life, 75
Hearts Unveiled; or, I Knew You Would Like Him, 75
Heartsease; or, My Brother's Wife. 2 vols. 1 50
Heir of Redclyffe. 2 vols. cloth, 1 50
Heloise; or, The Unrevealed Secret. 12mo. 75
Hobson. My Uncle and I. 12mo. 75
Holmes' Tempest and Sunshine. 12mo. 1 00
Home is Home. A Domestic Story, 75
Howitt (Mary). The Heir of West Wayland, 50
Io. A Tale of the Ancient Fane. 12mo. 75
The Iron Cousin. By Mary Cowden Clarke, 1 25
James (G. P. R.). Adrian; or, Clouds of the Mind, 75
John; or, Is a Cousin in the Hand Worth Two in the Bush, 25

JULIA KAVANAGH'S WORKS.

Nathalie. A Tale. 12mo. 1 00
Madeline. 12mo. 75
Daisy Burns. 12mo. 1 00

Life's Discipline. A Tale of Hungary, 63
Lone Dove (The). A Legend, 75
Linny Lockwood. By Catherine Crowe, 50

MISS McINTOSH'S WORKS.

Two Lives; or, To Seem and To Be. 12mo. 75
Aunt Kitty's Tales. 12mo. 75
Charms and Counter-Charms. 12mo. 1 00
Evenings at Donaldson Manor, 75
The Lofty and the Lowly. 2 vols. 1 50

Margaret's Home. By Cousin Alice,
Marie Louise; or, The Opposite Neighbors, 50
Maiden Aunt (The). A Story, 75
Manzoni. The Betrothed Lovers. 2 vols. 1 50
Margaret Cecil; or, I Can Because I Ought, 75
Morton Montague; or, The Christian's Choice, 75
Norman Leslie. By G. C. H. 75
Prismatics. Tales and Poems. By Haywarde, 1 25
Roe (A. S.). James Montjoy. 12mo. 75
" To Love and to Be Loved. 12mo. 75
" Time and Tide. 12mo. 75
Reuben Medlicott; or, The Coming Man, 75
Rose Douglass. By S. R. W. 75

MISS SEWELL'S WORKS.

Amy Herbert. A Tale. 12mo. 75
Experience of Life. 12mo. 75
Gertrude. A Tale. 12mo. 75
Katherine Ashton. 2 vols. 12mo. 1 50
Laneton Parsonage. A Tale. 3 vols. 12mo. 2 25
Margaret Percival. 2 vols. 1 50
Walter Lorimer, and Other Tales. 12mo. 75
A Journal Kept for Children of a Village School, 1 00

Sunbeams and Shadows. Cloth, 75
Thorpe's Hive of the Bee Hunter, 1 00
Thackeray's Works. 6 vols. 12mo. 6 00
The Virginia Comedians. 2 vols. 12mo. 1 50
Use of Sunshine. By S. M. 12mo. 75
Wight's Romance of Abelard & Heloise. 12mo. 75

www.ingramcontent.com/pod-product-compliance
Lightning Source LLC
LaVergne TN
LVHW050009180826
845678LV00021B/13

* 9 7 8 0 3 5 3 5 3 1 5 6 7 *